THE PRESIDENT AND THE PROVOCATEUR

Oldcastle Books

oldcastlebooks.com

OTHER BOOKS BY ALEX COX

10,000 Ways to Die: A Director's Take on the Spaghetti Western
X Films: True Confessions of a Radical Filmmaker

THE PRESIDENT
★ ★ ★ ★ ★ AND ★ ★ ★ ★ ★
THE PROVOCATEUR

ALEX COX

Oldcastle Books

First published in 2013 by
Oldcastle Books Ltd, PO Box 394,
Harpenden, Herts, AL5 1XJ, UK

Oldcastlebooks.co.uk
@OldcastleBooks

Editor: Laura Smith

A CIP catalogue record for this book is available from the British Library.

ISBN
978-1-84243-941-8 (print)
978-1-84243-942-5 (epub)
978-1-84243-943-2 (kindle)
978-1-84243-944-9 (pdf)

2 4 6 8 10 9 7 5 3 1

Typeset by Elsa Mathern, in Ionic 8.5pt
Printed in Great Britain by Clays Ltd, St Ives plc

This is dedicated to Mark Lane

CONTENTS

ST. CECILIA'S DAY

★　★　★　★　★　★　★　★　★

"The memory carried him to another: how, when he had traveled in the big cities and the crowds had lined the sidewalks, and overspilled into the roads, he could look up to the windows of the office buildings and there, above the cheering street mobs, see the white-collared executives staring down at him. And in city after city, as if by common instinct, they were all giving him the universal bent-arm, clenched-fist gesture of contempt and formally forming on the lips a curse that he could read above the shouting."

—Theodore H. White, *The Making of the President* 1960

"Kenneth O'Donnell, friend and associate of President Kennedy, [said] on the morning of November 22, 1963... the President remarked to him and Mrs. Kennedy that 'If anybody really wanted to shoot the President of the United States, it was not a very difficult job—all one had to do was get on a high building some day with a telescopic rifle, and there was nothing anybody could do to defend against such an attempt.'"

—Anthony Lewis, *On The Release of the Warren Commission Report*

The story which follows takes place in the mid-twentieth century.

While some of these events remain vivid to people still alive, for most of us, these are old, somewhat legendary occurrences, subject to controversy, which happened a long time ago.

I was eight years old when President Kennedy and Lee Harvey Oswald were murdered. I'd only the vaguest idea of America as the place where comic books came from. We did not live in a media-rich environment in 1963. My parents read a right-wing national paper, the *Daily Mail*, and our local rag, the *Liverpool Echo*, which contained one American comic strip, *Flash Gordon*. There was no such thing as 24-hour TV, no Internet, no cable, no satellite broadcasting. Instead there were two TV channels, broadcasting in black and white for about six hours a day. There were some "schools broadcasts" in the afternoon, but otherwise TV kicked off around 5 p.m., and shut down well before midnight. Nevertheless, what happened on November 22, 1963 was singularly strange. My family was gathered in the front room, to watch a popular comedian, Harry Worth, in his scheduled weekly show. Instead, the news of the president's murder was announced, and then... the broadcast ceased.

This was before the days of "rolling news" but the assassination of John Kennedy was a live, breaking news story of enormous importance: perhaps the most important piece of news since the end of the Second World War. For the BBC to go off the air in this way seemed strange. This President Kennedy was apparently an important man, his murder a matter of significance. So why were we staring at a black screen?

BBC television stayed off the air for several hours. The next day, the news was that a suspect had been arrested. The day after that, we learned the suspect had been killed in custody. The new president, in whose home state Kennedy had been assassinated, set up a blue-ribbon panel to investigate the murder. The panel, named the Warren Commission after its chairman, the chief justice, declared that Lee Harvey Oswald was the murderer, and that he had acted alone.

So that was that. What I didn't know at the time (because these things were never mentioned by the BBC, or the *Daily Mail*, or the *Liverpool Echo*) was that a number of prominent figures in England were skeptical about this "official" story. Britain's most eminent philosopher, Bertrand Russell, her most famous historian, Hugh Trevor-Roper, the politician Michael Foot, the publishers Victor

Gollancz and John Calder, the authors J.B. Priestley and Compton Mackenzie, and the film director Tony Richardson—among others—set up a *Who Killed Kennedy Committee*. It was ignored by the media; nothing came of it. Looking back on my childhood, I think there must have been a statewide effort to purge the presence of Russell—an atheist, a pacifist, and a freethinker—from the national mind. Religion was enforced within the English school system, and while at grammar school I read his *History of Western Philosophy*; but I had no idea that Russell was also the author of an excellent pamphlet entitled *Why I Am Not A Christian*. And I certainly didn't know that he and other eminent Britons had challenged the "official" version of the Kennedy murder.

Around the age of 15, I encountered in a bookshop a "Jackdaw" about the assassination.[1] Jackdaws were pretty cool aids to education. They were folders containing reproductions of historical documents: for example, the one on the English Civil War containing writings by Cromwell and the death sentence of the King. Unusually, this Jackdaw was full of contemporary material.

It was put together by the author Len Deighton, based on Mark Lane's best-selling book *Rush to Judgment*. It contained the WANTED FOR TREASON handbill distributed prior to the president's murder, a selection of autopsy photographs, and—most wonderful of all—a cardboard model of Dealey Plaza, where the assassination had occurred. Once you had constructed the little cardboard buildings—the Texas School Book Depository, the Dal-Tex Building, and the County Records Office—you could with strands of cotton plot the trajectories of the hail of bullets which killed the president and wounded the Governor of Texas. Your attention was naturally drawn to the railroad overpass, which offered limitless scope to a concealed assassin, and to the celebrated Grassy Knoll.

(Though we didn't know it at the time, the American Embassy in London, disturbed by Hugh Trevor-Roper's involvement in the *Who Killed Kennedy Committee*, asked FBI director J. Edgar Hoover to respond to an article the historian had written. Hoover refused, so the Embassy arranged for a "friendly press source"—John Sparrow, later Warden of All Souls' College, Oxford—to write an article defending Hoover and the Warren Commission. Airtels from 'Legat, London' to the FBI director give the impression that the American Embassy was *running* Sparrow. When Mark Lane challenged him to a debate in

London, "Embassy officials talked with SPARROW, and SPARROW then decided that he would not participate in such a debate as it would only lend dignity to LANE's position." Dignity, indeed.)[2]

An incipient conspiracy theorist, I read *Rush to Judgment*, an impressive work of investigatory scholarship which derailed the Warren Report. Over the next forty years I spent a lot of time learning about the subject. I subscribed to journals, including *The Third Decade*, *The Fourth Decade*, *The Grassy Knoll Gazette*, and *Probe*. I studied the *Forgive My Grief* trilogy of Penn Jones, a Texas newspaper editor who refused to let the "official version" stand. I read pretty much every book I could lay my hands on, including Thomas Buchanan's *Who Killed Kennedy?* (which predates *Rush to Judgment* and seems to have been based on foreign intelligence reports) and *Farewell America*, a pseudonymous text, allegedly created by French intelligence, which pins the murder on Texas oil men. I read the Gemstone File, a photostat which claimed Onassis was behind the murder. I read books which said the Mafia did it. I read books about Jim Garrison's investigation (including Garrison's *Heritage of Stone* and *On the Trail of the Assassins*) which said a gay CIA man in New Orleans did it. I read books which pinned the murder on the CIA (*Rush to Judgment* is the first of these, and Mark Lane never wavered on that issue) and books which catalogued Oswald's numerous intelligence connections—Philip Melanson's *Spy Saga* and John Newman's *Oswald and the CIA*. I read books by Michael Eddowes and Edward Jay Epstein which claimed Oswald was a Russian secret agent (there's a variant on this theme which claims Oswald was *replaced* by a Russian agent—see R.B. Cutler's *Alias Oswald*). I read books which supported the Warren Report and claimed Oswald acted alone: Gerald Posner's *Case Closed* relied on interviews which did not take place and bogus physics, and was enthusiastically received by the mainstream press. Vincent Bugliosi's massive *Reclaiming History* was a prosecutor's brief which ignored all the evidence which didn't fit the prosecution's case. I read Carl Oglesby's *Yankee and Cowboy War*, which saw the assassination and the events of Watergate as a struggle for national domination between old-money, East-Coast interests and the new oil/military money of the sunbelt. I read the Torbitt Document, which is some kind of disinformation claiming a Nazi cabal within NASA killed the president. I read the detailed and poetic works of Peter Dale Scott, who persuasively interprets the Kennedy murder as a form of elite system maintenance, in which the financial ambitions of the oligarchy and its proxies in the foreign policy establishment are constantly "adjusting" things so as to keep their show on the road.

A number of the later books point to the "military/industrial" establishment as the culprit. The best of these are James W. Douglass' *JFK and the Unspeakable*—a passionate book which also deals with Kennedy's and Khrushchev's efforts to reach a nuclear arms agreement—and *Brothers* by David Talbot. Both are fine books, but I can't forget what Mark Lane said to me regarding the movie *JFK*: "We have concrete evidence of CIA involvement. They are abandoning it in favor of vague finger-pointing at the military-industrial complex. How does that help solve the case?"

Lane—the attorney who represented Marguerite Oswald before the Warren Commission—concluded that the evidence in the Kennedy murder pointed to the CIA. Interviews conducted by Louisiana academic Michael L. Kurtz for his book *The JFK Assassination Debates* identify two CIA assets, Michael Jelisavcic and Hunter C. Leake, as Oswald's paymasters, in Minsk and New Orleans. The Agency provided photographic evidence that Oswald was being impersonated. And John Newman—an expert researcher with 20 years' experience in military intelligence—concluded that CIA was "spawning a web of deception about Oswald weeks before the president's murder."

Yet... would an intelligence agency, plotting a murder, implicate one of its own assets as the guilty party? It might if that agency were sufficiently compartmentalized, and secretive. Or else some *other* entity, plotting the same crime, might choose as its patsy someone with an "intelligence-rich" background. What of the most obvious beneficiary of the assassination, the incoming president, Lyndon Johnson? Within Texas, Johnson was long accused of being behind the murder. Books including Joachim Joesten's self-published *Case Against Lyndon B. Johnson*, and Glen Sample and Mark Collom's *Men on the Sixth Floor* make the case against LBJ. E. Howard Hunt's "death-bed" confession also pointed to Johnson. Nigel Turner's documentary *The Guilty Men*, screened on the History Channel in 2003, names LBJ's attorney, Edward Clark, as the intellectual author of the plot.

Now I too have written a book about the murder of the president. What does it add? What purpose does it serve? Some purpose, I hope, because John Kennedy wasn't the only victim in Dallas. A policeman died in mysterious circumstances the same day. And a bizarre young man, who claimed to be a communist but moved exclusively in right-wing circles, was murdered two days later, and found guilty of both killings, without a trial.

Bugliosi notwithstanding, no jury could have found Lee Harvey Oswald guilty. The only compelling evidence against him came from two sources: his own wife, held in the coercive custody of the U.S. government; and a couple of Dallas-based, intelligence-connected "friends." Had Oswald gone to trial, his wife could not have testified against him, and he would have walked free. A human life is a human life—whether it's the life of a wealthy president or an ascetic, spooky misfit, both are of equal value. So in this book I trace the parallel lives of two individuals, John Kennedy and Lee Oswald, whose lives were suddenly cut short that horrible weekend.

Who cares? the busy reader may enquire. These are events which happened a long time ago. Yet they are of immeasurable importance. When Jack Kennedy was assassinated, violence usurped democracy. The will of the electorate was rendered invalid, and the "election" of 1963 put Lyndon Johnson in the White House and embroiled America in the Vietnam War. Such a thing happened again in 2000, when the Supreme Court "elected" George W. Bush. Arguably that was a worse injustice, with even more disastrous consequences. But two wrongs don't make a right. And I suspect that the cavalier way in which the assassins got away with it enabled other assassinations to occur, and convinced the true holders of power that, one way or another, they could never lose.

In the background as these two men's stories unfold is worldwide military and economic struggle: the United States becoming the world's preeminent military power following the exhaustion of Britain and France, and the destruction of Japan and Germany.

The implosion of British and French colonial control created what an imperialist would view as vacuums. The United States rushed to fill them, and became an imperial power. From the mid-1940s to the late 1980s the U.S. confronted the Russians, who had acquired an empire of their own. At the time, the Russian empire was called the Union of Soviet Socialist Republics, or the USSR, or CCCP in Cyrillic, and the Russians who called themselves communists were also known as Soviets. Communism is mostly gone, now, yet the proxy confrontations, layers of distrust, and nuclear face-off between the Americans and the Russians continue. So I assume this period was just part of a long-term cold war between the giant American state and the giant Russian one. This still continues, and miraculously it has not yet killed us all.

Throughout this book I will simply refer to Russians as Russians, not as Soviets, and Russia as Russia, rather than its various acronyms; quotes may use the earlier forms. Regarding acronyms, I use HSCA to refer to the House Select Committee on Assassinations, which investigated two assassinations and concluded the killing of Jack Kennedy was by a conspiracy; ARRB to refer to the Assassination Records Review Board, which ordered the release of additional documents in 1998; HUAC to refer to the House Committee on Un-American Activities; NSRP to refer to the National States Rights Party; TSBD for the Texas School Book Depository; and FPCC for the Fair Play for Cuba Committee.

Certain abbreviations are more famous than others. I imagine the reader knows that the FBI is the Federal Bureau of Investigation (the U.S. domestic intelligence and national police agency), that the KKK is the Ku Klux Klan (a white racist organization), and that CIA is short for Christians In Action, or Cocaine Importers of America. Writers who really know their stuff don't use the definite article when referring to (the) CIA: I shall try and do likewise.[3]

I am entirely in the debt of all the writers and researchers who have gone before me. The research community is broad and deep, and I am grateful to them all. In particular, I would like to thank Mark Lane, Dick Russell, Jim Marrs, Gary Shaw, Tom Miller, Bob Cutler, Lisa Pease, Carl Oglesby, and Walter Bowart, for sharing their insights and vast accumulated knowledge, and Robin Ramsay, Tony Frewin and Simon Tams for reading this manuscript and giving me their thoughts.

As a filmmaker, I'm naturally drawn to the "visual effects" aspect of the assassination, and the manipulation of images to help create the lone-assassin legend. The photographic forgeries presented here, used at the time to support the "official" version of a leftist, loner, killer-malcontent, may seem crude today. But in 1964, these unsubtle photomontages helped to convict a dead man, who had no supporters, and who—had he enjoyed the luxury of a trial—would have walked free, for sure.

notes

1 Jackdaw no. 725—*The Assassination of President Kennedy*—was reissued in 2004 by Golden Owl Publishing, Amawalk, NY: ISBN 1-56695-263-3.

2 Anthony Frewin, *The Federal Bureau of Investigation's London File on The Assassination of President John F. Kennedy Calendared & Glossed*, Last Hurrah Press, Williamsport, PA, 1995, pp. 18–19.

3 A more complete list of acronyms, I hope helpful as the reader navigates this tome, is provided by Simon Tams as an appendix.

CHAPTER 1

JACK KENNEDY AND FAMILY

Early Exemplary History, Military and Political Career

★ ★ ★

John F. Kennedy was born on May 29, 1919. He was a second son, a child of good luck and bad. Good luck, because it is usually better to be born rich than poor. Bad luck, because he was a child of weak health, and unfortunate parents.

His mother, Rose, we would today describe as totally checked out. His father had a bad reputation, even among rapacious capitalists. Joseph Kennedy Sr.—banker, bootlegger, film producer, and political bagman—was spoiled, corrupt, narcissistic and cruel: a powerful father figure, and the worst possible role model.

Like many wealthy men, Joe Kennedy aspired to serve the public via a political career. From his own funds he bankrolled Franklin D. Roosevelt's campaign in 1932; he persuaded William Randolph Hearst, the newspaper baron, to back his candidate. Roosevelt won the presidency, but Joe failed to receive a cabinet post. He was generally disliked by people wealthier and more established than himself. Partially this was due to his character, his aggressive sexuality, and his unscrupulous ways, but there was another factor. The Kennedys were Roman Catholics, and, in a nation where the oldest, richest, most respected families were all Protestants, this was a black mark against them. The fact that they were of Irish ancestry was another problem, but that might have been dealt with: it was Catholicism that marked Joe and his clan as *the other*, in elite circles. Then, as now, the media took their cues from the one percent which owned them: and so, whenever a Kennedy aspired to public office, the newspapers would raise the issue of his religion as a serious obstacle to his candidacy—in the same way as Barack Obama's *blackness* had to be debated and decorously discounted by the media, before he might aspire to presidential heights.

Joe Kennedy failed to achieve a serious political career. FDR made him head of the Security and Exchange Commission, and let it be known that he was considering Joe as his vice president. But such musings were never serious. As the Second World War drew closer, Joe became increasingly enamored of Hitler. He was by no means alone in this. General Motors retained warm business relations with Nazi Germany till the bitter end, and Henry Ford wrote and published an anti-Semitic diatribe entitled *The International Jew*. But Ford and the gray executives of GM were establishment figures, Protestants. Their misdeeds, unlike the Kennedys', tended to be ignored. When elite interests—including members of the billionaire duPont family—attempted a *coup d'état* against FDR, the conspiracy was unmasked by a popular war hero, General Smedley Butler, yet the story barely made the newspapers.[1]

Then, as now, malfeasant millionaires might be newsworthy, but the beastliness of billionaires was rarely exposed. To reward his supporter and simultaneously keep him out of the way, President Roosevelt made Joe Kennedy his Ambassador to the Court of the English King.

Joe Kennedy's oldest sons, Joe Jr. and Jack, accompanied him on the sea voyage to London. There, Joe Sr. associated with the pro-fascist faction of the British aristocracy, while Jack toured Europe, Russia, and the Middle East. He returned to London on September 1, 1939—the day Germany invaded Poland, and Britain declared war. Jack flew back to the U.S. to continue his education; Joe Sr. remained in London, where he predicted a Nazi victory, not only over the U.K., but over the U.S. as well.

Lee Harvey Oswald was born at French Hospital, New Orleans, on October 18, 1939. His father had already died. Potentially of no account, Lee rapidly developed into a unique individual, displaying, from an early age, the ability to be in two places at once.

In 1940, Lee's mother, Marguerite Oswald, applied for Aid to Dependent Children, and Jack Kennedy completed his thesis at Harvard. Joe Kennedy, transferring his political energies to Joe Jr., resigned his Ambassadorial post and began running his oldest son's campaign for Congress. Left to his own devices, Jack might have pursued a career as a writer, or an academic—maybe even a journalist. But Joe Sr. kept a sharp eye and a tight rein on his kids. He encouraged Jack to publish his thesis, rewritten by a ghost, under a new title: *Why England Slept*. Joe got his friend Henry Luce, the publisher of *Time*, to release the book, and many copies were sold. Its title invited comparisons with Winston Churchill's book *While England Slept*. The invitation was not coincidental.

In 1941, Jack Kennedy volunteered for the U.S. Army. He was rejected, on account of chronic back problems, and turned down for health reasons by the Navy, too. His health was indeed terrible, with many chronic problems exacerbated by the use of steroids. But Joe, though opposed to war with Germany, pulled strings—and Jack was accepted by the Office of Naval Intelligence. Assigned to a desk job in Washington, DC, he found himself in competition with his father for the affections of a beautiful, Danish-born socialite/journalist, Inga Arvad. Arvad was also being watched by British Intelligence, who shared their information with the FBI. Ms. Arvad, the British said, was on excellent terms with high-ranking German Nazis: possibly she had slept with Hitler. J. Edgar Hoover, director of the FBI, liked to have the goods on up-and-coming journalists and politicians. By continuing his affair with Arvad, Kennedy handed Hoover his goods. In January, 1942, the journalist Walter Winchell publicized the affair.

The same month, Marguerite Oswald put her two older sons, John and Robert, in the care of the Bethlehem Orphans Asylum, in New Orleans. She attempted to give up baby Lee, as well—but he was rejected, being too young. On and off over the next year, Lee was cared for by his aunt, Lillian Murret. In December, 1942, Marguerite applied again to give Lee to an institution, and on the day after Christmas the lad joined his brothers in the Orphans Asylum. He was three years old.

The Navy moved its young ensign to South Carolina; Kennedy and Arvad relocated their affair to a hotel in Charleston, where they were surveilled and tape-recorded by the FBI. To put an end to the tryst, Joe Kennedy arranged for his son to see service abroad—first in Panama, and then in the Pacific. There, Jack made lieutenant, and was put in charge of a "PT" boat. These were small, light, maneuverable vessels, which many young officers were anxious to command. Jack managed the distinction of being rammed by a Japanese destroyer—the only time a PT boat was struck by an enemy vessel during the entire War. As his ship sank in flames, he demonstrated real heroism: rallying the survivors, and towing a badly burned crewmate several miles to shore, with the man's lifejacket strap clenched between his teeth. For this and other brave acts he received the Navy and Marine Corps medal.

Up to this point—August 2, 1943—it was possible to dismiss Jack Kennedy as a wealthy, womanizing party-boy. Allowing his fast little boat to collide with a Japanese warship was a mistake he should not have made, but Jack's selflessness and sense of responsibility, in the worst of circumstances, were indisputable. The incident showed that he was reckless, but also that he was calm under pressure and looked out for other people. There are worse qualifications.

Joe Sr. made sure the news of Jack's bravery was spread abroad. A laudatory article in the *New Yorker* was republished in the *Reader's Digest*, then reprinted as a pamphlet. Jack saw further action aboard PT boats, and won various other medals including the Purple Heart. But his experiences in the Pacific instilled in him a profound distrust of admirals and generals. Like many in the lower ranks, he thought Douglas MacArthur—the "American Caesar"—inept and uninterested in the welfare of his men; the admirals he met seemed vainglorious and ignorant. In reaching these conclusions, he made his first serious break with his father. Joe Sr., who had avoided military service and was always deferential to high-level brass. Jack, having volunteered, felt differently.

Marguerite Oswald, meanwhile, took Lee Harvey out of the Orphans Asylum, and moved to Dallas, Texas.

On June 13, 1944, the first flying bombs landed on London. They were called V-1s—Hitler's "Vengeance" weapons. This was new technology warfare: the doodlebugs were not artillery shells, but pilotless missiles, the ancestors of today's Predator and Reaper

Drones. They were the brainchild of the Nazi rocket genius Wernher von Braun.

The U.S. response was Project APHRODITE. Intended as a cruder form of "flying bomb," it entailed packing an American aircraft with high explosives, and flying it toward a target, with the crew bailing out before impact. The APHRODITE bomb was intended to reach its final destination as a "drone" guided by radio control from other U.S. planes. Army and Navy experiments with such tactics, using B-17 and B-24 aircraft, had ended in failure and the death of test pilots. Still, it was felt the German flying bombs demanded a response *in kind*.

Joe Kennedy, Jr., was a bomber pilot, overdue for leave. He had completed more B-24 combat missions than any other pilot, which qualified him both for a vacation and for an APHRODITE mission: a raid on one of the V-2 launch sites, in Mimoyecques, France. Joe Jr. chose the latter, and, despite bad weather, went ahead with it. His B-24, loaded with explosives, took off on August 12, 1944. The Americans turned off their radar so as not to detonate the bombs prematurely via radio waves; the British, unaware of the mission, tracked the aircraft with their ground-based radar. Twenty-five minutes into its flight, still over British soil, the B-24 exploded. Joe Jr., his copilot, and navigator were killed.

A month later, the first V-2 rocket bombs landed in London, causing great alarm. The V-2 was an even more fearsome weapon than the V-1: rocket-powered, traveling faster than the speed of sound, its explosion followed by a sonic boom. More than a thousand fell on England; still more were fired into Belgium. But von Braun's rocket bombs came too late, and were too few, to change the course of the War.

Posthumously, Joseph Kennedy, Jr. received the Navy Cross. His death left his younger brother with little choice as to his life's direction. In old Joe's eyes, Jack—his second son—was now the family's principal politician, and presidential candidate. Jack's health worsened, and he was discharged from the Navy early in 1945.

As the Nazi state collapsed, von Braun and his fellow rocketeers abandoned their slave camp at Dora, where the rocket bombs had been made. The rocket factory was running out of materials; it had also run out of food, and the slave laborers were starving faster than they could be hung. Von Braun, his brother Magnus, and other Nazi scientists evacuated themselves to a resort town on the

Austrian-German border. There, on May 2, 1945, they surrendered to the 44th U.S. Infantry Division, five days before the end of the European war. Von Braun acted like a celebrity and posed for photos with his captors, attracting the attention of Richard Porter, a U.S. intelligence operative. Porter was tasked to recruit former Nazi scientists in an operation which would come to be known as PAPER CLIP. Meanwhile, in another secret deal—Operation RUSTY— the Americans acquired the Nazis' secret police network and its spymaster, Reinhard Gehlen. Gehlen and six of his top aides were brought to Washington on August 24, and provided with a military butler and several white-jacketed orderlies.

Operation RUSTY remained top secret for many years. The acquisition of the rocket scientists, on the other hand, was something to boast about, and on October 1, 1945, the U.S. War Department's Bureau of Public Relations issued a press release:

OUTSTANDING GERMAN SCIENTISTS BEING BROUGHT TO U.S.

The Secretary of War has approved a project whereby certain outstanding German scientists and technicians are being brought to this country to ensure that we take full advantage of those significant developments which are deemed vital to our national security.

Interrogation and examination of documents, equipments and facilities in the aggregate are but one means of exploiting German progress in science and technology. In order that this country may benefit fully from this resource a number of carefully selected scientists and technologists are being brought to the United States on a voluntary basis. These individuals have been chosen from those fields where German progress is of significant importance to us and in which these specialists have played a dominant role.

Throughout their temporary stay in the United States these German scientists will be under the supervision of the War Department but will be utilized for appropriate military projects of the Army and Navy.

Among the "carefully selected scientists" were von Braun and over 120 colleagues, many of them veteran organizers of slave labor camps.

Technically prisoners of war, they were comfortably housed at Fort Bliss, Texas. By April, 1946, the German scientists were participating in V-2 launches at White Sands, New Mexico, and planning U.S. rocket development with representatives of General Electric.

Back home, Jack Kennedy suffered from bouts of malaria, and a stomach ulcer; on a trip to London, he collapsed and was diagnosed with Addison's disease. He was clearly in need of rest. No matter: Joe Sr. had his son's Congressional campaign already planned. He leaned on one of his cronies, U.S. Representative James Michael Curley, to vacate his seat. Curley, under investigation for corruption, was happy to run instead for mayor of Boston. Old Joe ran Jack's bid to replace Curley in the Democratic primaries which followed; he was both Jack's campaign manager and his financier. The scheme infuriated some: the *East Boston Leader* characterized Jack's candidacy as "Congress Seat for Sale—No Experience Necessary—Only Millionaires Need Apply." But the district was overwhelmingly Democratic, and the young war hero won with 71.9 percent of the vote. On November 12 Jack filed a report with the Massachusetts secretary of state certifying that *no money* had been collected for, or spent on, his campaign. According to Democratic veteran Tip O'Neill, Joe Sr. had spent $300,000 to win the election, a "staggering sum" for a 1946 congressional campaign.

Lee Harvey Oswald spent the summer of 1946 at Covington, Louisiana, and began school there in the fall. The following year, Marguerite Oswald returned to Texas, and Lee attended first grade in Fort Worth. In Washington, President Truman asked Congress to approve the creation of an international intelligence-gathering bureaucracy, to be called the Central Intelligence Agency. Representative Kennedy was absent for the vote which authorized the creation of CIA, in 1947, but voted in favor of a bill funding the Agency the following year.

Frank Wisner, a Wall Street lawyer who had conducted negotiations with Reinhard Gehlen, was quickly made director of the Office of Policy Coordination, CIA's espionage and counterintelligence branch. Wisner set into motion Operation MOCKINGBIRD, a program designed to influence domestic American media, and picked Philip Graham, publisher of the *Washington Post*, to help him run it. CIA soon "owned" reporters at the *New York Times*, *Newsweek*, and CBS. Among the journalists the Agency co-opted were Joseph Alsop, Ben

Bradlee, C.D. Jackson, and Walter Pincus. News directors and publishers became part of the program, including William Paley of CBS, Henry Luce of *Time* and *Life* magazines, Arthur Hays Sulzberger of the *Times*, and Joseph Harrison of the *Christian Science Monitor*. "You could get a journalist cheaper than a good call girl," another CIA man recalled, "for a couple of hundred dollars a month." MOCKINGBIRD's media agents helped, when asked, to play up the Russian threat, or to promote the urgent need for new, intercontinental ballistic missiles, based on Wernher von Braun's designs.[2]

Mining this vein, Reinhard Gehlen tried in 1948 to convince his new employers that the Russians were about to launch a war against the West, and that the U.S. should preempt it using its atomic weapons. Though he won the support of General Lucius Clay, the U.S. commander in Germany, and of Truman's secretary of defense, James Forrestal, who also favored a "preemptive" nuclear strike, Gehlen's counsel was apparently distrusted. Nevertheless Wisner and CIA continued to rely on his intelligence, spending some $200 million and employing 4,000 people full-time to resurrect Gehlen's Nazi intelligence Org.[3]

The following year, Forrestal suffered a mental breakdown and committed suicide at Bethesda Naval Hospital. The North Atlantic Treaty Organization (NATO), a Gehlen-inspired grand alliance against Russia, was created by the Americans. West Germany and Britain would prove enthusiastic, nuclear-equipped junior partners. France would soon leave. Spain, still a fascist country, was not allowed to join.

In 1950 an American General, Dwight D. Eisenhower, was given the modest title of Supreme Commander, NATO, and put in charge of its offices in Paris. The same year von Braun's group took up residence at the Army's Redstone Arsenal in Huntsville, Alabama. Located in the heart of the unreconstructed, racist South, this was the new home of the Army Ballistic Missile Agency—and the group's first assignment was designing and developing nuclear-tipped Redstone and Jupiter missiles. Later the facility would be renamed the George C. Marshall Space Flight Center.[4]

The name change is instructive. All the Nazi rocketeers claimed their primary interest was in space travel, and in von Braun's case it was probably true. The intercontinental ballistic missiles (ICBMs) which they designed were *dual-use* technology: the same massive multistage rockets could send a man to the Moon, or a hydrogen bomb to Moscow. It was Gehlen and his American supporters who advocated nuclear war. Von Braun's preference, all things being equal, was for space exploration. But, as Tom Lehrer later put it,

"Once the rockets go up, who knows where they come down?
That's not my department, says Wernher von Braun."

Though liberal on domestic issues, Representative Jack Kennedy established himself as a hawk in foreign affairs. He spoke out against communism and called Russia "a slave state of the worst sort... embarked upon a program of world aggression." 1950 saw him vote in favor of the McCarran Act, which required the registration of communists, and their arrest and internment in the event of a national emergency. President Truman vetoed the legislation, but Kennedy had nothing to lose from an increasingly strident anticommunist crusade. In the late '40s and early '50s, every aspiring politician was an anticommunist, just as up-and-coming pols must condemn Muslim extremism today. A poll taken in 1949 revealed that 83 percent of Americans favored the registration of communists; 80 percent believed that union leaders should be required to sign loyalty oaths. The Korean War, a domestic matter which concerned the two halves of a divided country, became pressing American business. Did the U.S. go to war to promote the anticommunist cause? Or did the cause drive America? From June 1950 until July 1953, U.S. troops were poured into a maelstrom involving far greater numbers of Koreans and Chinese, and were killed more or less proportionately, while U.S. air power burned the country to the ground.

In this new climate, Americans got into serious trouble for visiting Russia, or associating with communists. An example was made of the black actor and civil rights activist Paul Robeson. Robeson was denied a passport by the State Department: he and his lawyers were told that "his frequent criticism of... the United States should not be aired in foreign countries." Unable to travel abroad, Robeson was blacklisted at home. His health suffered, but he remained resolute in his beliefs. Others were made of more flexible stuff. Representative Kennedy fell in with Joe McCarthy, the Republican senator from Wisconsin, a friend of his father's. McCarthy claimed that the State Department had been infiltrated by homosexual communists. He tended to be vague about names, and inconsistent as to numbers. But his bourbon-fueled protests were in tune with the times: Jack praised McCarthy for his energy, intelligence and patriotism, while younger brother Bobby went to work for the House Committee on Un-American Activities, investigating European shipping lines for supplying weapons to China and North Korea.

This was the atmosphere which inspired Arthur Miller's play about witch-hunts, *The Crucible*. In '50s America, as in Puritan New England, innocent people were ruined, while "guilty" ones turned informer and wrecked more innocent lives. Older politicians professed to be disturbed by the witch-hunt; younger pols—Jack Kennedy and Richard Nixon, among them—took to it like fish to water, and, for a while at least, swam by its rules.

At the same time, Jack Kennedy embraced new, Congressional opportunities for foreign travel, revisiting Europe, then traveling to Israel, Iran, Pakistan, India, Japan, and an area still known as "French" Indochina: Vietnam.

In 1951, the Russians began sending their captured German scientists home. As a point of pride, they had decided to build their rockets without Nazi assistance. As the war in North Korea swung in favor of the communists, President Truman authorized the use of nuclear weapons by the U.S. military—just as he had against Japan. But the nukes were not, ultimately, deemed necessary: when every town and city had been napalmed, there was almost nothing left to destroy.[5]

Joe Kennedy, meanwhile, decided his son was ready for the Senate. This was a natural stepping-stone to a presidential bid. It was also a bold move for the Kennedys: for the first time, the clan would be pitting itself against one of the old-money, long-established families of the United States. For Joe had set his and Jack's eyes on the Senate seat of Henry Cabot Lodge, an American oligarch with presidential aspirations of his own.

Spring of 1952 saw a Texas oil millionaire, Sid Richardson, fly to Paris to visit General Eisenhower. He brought with him a letter from another Dallas oil man, Clint Murchison Sr. Richardson and Murchison both urged Eisenhower to run for president, as a candidate for either party. The oil men detested Truman for vetoing legislation which favored their business, and for opposing big oil's exceptionally generous "depletion allowance." Fearing the liberal Adlai Stevenson might otherwise win the nomination, Murchison asked Eisenhower to run as a Democrat. Later that year Eisenhower spent ten days at Murchison's Hotel Del Charro in La Jolla, California. When he agreed to run for president—as a Republican—the oil men invested heavily in a "Draft Eisenhower" movement.[6]

(The "Draft Eisenhower" campaign is an early example of what we now call *astroturf*: a fake grassroots movement funded with serious money, usually in secret, by big-business interests. An earlier instance of such a false-front operation was the American Liberty League, funded by the duPonts, Morgans, Pews, and Rockefellers, to oppose FDR's policies and the New Deal. The League went further than its sponsors intended, fragmenting into a dangerous constellation of smaller, violent groups.)

In the run-up to the election, Joe Kennedy again ran and paid for his boy's show. Jack had asked Mark Dalton, the nominal head of his 1946 campaign, to be his campaign manager; Joe Sr. fired Dalton, hiring Jack's younger brother, Bobby, as his replacement. The family worked hard, Jack campaigned hard, and the Kennedys outspent the Lodges. Jack won a narrow victory—still an impressive one, given the previous Republican majority—at a cost, to Joe, of several million dollars. The same election saw Eisenhower, who had run as a Republican, elected president. Election day also saw the creation, by order of Harry Truman, of the National Security Agency—a secretive government agency, run by the military, and charged with a task which CIA had so far flubbed: signals intelligence. Within a few years NSA would have a larger budget than any other intelligence agency, CIA included, and would be undertaking active operations of its own.

As a Senator, Jack Kennedy focused on foreign policy. He railed against the Russians and criticized the French for their response to nationalist insurgencies in Cambodia, Laos, and Vietnam. His biographer, Robert Dallek, wrote: "he spoke to them [the French] in the belief that America's financial stake in the fighting, which was at 40 percent and rising, entitled the United States to recommend changes that held out greater hope of success than the stumbling French policy."

The Korean War "officially" ended in July 1953, with an armistice which confirmed a stalemate, based around the original, disputed border.[7] In September, Jack Kennedy married Jackie Lee Bouvier, a beautiful socialite. The following year, irritated by McCarthy's attacks on the military, Eisenhower demanded hearings into his activities. Live television coverage of his Army hearings spotlit the drunken Senator, who quickly fell from grace. A special Senate committee recommended that he be "condemned" for breaking Senate rules and abusing an Army general. The Senate voted—along party lines—to condemn McCarthy, and Jack Kennedy was the only Democrat not to vote. His supporters have rationalized this failure in two ways: his father's influence, and McCarthy's popularity with Catholic voters. But it reflected badly on Jack.

As McCarthy's career declined, two of his friends, Sid Richardson and Clint Murchison, invited him to spend more time at their expanding resort, where Eisenhower had recently stayed. The oil men were in the process of buying a racetrack, the Del Mar Turf Club, adjacent to the Hotel Del Charro. The track owners were at first reluctant to sell, until the FBI started leaning on them to move. FBI director Hoover was a good friend of the oil men, and of the disgraced Senator, and to make things right and tight, the Texans announced to the press that they were buying the track for charity. Henceforth, all the Turf Club's profits would go to a tax-free foundation called Boys, Inc., whose goals were to "instill virtue in boys and fight juvenile delinquency." J. Edgar Hoover and John Connally, Richardson's lawyer, were made directors of the charity.[8]

Over the years, the Hotel Del Charro and the track at Del Mar would provide hospitality to politicians, lawmakers, movie stars, and *mafiosi* of the highest repute. Its impact on delinquency and the virtue of boys is less clear. The same year—1954—Texas Governor Allan Shivers tried to enact a state law making membership of the Communist Party a crime punishable by death. Despite the oil men's backing, the law was not passed.

In 1955, Wernher von Braun and his colleagues became U.S. citizens in a mass ceremony. Jack Kennedy's health worsened. Severe back pain sometimes hospitalized him; he also suffered from chronic abscesses, colitis, arthritis, abdominal cramps, muscle spasms, dehydration, urinary tract infections, and diarrhea. During one of several convalescences, he published a book, *Profiles In Courage*. The book depicted eight occasions on which U.S. Senators, not unlike himself, had performed nobly. It became a national best-seller and won the 1956 Pulitzer Prize, raising Jack's own profile still higher, before backfiring in a squabble over its authorship. It was widely believed that Kennedy had employed a ghostwriter, probably his gifted aide Ted Sorensen. But when columnist Drew Pearson said so publicly, Kennedy hired a Washington attorney, Clark Clifford, to demand a retraction. Pearson complied. The same year, Jack failed to secure the vice presidential place on Adlai Stevenson's democratic ticket; this worked in his favor when Eisenhower won a second term.

Robert Kennedy, serving as counsel for a Senate subcommittee, opened an investigation into labor racketeering. When this focused on the Teamsters Union, Joe Kennedy was alarmed. Old-style democrats like Joe counted on the support of labor unions at election time (though the Teamsters were unique, being the only significant union to support the Republicans). But Jack sided with Bobby, and became a member of the subcommittee. Politically, he was positioning himself on the right wing of the Democratic Party—while staying in the public eye. He won reelection to the Senate with little difficulty, at a cost to his father of 1.5 million dollars. Meanwhile, the U.S. Air Force approached Dr. Leonard Reiffel, of the military-backed Armor Research Foundation in Chicago, with a novel proposal: to fire one of von Braun's ICBMs at the Moon. The idea, they explained, was to explode a hydrogen bomb there.

"It was clear the main aim of the proposed detonation was a PR exercise and a show of one-upmanship. The Air Force wanted a mushroom cloud so large it would be visible on earth," Reiffel later said. "The explosion would obviously be best on the dark side of the Moon, and the theory was that if the bomb exploded on the edge of the Moon, the mushroom cloud would be illuminated by the sun."[9]

Dr. Reiffel protested that the H-bomb blast would destroy the pristine Lunar environment: a disaster for scientists. "But the USAF were mainly concerned about how the nuclear explosion would play on earth." Reiffel investigated the possibilities of such an explosion via a top secret project, A119: A Study of Lunar Research Flights. (Carl Sagan was one of the scientists involved in mathematical modeling of the dust cloud, and the insane plan—never implemented—was revealed by one of his biographers in 2000.)

September 1957 saw white riots in Little Rock, Arkansas. The state governor, Orval Faubus, facing a tough re-election fight, had donned the mantle of white supremacy, and defied a federal court order to integrate the Central High School. Faubus called out the National Guard to keep nine black children from attending classes; emboldened whites attacked a group of black journalists and threatened to lynch the children. Eisenhower, in one of his most decisive acts as president, sent in the troops. Even though his Attorney General advised using federal marshals rather than the military, Eisenhower was adamant. On September 25, two weeks after the president had signed a Civil Rights Act, a convoy of 26 Army vehicles rolled into Little Rock to support it. Faubus fumed, but the school was integrated. Commander of the Arkansas Military District, in charge of the integration action, was General Edwin A. Walker.

The appearance of extreme right-wing groups around this time is often ascribed to a fear of communism. No doubt the Korean War, with its multiple horrors and deaths, contributed to that fear. But for most Americans, anticommunism was still an abstraction. Who knew a communist? One thinks of the postwar United States as a prosperous place, and for many people it was. But there were also a lot of poor whites, and many poor minorities, and in areas where jobs were few, it was easy to play the race card. So 1958 saw the birth not only of the John Birch Society, but also the formation of the National States Rights Party. The John Birch Society was another "astroturf" movement, opposing communism and civil rights, funded by business interests. Among these were a candy magnate, Robert Welch, and a Texas oil man, Fred Koch. Koch's children would later become famous for financing the right-wing "Tea Party" movement against President Obama. The focus of the Birchers was not overtly racist: they opposed civil rights because the movement was infiltrated by communists; they opposed the United Nations because it was infiltrated by communists; and so on. The NSRP, brainchild of a former American Nazi, Edward Fields, was explicitly white-supremacist. Founded in Knoxville, Tennessee, in July 1958, it moved its headquarters between various southern cities including Birmingham, Alabama, and Savannah, Georgia. Members wore a uniform consisting of a white shirt, black tie, Sam Browne belt, "NSRP pin centered above the pocket on the right side" and an armband depicting the party emblem, a thunderbolt superimposed over the Confederate flag.

Present at the NSRP's birth was a right-wing military man, Captain John G. Crommelin, who had been forced to resign from the Navy in 1950, after briefing journalists against the unification of the armed forces. Some other NSRP founders had bombed a black church in Birmingham the previous month: among them, one Jesse Benjamin Stoner, who would shortly become the group's legal counsel (Stoner was arrested for the bombing in 1977, and convicted in 1980). Five NSRP members were arrested after the bombing of an Atlanta synagogue in October 1958; three would be tried twice, but acquitted. Two of the accused were associates of Admiral Crommelin, who paid the costs of their defense.[10]

The NSRP would soon claim to be the third-largest political party in the United States, with as many as 100,000 members. It also claimed a mailing list of 2,500 names, and a print run of 15,000 copies for its tabloid newspaper, *The Thunderbolt*. An FBI monograph, dated August 1966, estimated the actual membership at less than 100. One of the benefits of membership, according to a membership form reproduced by the FBI, was "Legal protection: NSRP furnishes legal aid to any member persecuted [sic] in the line of authorized Party duty, anywhere in America. We are the only right-wing organization to offer such a plan."[11]

This may sound ludicrous, but the FBI took the NSRP seriously— perhaps because its leaders identified J. Edgar Hoover's police force as a prime adversary. "The NSRP has consistently and pointedly advocated a policy of force and violence," the monograph reported. "Spokesmen for the NSRP have made numerous inflammatory statements which could incite some listener to precipitate an act of violence. Its publications have regularly advised their readers to obtain rifles..."[12]

In October 1958, President Eisenhower created the National Aeronautics and Space Administration—NASA—a separate agency to compete with the Russians in space. But he was not keen on von Braun's proposal to send Americans to the Moon and Mars. Still, von Braun promoted his plans—and himself—relentlessly. He appeared on the cover of *Life* and was *Time*'s "Man of the Year." He made three television shows for Walt Disney, promoting the conquest of space.

In June 1959 a reporter named Fletcher Knebel broke the news that Jack Kennedy had Addison's disease; Knebel claimed to be publishing it in response to "a whispering campaign aimed at discrediting Senator Kennedy as a presidential candidate." The Kennedys denied the story outright. In truth or in lies, in sickness or in health, all eyes were focused on the 1960 presidential election, where the Republicans' candidate would be the vice president, Richard Nixon—frequent visitor to the Hotel Del Charro, and friend of the Texas oil fraternity. In October, President Eisenhower promoted Edwin Walker to the rank of Major General, and made him commander of the Twenty-Fourth Infantry Division—the "Screaming Eagles"—in Germany.

notes

1   Jules Archer, *The Plot to Seize The White House*, Hawthorne Books, NY, 1973; Clayton E. Cramer, "An American Coup d'État?", *History Today*, Nov. 1995.
2   Carl Bernstein, "The CIA and The Media," *Rolling Stone*, Oct. 20, 1977; Deborah Davis, *Katherine The Great*, Sheridan Square Press, New York, 1991, pp. 129–131, Lisa Pease, "The Media and The Assassination", *The Assassinations*, pp. 301–303; Alex Constantine, "OPERATION MOCKINGBIRD: The CIA and the Media", *Prevailing Winds Magazine*, No. 3, pp. 17–23.
3   Christopher Simpson, *Blowback*, Collier, NY, 1988, pp. 42–53, 61.
4   Today the Von Braun Complex at Redstone Arsenal is one of the largest military facilities in the United States, home to the Missile Defense Agency and the Army Space and Missile Defense Command. Kenneth Kesner, "Is Huntsville Becoming A Pentagon of the South?", *Huntsville Times*, Jan. 1, 2012.
5   Bruce Cummings, *The Korean War: A History*, Modern Library, NY, 2010, pp. 156–157.
6   Anthony Summers, *The Secret Life of J. Edgar Hoover*, Simon & Shuster, 1993, pp. 205–7, Jane Wolfe, *The Murchisons*, St. Martin's Press, NY, 1989, pp. 194–6.
7   Cummings, *The Korean War*, p. 35.
8   Jane Wolfe, *The Murchisons*, St. Martin's Press, NY, 1989, p. 194.
9   Antony Barnett, "U.S. Planned One Big Nuclear Blast For All Mankind," *The Observer*, May 14. 2000.
10 Jerry D. Rose, "J.B. Stoner: An Introduction," *The Fourth Decade*, Vol. 3, No. 1, Nov 1995, pp. 25–29; "J.B. Stoner, White Supremacist, 81: Bombed Black Church," *Los Angeles Times* obituary, April 28, 2005. Clive Webb, *Rabble Rousers: The American Far Right in the Civil Rights Era*, University of Georgia Press, 2010, p. 127.
11 FBI monograph, *National States Rights Party*, August 1966, p. iv. The biography of Fields in this monograph contains an entire page of blacked-out material; the biography of Stoner is also redacted. One possible explanation for this is that the NSRP leaders were in close proximity to FBI informants/provocateurs, whose identities are concealed by the redactions. Another is that Fields was an FBI informant/provocateur himself.
12 FBI monograph, *National States Rights Party*, August 1966, p. iv.

CHAPTER 2

LEE HARVEY OSWALD AND FAMILY

His *Dubious* Youth, Military Service, and Defection

★ ★ ★

I have tried thus far to record these events chronologically. Now we must backtrack. The life of Lee Harvey Oswald, brief though it was, is so complex, and contradictory, that it demands unique attention. When Lee was 13—the year was 1952—his mother moved him from Texas to New York. She claimed this was so they could be close to John Pic, her oldest son from a previous marriage. But John told the Warren Commission that neither he nor Marguerite's other son, Robert, could stand her, and that they saw little of each other.

What teenage Lee got up to in New York is a mystery. The FBI would later claim he went to Trinity Evangelical School in the Bronx—many miles from his residence in Manhattan. But Trinity School has no record of his presence, and John Pic testified that Lee attended school a mere two blocks from his apartment. The Warren Commission records contradict themselves as to the number of days he attended school, his record as a truant, and his height. Only one photograph of Lee exists from his New York days: when John Pic saw it, he said it was not his brother.[1]

Meanwhile, a youth calling himself Harvey Oswald surfaced in North Dakota. Harvey claimed to hail from New York, to have traveled widely, and to have been a juvenile delinquent. William Timmer, of Stanley, ND, told the FBI he had been friends with the young Oswald, who on one occasion produced a pamphlet on Marxism, declaring "I'll bet you've never seen anything like this."

In 1964 several State Department officials told a Senate sub-committee investigator that Oswald had lived in North Dakota; Oswald himself told an American journalist, in 1959, that "we moved to North Dakota." The Warren Commission simply ignored these stories, preferring Marguerite's testimony that she and Lee remained in New York for one and a half years.[2]

(The critical reader may interject here, or later: *so what?* Just because some guy called Trimmer, or a State Department person whose name has been redacted, or even Lee Harvey Oswald himself, said he was in North Dakota, doesn't make it true. This is quite correct. I don't mean to assert that every claim reported in this book is accurate. What I am trying to do is to point out that the "historical" version of these events, enshrined by the Warren Commission, which mainstream media continue to promote, is an obvious fiction: riddled with similar contradictions and outright forgeries, prejudiced and selective in its choice of evidence, closing its eyes to the darker aspects of state and money power. If the truth matters, then all potential evidence must be considered.)

One exhibit of the Warren Commission shows 14-year-old Lee Harvey Oswald attending Junior High #44 in New York for 62 days in fall 1953. Another exhibit shows Lee Harvey Oswald attending Beauregard Junior High School in New Orleans for 89 days in fall 1953. One boy, even a remarkable boy, cannot be simultaneously in two places. So, which record is correct? Which one was Lee?

In 1954, in the playground at Beauregard, Lee Oswald got in a fight and had a tooth knocked out. A friend took a picture of him grinning toothlessly, and, years later, sold it to *Life* magazine, which published the picture. The body of Lee Oswald buried in Fort Worth has a full set of teeth. Which one was Lee?

John Armstrong has done an enormous amount of research into testimony regarding Oswald, his employment history, and the various "Oswald" sightings. His conclusion is that there were two boys using the name "Lee Harvey Oswald," one tall, one short, superficially similar in appearance, as part of a particularly bizarre, long-term intelligence operation.[3]

Armstrong points out that the Russian spy service recruited agents as young as nine to practice espionage abroad; there's no reason to assume "our" spooks might not do likewise. Armstrong's thesis is bolstered by John Newman's reporting of dual intelligence files on Oswald. But obsessive secrecy and duplicity could also explain the dual files. Was Lee Harvey Oswald a mysterious individual who, like a character from a Latin American novel, possessed the power to be in two places at once? Or was he invented/impersonated by others, for their own purposes?

Oswald either remained at Beauregard, or moved to Fort Worth, Texas, where he studied at Stripling Junior High. Again, the evidence says that he attended both schools, full-time, at the same time. In 1955 and 1956, according to the Warren Commission, Oswald held a series of jobs in New Orleans. But Armstrong points out that there is almost no hard evidence for any of these jobs: no employment applications, no canceled payroll checks, no monthly or quarterly tax statements, no FICA withholdings, no W-4s or W-2s. There *is* evidence that, on July 27, 1955, Oswald joined the Civil Air Patrol, a sort of air-based Boy Scouts, and purchased a cadet's uniform; his platoon leader was a local air ace, David Ferrie.[4]

The "official" version of Lee Oswald's history—the Warren Commission Report—tells us that as a teenager in New Orleans, he began to read communist literature, at the public library. According to the Report, the young Oswald would praise Russian president Nikita Khrushchev, and told a witness "that he would like to kill President Eisenhower because he was exploiting the working class." Several witnesses testified that Oswald lived and worked in New Orleans through 1957, and 1958.[5]

This testimony had to be discounted, since Lee Oswald—despite his communist leanings and murderous desires—joined the Marines in October, 1956. Shortly before enlisting, he mailed the following letter to the American Socialist Party:

Oct 3 1956

DEAR SIRS
I am sixteen years of age and would like more information about your youth league. I would like to know if there is a branch in

THE PRESIDENT AND THE PROVOCATEUR

my area, how to join, ect. [sic] I am a marxist, and have been
studying socialist principles for well over fifteen months. I am
very interested in your Y.P.S.L.
Sincerely,
Lee Oswald [6]

1957 saw an increase in international tensions, as the Russians began
testing their own ballistic missiles, and the CIA's top secret U-2
spy plane was tasked to monitor the tests. Flying at high altitude,
the U-2 was believed to be beyond the range of Soviet missiles or
aircraft. In April, CIA opened a top secret base for U-2 missions at
Atsugi, Japan.

In August 1957, having attended radar school in Biloxi, Mississippi,
Lee Oswald was shipped to Japan. He arrived at the Atsugi Naval
Air Station on September 12. Twenty-two days later, the Russians
fired off one of their dual-use rockets and launched the first man-
made satellite, *Sputnik*, into orbit around the earth. This was viewed
by the Americans as a crushing blow. When the first U.S. attempt
to launch a satellite failed, alarmists warned of a "missile gap"—a
theme seized upon by Gehlen and the German rocket scientists,
and developed by ambitious right-wing politicians, Jack Kennedy
among them. [7]

On October 27, Lee Oswald shot himself—slightly. The .22 bullet
merely grazed his left arm. His Marine buddies thought he was
trying to avoid being shipped to the Philippines. Lee's gun was a
two-shot, silver-plated Derringer which he claimed to have obtained
by mail order from the United States. It was illegal for enlisted men
to own private firearms, but Oswald got off lightly. He spent three
weeks recuperating in a U.S. Navy hospital in Japan, then returned
to his unit. He was 18 years old.

In November the Russians launched *Sputnik 2*, carrying a dog,
Laika, into space. Laika died on re-entry, no provision having been
made for her return alive. In the odd logic of scientists and the media,
this was viewed as a second great triumph for the communists,
rather than something cruel and insane. The same month, President
Eisenhower suffered a stroke, and received the report of the Gaither
Panel, entitled *Deterrence and Survival in the Nuclear Age*. This top
secret document warned of a missile gap which its authors claimed
would leave the U.S. defenseless against a Russian nuclear strike

within two years; they urged a massive military buildup, including an 800 percent increase in the number of American ICBMs, and "a nation-wide fallout shelter building program to protect the civilian population." Appendix A to the report contained the claim that a surprise attack against Russia would be successful, destroying the enemy's retaliatory capacity, *if carried out within the next two years.* Eisenhower, despite his weakened state, rejected this invitation to thermonuclear war. He was able to do so, in part, because photographic intelligence provided by U-2 flights showed that the Russians had very few ICBMs in service. The so-called "missile gap" did not exist.

H. Rowan Gaither fell ill while his report was being prepared, and rejoined the study as a member of its advisory panel. Another panel member was John J. McCloy, former High Commissioner for occupied Germany, now the head of the Chase Manhattan Bank and attorney to the Rockefellers. Enormous sums of money were at stake here, and McCloy's clients, Texas oil companies among them, would profit richly from a 25-billion-dollar shelter-construction program, and a massive military buildup. But would a sober, establishment figure like McCloy—the man who supervised the building of the Pentagon— really give the nod to a sneak nuclear attack? What if U.S. intelligence was wrong, and some of the Russian bombers escaped an American first strike? It was insanity to wink at such things, and one wonders if the Appendices to the report were added, by persons unknown, after McCloy and Gaither signed off on the main document.[8]

That the president had accurate information about Russian missile strength, and could act sanely as a result, was thanks to Detachment C (the CIA U-2 spy mission), its brave pilots, and its skilled technicians—including radar specialist Lee Harvey Oswald, Private (First Class), USMC. At Atsugi, the young Marine was plotting U-2 overflights of communist territory on a big map board, using a grease pencil.

Oswald's unit left Japan for the Philippines in late 1957. On the island of Corregidor he became a mess cook, supposedly serving lunch on one occasion to the movie actor John Wayne, and getting his picture taken over the Duke's shoulder.

(This photo first appeared in Edward J. Epstein's book *Legend: the Secret World of Lee Harvey Oswald*. As with many snapshots of Oswald, one wonders if it is genuine. The accused assassin of the president photographed lurking behind Hollywood's greatest super-

Fig. 1: John Wayne and Lee Harvey Oswald?

patriot? It seems like a case of photomontage, or mistaken identity. But Epstein considered it authentic.) Beyond Corregidor, serious business was at hand. President Eisenhower had authorized CIA chief Allen Dulles to topple the left-leaning Indonesian president, Sukarno. In support of this, the Marines were meant to take part in "maneuvers" off that country's coast. But when a CIA plane with an American pilot was shot down, the president changed his mind, and told Dulles to disengage. On April 11, Oswald was court-martialed for illegal possession of a firearm: his Derringer. On June 27, Lee was court-martialed again, for pouring a drink over the head of a non-commissioned officer in a bar: he was sentenced to the brig. On his release he went with his unit to Taiwan, then was redeployed to Atsugi. At the end of the year, he was sent back to the States, to the naval base at El Toro, California, where he began studying Russian, and failed a language test. His interest in communism was not extinguished.[9]

To be a communist in America was a lonely thing. Newly-minted John Birchers claimed that a communist takeover of the United States was imminent, but there was little outward sign of it. The

Birchers also insisted President Eisenhower was a communist agent. In response, Eisenhower's National Security Council directed the U.S. military to educate troops and the public about the dangers of communism. As a counsel for the McClellan Committee, Bobby Kennedy participated in the propaganda offensive.

Somehow, in this environment Private Oswald thrived. As he later told a journalist, while in the Marines he "indoctrinated himself" in Marxism. He played Russian records and subscribed to socialist periodicals. He expressed support for revolutionary Cuba, where leftists led by Fidel Castro had recently overthrown a dictator. Lee's Marine buddies started calling him "Oswaldkovich."

Like the snapshot of Lee Harvey Oswald with John Wayne, this "official version" seems incredible. In Japan, Oswald had been court-martialed twice, for shooting himself with an illegally owned gun and for drunkenly provoking an officer. Yet he kept his high-security clearance, and was sent to foreign-language school. At a time when communism was viewed as a serious threat, why did the Marine Corps permit Comrade "Oswaldkovich" to indulge in activities which were potentially treasonous?

The former CIA Clandestine Services specialist Victor Marchetti said in an interview, "In 1959, the United States was having real difficulty in acquiring information out of the Soviet Union; the technical systems had, of course, not developed to the point that they are at today, and we were resorting to all sorts of activities. One of these activities was an ONI [Office of Naval Intelligence] program which involved three dozen, maybe forty, young men who were made to appear disenchanted, poor American youths who had become turned off and wanted to see what communism was all about.

"Some of these people lasted only a few weeks. They were sent into the Soviet Union, or Eastern Europe, with the specific intention the Soviets would pick them up and 'double' them if they suspected them of being U.S. agents, or recruit them as KGB agents. They were trained at various naval installations both here and abroad, but the operation was being run out of Nag's Head, North Carolina."[10]

Oswald, based at a U.S. naval installation, studied up on communism. In January, 1959, Marguerite Oswald told her doctor "that her son wanted to defect to Russia." The same month, President Eisenhower presented Wernher von Braun with the Distinguished Federal Civilian Service Award. In February, the first Discoverer satellite was launched, in strictest secrecy, by von Braun's team. Discoverer was part of the CIA's "Corona" Program, a series of strategic reconnaissance satellites carrying 70mm film cameras, to provide photographic surveillance of Russia and China.

In March, Lee Oswald applied to Albert Schweitzer College, in Switzerland, "in order to broaden my knowledge of German." He didn't speak German, but his application was accepted. In August, Lee requested an early release from the Marines on compassionate grounds, claiming his mother had been injured at work. The ever-indulgent Marine Corps discharged him three months early.

In September 1959, the Russian premier, Nikita Khrushchev, visited New York and Washington. Security was tight. A fleet of motorcycles and black Secret Service Cadillacs surrounded the convertible limousine bearing the two presidents into Washington. Riflemen were stationed on rooftops along the route; police helicopters hovered overhead. At the Capitol, Khrushchev met Senator Richard Russell, head of the Armed Services Committee and a close friend of CIA chief Allen Dulles: "I know of no appropriations anywhere for any subversive work in Russia," Russell assured the Russian leader.

In the late 1950s and early 1960s, the Agency ran an operation code-named LCIMPROVE. This was defined as "Counter-espionage involving Soviet intelligence services worldwide." It apparently combined efforts to infiltrate spies into Russia with a mole-hunt for Russian spies at home. As such, it would have been the remit of CIA's James Jesus Angleton, an alcoholic, paranoid, devoted anticommunist. Given Angleton's distrust of his colleagues and of other agencies, there's no chance that LCIMPROVE and any ONI fake-defector program were connected. But what happened next suggests that an intelligence agency was steering the malcontent ex-Marine.

Withdrawing $203 from his bank account, Oswald embarked on a roundabout journey to Moscow—a passage costing, at that time, more than a thousand dollars. He traveled to New Orleans and stayed three nights in a hotel. He purchased his ticket from an agency in the International Trade Mart. He sailed on a freighter from New Orleans to Le Havre, France, on September 20. He arrived in France, and entered England, on October 9. He left the next day. There was no direct flight to Finland on October 10, yet Oswald registered at a hotel in Helsinki that night. When the Warren Commission attempted to reconstruct his itinerary on commercial flights via different cities, they were unable to do so. So how did Oswald get to Helsinki? And why did he go? Helsinki was in Finland; Oswald had applied to attend college in Switzerland; he had told his mother he intended to defect to Russia. Yet he had no Russian visa. Oswald could not possibly have known of the Helsinki CIA station chief's memo, dated August 28, reporting that the Russian consul in Helsinki would issue visas "immediately and without Moscow approval." Or could he? If Oswald was part of an intelligence scheme to penetrate Russia, his handlers would have sent him via Helsinki because it was the *only* place a visa-less American could gain entry. At other embassies and consulates, the wait was weeks, if not months. In Helsinki, Oswald requested a tourist visa on October 12, and received it on October 14. He showed up in Moscow the next day.[11]

In autumn of 1959, Joe Kennedy boasted to reporters: "Jack is the greatest attraction in the country today. I'll tell you how to sell more copies of a book. Put his picture on the cover. Why is it that when his picture is on the cover of *Life* or *Redbook* that they sell a record number of copies? You advertise that he will be at a dinner and you will break all records for attendance. He can draw more people to a fund-raising dinner than Cary Grant or Jimmy Stewart. Why is that? He has more universal appeal." Joe was right. His politician son was famous, popular and well-positioned for his next move. Lee Harvey Oswald, previously unknown, was about to become famous, too.

Oswald told his Moscow tourist guide, Rima Shirokova, that he was a communist, and wanted to defect. He waited in his room at the Hotel Berlin for meetings with the appropriate authorities. A stout, balding official visited him, told him that Russia "was great only in literature," and advised him to go home. Radio Moscow interviewed him. October 18 was Lee's twentieth birthday. Rima gave him a copy of Dostoyevsky's *The Idiot*. Clearly the Russians distrusted him, and on October 21 Oswald received the news that his visa had expired and he had two hours to pack and leave. In response, he attempted suicide—but, as in the Marines, his self-inflicted wound did not prove fatal. Rima had him taken to a mental hospital, where he was incognito for a week. He emerged on October 28, assisted by *la Shirokova*, and moved from the Hotel Berlin to the Hotel Metropole.

He entered the U.S. Embassy in Moscow on a cold Saturday morning. It was Halloween. Oswald had no hat, no coat, yet wore white gloves, such as a dandy might take to the opera. Were they his dress gloves from the Marine Corps? He announced to a secretary that he wanted to renounce his citizenship; she passed him to the American consul, Richard Snyder. Oswald told Snyder the same thing: he wished to renounce his citizenship and give up his passport. Snyder thought Oswald had memorized his speech and started probing him. Oswald replied, "I was warned you would try to talk me out of defecting." Warned by whom? His words pointed to partners in his defection plan. According to Snyder's contemporary account, Oswald then declared his intention to betray the United States with an act of high-tech treason:

> "Oswald offered the information that he had been a radar operator in the Marine Corps and that he had voluntarily stated to unnamed Soviet officials that as a Soviet citizen he would make known to them such information concerning the Marine Corps and his specialty as he possessed. He intimated that he might know something of special interest."[12]

If Lee hadn't been in trouble before, he was in trouble now. At the U.S. Embassy in Moscow, he had just stated his intention to renounce his citizenship and betray the Corps. He claimed he had already offered the Russians top secret information—presumably about U.S. radar and U-2 surveillance systems, his areas of specialty. Snyder's telex to the State Department, relating Oswald's threats, was copied to FBI, CIA, and ONI; simultaneously the Naval Attaché in Moscow cabled the commander of Naval Operations in Washington. CIA and ONI opened files on him—assuming such files were not already open. Consul Snyder wondered, in an interview with John Newman, why Oswald had volunteered the information that he intended to become a traitor: was it because he thought the U.S. Embassy might be bugged, with Russian intelligence listening in, and drawing conclusions based on his performance?

Two weeks earlier, another American and former Navy man, Robert Webster, had defected in Snyder's office. Webster's case was even stranger than Oswald's: a high-tech plastics specialist, he was accompanied to the Embassy by his employers, Henry Rand and George Bookbinder—both former members of the OSS, and thus intelligence operatives themselves.[13]

According to Anthony Summers, in the 14 years prior to Webster's defection, only two Americans had defected to Russia; then, in a period of just 18 months, from 1959 to 1960, came a rash of defectors—including five Army men stationed in West Germany, two NSA specialists, a former Air Force major, and an ex-Marine named Oswald. The Russians were apt to be suspicious about so many pro-communist turncoats, and keen to keep the fake ones out.[14]

Newman treats Snyder as a career diplomat; his story rings true, although it may not be. Snyder, who insisted to FBI investigators and to Newman that he interviewed Oswald alone, was contradicted by another U.S. consul, John McVickar, who claimed to have been present throughout the interview. CIA documents show that Snyder joined the Agency as an employee in 1949; they record that he left the Agency in 1950, to work for the High Commissioner of Germany, John McCloy. Certainly the communists thought Snyder was a spy. *Who's Who in CIA*, a list of alleged U.S. intelligence operatives published in East Berlin in 1968, contains the following two entries:

Snyder, Richard E.
b.: 10.12.1919; L.: French, German, Japanese, Russian;
1940-46 Captain in G-2 of U.S. Army;
from 1950 in Department of State; from 1957 work for CIA;
    OpA: Frankfurt/Main, Munich, Kobe, Moscow, Nagoya,
    (Consul)

McVickar, John Anthony
b.: 22.5.1924; L.: Russian, Spanish;
1944-46 and 1951-52 in U.S. Navy;
from 1949 in Department of State; from 1966 work for CIA;
    OpA: New Delhi, Hongkong, Moscow, La Paz, Cochabamba,
    (Consul), Washington[15]

So it's possible that Snyder and McVickar were agents under diplomatic cover, and that they were handling Webster, Oswald and other false defectors. Either way, Snyder's drawing-out of Oswald during their interview led to a treasonous outburst which presumably enhanced the Marxist ex-Marine's potential value to the Russians. And Snyder did Oswald another favor, by refusing to let him sign his renunciation papers. The Embassy had closed at noon, the consul explained, and Oswald would have to return on a weekday if he really wanted to renounce his citizenship. Oswald acted furious, abandoned his passport, and marched out. Yet he did not return.

Snyder called the UPI bureau chief and suggested that he interview Oswald. Oswald refused to speak to him, but willingly opened the door of his Metropole Hotel room to a woman reporter, Aline Mosby. Among other things, Oswald told Mosby that he had lived in North Dakota. Her short article ran in the Fort Worth newspapers, and within hours his mother and brother were besieged by reporters. Marguerite and Robert tried to contact Lee in Russia, but he did not respond. Both Oswalds were living in Dallas, Texas, a city which did not look kindly upon communists, traitors, nor their relatives.

notes

1   John Armstrong, "Harvey & Lee: The Case for Two Oswalds," published in *The Assassinations*, Feral House, Los Angeles, 2003, pp. 94–97.

2   Armstrong, "Harvey & Lee," *The Assassinations*, pp. 97–99.

3   Armstrong, "Harvey & Lee," *The Assassinations*, pp. 91–92.

4   "Captain" Ferrie was viewed by some researchers as the "criminal mastermind" behind the assassination. Jim Garrison called him "one of the most important individuals in history." After fifty years of information and speculation, Ferrie seems more peripheral today: a possible getaway pilot, or a potential patsy. There is more about Ferrie and his New Orleans circle in Edward T. Haslam's *Mary, Ferrie & The Monkey Virus: the Story of an Underground Medical Laboratory*, Wordsworth, Albuquerque, NM, 1995.

5   Armstrong, "Harvey & Lee," *The Assassinations*, pp. 103–112.

6   Warren Commission Hearings & Exhibits (WH), Vol. 20, p. 25—Gray Exhibit No. 1.

7   Simpson, *Blowback*, note, p. 64.

8   *Deterrence and Survival in the Nuclear Age (The Gaither Report)*: Security Resources Panel of the Science Advisory Committee, Washington, Nov. 7 1975; David Lindsey Snead, *Eisenhower and the Gaither Report: The Influence of a Committee of Experts on National Security Policy in the Late 1950s*, Dept. of History, University of Virginia, 1997.

9   Edward J. Epstein, *Legend: the Secret World of Lee Harvey Oswald*, McGraw-Hill, 1978, opp. p. 192.

10 Anthony Summers, *Conspiracy*, McGraw-Hill, NY, 1980, pp. 173–175.

11 John Newman, *Oswald and The CIA*, Carroll & Graf, NY, 1995, pp. 3, 4, 155.

12 FSD-234, p. 2 (Consul Snyder's report to the State Department).

13 Gary Hill, "The Webby N'Ozzie Parallax," *The Fourth Decade*, Vol. 2, No. 5, July 1995, pp. 49–52; Gary Hill, "Webby N'Ozzy: The Saga Continues," *The Fourth Decade*, Vol. 2, No. 6, Sept. 1995, pp. 31–35.

14 Summers, *Conspiracy*, pp. 176–178.

15 Dr. Douglas Mader, *Who's Who in CIA*, Panorama DDR, Berlin, 1968.

CHAPTER 3

1960
Election Year

★ ★ ★

U-2 overflights of Russia continued into the new year. The Corona rocket launches went on, bearing more Discoverer satellites aloft. As yet none of the satellites had succeeded in its mission: the rockets malfunctioned on launch, or the satellites failed to achieve orbit. But von Braun and his colleagues remained optimistic.

Lee Harvey Oswald vanished from the radar for an entire year. The only written record of his activities in 1960 is his mysterious "historic diary": a document which even the Warren Commissioners found problematic—it seems to be a fake journal written some time after the dates it purports to cover, in a couple of sittings, by someone whose written English was a lot cruder than Oswald's. According to its account, after greeting the new year in Moscow, Lee took the train to Minsk, in Byelorussia, where here he was given a free apartment with a river view, a substantial amount of money, and a job in a radio factory. Norman Mailer, researching his book about Oswald, interviewed a man who claimed to have been the

KGB's counterintelligence chief in Minsk. Mailer called him Igor Ivanovich Guzmin, though other sources say his name was Golubtsov. According to Guzmin/Golubtsov, the KGB had several theories about Oswald: 1) that he was an American spy; 2) that he was a genuine defector; 3) that he was "not proficient in Marxist-Leninist theory" and therefore suspect; and 4) that he understood Russian better than he let on. In Minsk the KGB assigned Oswald a case officer, Alexander Fedorovich Kostikov (Mailer gives him the pseudonym of "Stepan Vasilyevich Gregorieff"), and kept him under constant surveillance. According to the KGB men, Oswald was first assigned to the factory's experimental shop, which produced electronic components for the Russian military and space program. To put a potential spy in such an environment seems like a deliberate test: Oswald presumably passed by showing no interest, and after six weeks he was moved to a lathe elsewhere in the factory. The KGB told Mailer Oswald didn't drink or smoke; he went to the cinema, read Russian newspapers, ate pastries, wandered around stores without buying anything, and dated girls.[1]

Jack Kennedy's trajectory in 1960 is more thoroughly accounted for. He announced his Presidential candidacy to an audience of supporters in the Senate Caucus Room, on January 2: a slow news day, gaining him maximum publicity. Joe might have been right that Jack was the most attractive candidate, but the odds were still against him. A Gallup poll late in 1959 suggested that either Richard Nixon or Nelson Rockefeller would beat Kennedy in a presidential contest. And there was strong opposition to him within his own party, where he was viewed as a lightweight, subservient to his dad, with a "Catholic problem." Liberals saw Jack as a right-winger and preferred Adlai Stevenson, who had already run for president twice. To counter this, Kennedy began tacking in a liberal direction. This infuriated at least one of his rivals, Hubert Humphrey, whose Senate voting record suggested he actually *cared* about civil rights.

In politics, sincerity counts for a lot less than money, and Joe Kennedy won the initial primaries simply by outspending Humphrey. Both sides ran dirty campaigns: Humphrey's theme song, "Give Me That Old-Time Religion," emphasized his Protestantism; Jack's team was accused of sending anti-Catholic propaganda to Catholics, in order to get out the vote. But money spoke loudest. Jack was the first candidate to have his own private jet—a Convair named

Caroline—which Joe had purchased for $385,000 the previous year. On the ground, Jack rode in a Cadillac with a car phone. Humphrey traveled in his campaign bus.

The morning of May 1 saw Kennedy and Humphrey campaigning in the Appalachians. The U-2 news came as a shock, perhaps, to politicians who had been denied security clearance. But suddenly the top secret program was secret no longer: a U.S. spy plane overflying Russia had been shot down, its pilot captured, its high-tech secrets in communist hands. This was an embarrassment for Eisenhower, who had authorized CIA to build the spy plane, and signed off on multiple violations of Russian air space. And it was an embarrassment for CIA, which had insisted that the U-2 flew higher than Russian fighters or missiles could reach.

Three days later, Robert Webster showed up at the American Embassy in Moscow and told a consul he wanted to return to the United States. The atmosphere was thick with talk of sabotage, of double-agentry. CIA chief Dulles was convinced that the pilot, Gary Francis Powers, was a double agent who had crashed his plane deliberately. What of Lee Oswald, who'd threatened to reveal secrets in Moscow, then disappeared? Had he spilled all he knew about the U-2, its capacities and flight paths? And how had that helped the Russians, if the secret aircraft flew beyond their missiles' range? Powers, in later years, blamed Oswald for his plane's downing. Russian outrage grew as American denials continued. Theodore White wrote,

> "From May 5, when Mr. Khrushchev gloatingly told his Soviet Congress of the shooting down of the U-2, until July 11, when the Democratic Convention opened in Los Angeles, American statecraft reeled through a period of chaos and humiliation..."[2]

And the Democrat candidates made the most of it. All of them, including Kennedy, played up the theme of American military weakness. From Appalachia, Kennedy declared, "The Soviets have made a spectacle before the world of the U-2 flight and the trial of our pilot, and have treated this nation with hostility and contempt." Citing the missile gap, the U-2 incident, Cuba, the Congo, and space travel as areas where the U.S. lagged behind Russia, Jack captured the Democratic nomination.

In fact, thanks to the Corona Program, the U.S. was well on the way to achieving much higher-quality photographic intelligence than the U-2s could provide. And the Air Force and CIA were already working on a successor to the U-2, a black, jet-powered American spy plane which would fly even higher, and faster: the SR-21 Blackbird. Just as there was no missile gap, there was no U-2 gap, something Eisenhower and Nixon both knew. After Kennedy won the Democratic nomination, President Eisenhower sent CIA director Dulles to brief him on the "commanding military strength" which the United States secretly enjoyed. Dulles, instead, gave Jack the impression that the missile gap was genuine.

Like Dulles, J. Edgar Hoover opposed a prisoner exchange to free the U-2 pilot. The FBI chief declared, "It would be catastrophic if the U.S. arranged for Powers' release and he then refused to come home." Nikita Khrushchev was in no hurry to release his CIA prisoner, either. So Powers languished in a Russian jail. Lee Oswald was still missing behind the Iron Curtain, but news of his ability to be in two places at once reached the FBI director. In June 1960, Hoover sent a memo to all field officers, warning them an impostor might be using Oswald's birth certificate. Though 1960 saw few reported sightings, Oswald doubles would emerge again the following year.

On July 28, Tass, the Russian news agency, reported that John Joseph Dutkanicz, a U.S. Army intelligence specialist, had defected. On August 5, Robert Webster applied to the Russian government for his exit visa. A few days later, a Discoverer satellite—number 18—was recovered by the Americans with its camera intact. At last the Corona program had paid off, and the U.S. had the best-quality photographic intelligence possible, revealing all visible activity in Russia and China—and confirming, once again, the communists' lack of nuclear-capable missiles, and their shortage of bomber planes.

Gary Francis Powers was tried for espionage in Moscow on August 17 and 18. Was Oswald there? He suggested as much to his brother Robert, writing that Powers "seemed to be a nice, bright American-type fellow, when I saw him in Moscow." When could Oswald have seen Powers, if not at his trial? On a private visit to see him in prison? As a stateless foreigner Lee needed permission to travel between cities, though he was able to violate that rule, as we shall see.[3]

As the U.S. presidential campaign progressed, then as now there was little to distinguish the candidates on the issues. Both

Richard Nixon and Jack Kennedy favored an aggressively right-wing foreign policy; both paid lip service to the civil rights movement at home. Eric Sevareid, the newspaper columnist, complained that Kennedy and Nixon were the same: like passionless, buttoned-down, ambitious junior executives, "wearing the proper clothes, thinking the proper thoughts, cultivating the proper people." When the two candidates debated, the TV audience thought Kennedy—who looked better than Nixon on television—had won the debate; the radio audience judged Nixon the winner.

But Kennedy, despite his health problems, seemed increasingly relaxed as the election approached, Nixon increasingly tense. Religion remained an issue which helped Nixon and hurt Kennedy, especially when anti-Catholic flames were fanned by journalists like Fletcher Knebel. But the press in general approved of Kennedy, and disliked Nixon. Attempts by Nixon's camp to steal Jack's medical records, and reveal his perilous health, proved unsuccessful.

In September 1960, Kennedy and his running mate, Lyndon Johnson, visited Texas—Johnson's home state. They rode in a parade through Dallas, and the candidate gave a speech at the Memorial Auditorium. In October, the Kennedy campaign issued a statement suggesting that Jack favored unilateral intervention to overthrow the Castro government in Cuba. But the idea of an American invasion of the neighboring state—an act of aggression illegal under international law—wasn't popular, and the issue was dropped. Ironically, CIA-Pentagon plans to invade Cuba had been approved by Eisenhower in March, and were well known by Kennedy's rival, vice president Nixon. The same month, the State Department sent Richard Bissell, Director of Plans at CIA, a list of 12 "Americans now living in [communist] bloc countries who might be called 'defectors.'" State wanted the Agency "to verify and possibly expand this list," which included two Army sergeants, one of them Dutkanicz; an Air Force sergeant who had defected in East Germany; two NSA employees; plus Robert Webster and Lee Harvey Oswald. The list described Oswald and Webster as "tourists." State was not yet aware that Webster wanted to come home. Webster's request for an exit visa was denied on October 24: the Russians told him he could reapply in a year's time.[4]

CIA responded obliquely to the State Department's request, providing additional information about some defectors, but revealing no other names. Their Oswald response was separate from the information about the others, and—as frequently happened with his intelligence files—they got his name wrong. Lee *Henry* Oswald, CIA reported, "renounced his U.S. citizenship at the U.S. Embassy in Moscow, giving as his reason the plight of the American Negro and U.S. 'imperialism' abroad... OSWALD is reported to have stated that regardless of any material shortcomings he sees in the USSR, he will never return to the United States."

Meanwhile, director Hoover of the FBI contacted Bissell about another matter: "a source whose reliability has not been tested" had reported that a leading Chicago *mafioso*, Sam Giancana, was insisting to friends that Fidel Castro was shortly to be eliminated, probably by poison. Hoover was reporting to Bissell what Bissell already knew: CIA had, with Eisenhower's approval, engaged the American mafia to assassinate the Cuban president. It was by no means unique, this collaboration between U.S. intelligence and organized crime, but it was supposed to be a secret. Perhaps Hoover was reminding the Director of Plans that it was hard to keep secrets from the FBI. On October 27, Richard Gibson, head of the New York chapter of the Fair Play for Cuba Committee, was lured to the hotel room of a young woman, June Cobb. Gibson consumed half a bottle of whiskey and told Cobb about the structure of the FPCC—a small group, tied to the American Communist Party, which sought better relations with Cuba. He also told her about his colleagues in the group, and where it got its money. The FPCC, Gibson explained, was secretly funded in cash by Castro's government. In the adjacent room a group of CIA men tape-recorded Gibson's monologue. They shared their transcript with the FBI, and both agencies soon began active campaigns to monitor and infiltrate this new subversive organization (in due course, Gibson himself became a CIA informant).[5]

On November 4, Lyndon Johnson and his wife, Lady Bird, were jeered and spat on by a mob in Dallas, Texas. The incident occurred at the Adolphus Hotel, one of the city's oldest and most respectable premises. Ascribed variously to "Nixon supporters" and to the extreme right, the incident indicated a certain fury on the part of conservative Texans that one of their own had joined the Kennedy campaign. Most Americans did not share their anger. On Tuesday, November 8, more than 68 million of them voted. Kennedy won the presidency by a tight margin. As previously, Joe Kennedy spent an enormous sum to secure his son's success. In later years, it would be suggested that the Chicago mafia had also been enlisted on the Kennedys' behalf to 'deliver' the votes which won the election. In terms of vote-counting, this claim is false. Jack Kennedy won with 303 electoral college votes, to Richard Nixon's 219. Without Illinois' 27 electoral votes, he would still have won: 276 to 246.[6]

Yet accusations of mafia involvement in the Kennedy presidency would continue.

One can certainly see political corruption, and bribery, and broken campaign finance rules, in John Kennedy's rise to power. But actual links with organized crime have never been shown. The president-elect was friendly with the actor/singer Frank Sinatra, who had demonstrable mafia connections. But Jack would end their friendship after he became president, much to his colleagues' relief and Sinatra's dismay. And Richard Nixon, with his Hotel Del Charro/mafia/oil connections, was vastly more dubious in this regard. Kennedy's running mate, Johnson, was also problematic, being deeply involved with various corrupt lobbyists, led by a fellow Texan, Bobby Baker. Why did Jack pick Lyndon as his vice president? It was an act which disappointed many of his supporters. One 'official' explanation is that Johnson was a pragmatic politician who could deliver the South and West. Another is that Philip Graham, publisher of the *Washington Post* and a friend of both men, leaned on Kennedy to make Johnson his running mate. All three were obsessive womanizers—Kennedy most of all—and it is possible that Baker, who served as a pimp to many Capitol Hill politicians, applied some pressure of his own.

The NSRP, representing the racist extreme right, was on the ballot in several states. Its ticket paired Arkansas governor Orval Faubus and Admiral John Crommelin. NSRP candidates received 44,977 votes out of a total 68,838,005. Yet the white racist faction was encouraged when, on December 1, Jack Kennedy met with Senator Richard Russell in Washington. The president-elect, having greeted other senators in his own office, made a strangely submissive offer to come to Russell's office on Capitol Hill. Russell felt the venue inappropriate, and the two men met in Kennedy's office instead. But Kennedy, clearly intimidated by the senior senator, didn't raise the issue of civil rights. Prior to the election, Russell and his Southern caucus had feared that, whoever won the election, the cause of racial segregation was doomed. Now, suddenly, there appeared to be breathing space...[7]

After the Russell meeting, the president-elect went to Palm Beach, Florida to relax. He was followed by a retired postal worker, Richard Paul Pavlick, 73 years old, who had been stalking Kennedy for some months. Newspapers later claimed that Pavlick was an anti-Catholic activist, opposed to the buying of elections. Pavlick loaded his car with several sticks of dynamite, and lay in wait outside the Kennedy compound on the morning of Sunday, December 11. According to the press, he intended a suicide attack—ramming Jack's car and detonating his explosives when the family left for Mass—but changed his mind when he saw Jackie and the children entering the limo, and resolved to kill the president-elect another day. He was arrested on December 15, following a tip-off from the postmaster of his hometown, Belmont, New Hampshire, who had been disturbed by the tone of Pavlick's postcards, and the pattern of his travels. Pavlick would spend the next six years in mental institutions.[8]

On December 9, CIA opened a '201' file on Lee Harvey Oswald, under the name Lee Henry Oswald. In 1975, Angleton's successor, George T. Kalaris, wrote that the file was opened "as a result of his defection to the USSR on 31 October 1959 and renewed interest in Oswald brought about by his queries concerning possible reentry into the United States." As Newman observes, this is an "amazing statement"—since, officially, Oswald's whereabouts and intentions at this time were unknown. The opening of a 201 file on Oswald for this reason suggests that Mission Control was still in contact with the mysterious ex-Marine.[9]

Discoverer 18, a Corona satellite launched on December 7, was successfully recovered two days later. Its onboard spy camera provided a new trove of detailed photographic intelligence as to how weak America's enemies were.

notes

1 Norman Mailer, *Oswald's Tale: An American Mystery*, Random House, NY, 1995 pp. 69–75, 79, 87–96, 101, 133, et sequ.

2 Theodore H. White, *The Making of the President*, 1960, Athenium House, NY, 1961, p. 140.

3 Anthony Summers, *Conspiracy*, pp. 205–6.

4 Newman, *Oswald and The CIA*, pp. 170–173, 182–189.

5 Newman, *Oswald and The CIA*, pp. 236–240.

6 *EXTRA!*, Vol. 7, No. 3, July-Aug 1994, p. 15.

7 FBI monograph, *National States Rights Party*, August 1966, p. 10; Nick Bryant, *The Bystander: John F. Kennedy and The Struggle for Black Equality*, Basic Books, NY, 2006, pp. 193–195.

8 "Kennedy Death Plot Timed to Sunday Mass," AP, *Palm Beach Post*, Dec. 20, 1960.

9 George T. Kalaris memo, subject "Lee Harvey Oswald," Sept. 18, 1975, NARA, JFK files, RIF 1993.07.02.13:52:25:56030; Newman, *Oswald and The CIA*, p. 176.

CHAPTER 4

1961

Washington and Minsk

★ ★ ★

Jack Kennedy specified that tails and top hats should be worn at his inauguration. He, for most of the event, appeared bare-headed. It was a striking visual *coup*: the young, hatless president set against a backdrop of pompous Victorian stoogery. Jack was still a young man, and he wanted to emphasize that.

The excitement attending Jack Kennedy's inauguration was only surpassed by the enthusiasm for the election of Barack Obama 48 years later. Both men were disliked by a large minority of the population. Both had been stigmatized as *outsiders*: Kennedy for his religion, Obama for the color of his skin (and for his religion, since he was frequently accused of being a Muslim, though he wasn't). In both elections, a majority of the electorate voted for the minority candidate. This showed, I think, maturity and absence of prejudice on the part of those voters, which neither the media nor the political class shared.

There was another similarity. In each case, the new president was elected with a mandate for change. And both Kennedy and Obama disappointed their most enthusiastic followers by playing things extremely "safely." Each young president opted for "bipartisanship"— something the electorate had not asked for, and did not want. Obama kept a dismal Republican appointee, Robert Gates, as his Secretary of Defense; Kennedy's choices were arguably worse, as he retained both Dulles at CIA and Hoover as FBI director, while adding "moderate" Republicans to his cabinet in the shape of C. Douglas Dillon (Treasury Secretary) and Robert McNamara (Defense). Worse still was his desire to appease the reactionary forces in his own party: Southern racists like Richard Russell and James O. Eastland.

Presumably the president was briefed on the U-2 and Corona data, so he knew—at last—that there was no missile gap. In a series of meetings with Dulles and General Lyman Lemnitzer of the Joint Chiefs of Staff, Kennedy was briefed on CIA/Pentagon plans for an invasion of Cuba, to be spearheaded by Cuban expatriates. He approved a revised version of the invasion plan, and on January 16, the State Department announced that U.S. citizens were forbidden to travel to Cuba without the express permission of the Secretary of State. Kennedy's Cuba policy was thus a continuation of Eisenhower's, his predecessor having broken diplomatic relations with the island only two weeks before. It is unknown whether Kennedy was made aware of CIA plans to kill Patrice Lumumba, prime minister of the Congo, who was murdered on January 17.

On January 18, the president addressed Congress in apocalyptic terms. He spoke of "peril" and warned that "before my term has ended, we shall have to test anew whether a nation organized and governed such as ours can endure. The outcome is by no means certain." Why did he say this? The United States was at peace. Following his inauguration, the Russians had made friendly gestures, freeing the captured pilots of two American spy planes. But Kennedy, perhaps a prisoner of his previous hardboiled rhetoric and senatorial style, did not respond. The next day, Eisenhower visited him and proposed military intervention against the communists in Laos—advice Kennedy didn't take. Eisenhower also demonstrated the use of an "emergency button" which would summon a helicopter to the White House lawn so as to evacuate the president in an emergency.

In Minsk, Lee Harvey Oswald proposed marriage to one of his girlfriends. She turned him down. He became homesick. His "historic diary" for the period January 4–31 inclusive reads:

"I am starting to reconsider my disire about staying the work is drab the money I get has nowhere to be spent. No night clubs or bowling allys no places of recreation acept the trade union dances I have had enough."

In January 1961 someone calling himself Lee Harvey Oswald showed up at the Bolton Ford Truck dealership in New Orleans and enquired about buying a fleet of vehicles to be sent to Cuba. He claimed to be working for an outfit called the Friends of Democratic Cuba. A few weeks later this person, or someone like him, appeared again, at the Dumas and Milnes Chevrolet dealership in New Orleans, to discuss the purchase of a 1958 Chevrolet. He showed the salesman a Texas driver's license bearing the name Lee Harvey Oswald. According to his "historic diary," Oswald was still in Russia; according to the Warren Report, he didn't know how to drive.[1]

To establish himself, early on, as an activist president, Jack Kennedy signed an Executive Order to increase food distributions to unemployed Americans. This stirred an expectation among his supporters that he would use Executive Orders to override Congressional objections, and actively promote civil rights. But Kennedy didn't do this. It seems strange today, but since the Civil War the South had been solidly Democrat: even in the 1960s, the GOP was still viewed by conservative white Southerners as the party of Abraham Lincoln. Unwilling to tangle with the right-wing, racist faction dominated by Russell and Eastland, Kennedy backpedaled on equal rights for black Americans—just as his predecessors had done. Instead, he appointed blacks to certain uncontroversial posts, and set up a Committee on Equal Employment Opportunity (CEEO) to eliminate racial discrimination in the hiring of federal employees. He tasked Lyndon Johnson to chair the committee. Johnson viewed the job as a poisoned chalice: he came from Texas and didn't want to antagonize Southern colleagues. Yet it would be Johnson, rather than Kennedy, who proved the domestic champion of civil rights.

Kennedy did not respond to his first foreign-policy challenge: a military coup in El Salvador on January 25. Given the United States' somewhat dominant position in Central America, it would have been easy for Kennedy to apply political pressure to restore the "reformist" civilian-military junta, or, even better, to guarantee fair elections. But he made no such moves.

On January 26, Lee Oswald's mother flew to Washington, DC. There she made a personal visit to the State Department, which an FBI report described thus:

> "She [Marguerite Oswald] advised that she had come to Washington to see what could be done to help her son, the subject. She expressed the thought that perhaps her son had gone to the Soviet Union as a 'secret agent' and that the State Department was not doing enough to help him. She was advised that such was not the case and that efforts were being made to help her son."[2]

On February 5, Lee wrote to the American Embassy, asking why there had been no response to a previous letter, mailed in December. In that letter —no copy of which exists, though CIA had opened his 201 file in response to it—Oswald had apparently asked to return home. This letter reached Richard Snyder in Moscow on February 13. Snyder wrote back that Lee should come to Moscow to discuss his case.

In February, the CIA expanded its program of domestic spying on the FPCC. James McCord, of the Agency's Security Research Service (the same James McCord who would later be embroiled in the Watergate scandal) authorized the surveillance of a student, Court Wood, who had recently returned from Cuba under FPCC sponsorship. In charge of the operation was a counterintelligence specialist from Texas, David Atlee Phillips. The operation continued for months but netted little information other than the news that Wood was a wealthy, naive youth who grew a beard in emulation of his Cuban heroes.[3]

On March 1, by Executive Order, President Kennedy created the Peace Corps. The idea has been attributed to Hubert Humphrey and to Sargent Shriver, Kennedy's aide: groups of young American volunteers, working alongside native people in the third world to improve their lives, would create a better impression of America, and counter communist propaganda.

On March 13, Kennedy proposed an *Alianza para Progreso*—an Alliance for Progress: "a vast cooperative effort, unparalleled in magnitude and nobility of purpose, to satisfy the basic needs of the [Latin] American people for homes, work, and land, health and schools." Like the Peace Corps, the Alliance was meant to counter the influence of the Cuban revolution. Neither succeeded: the Peace Corps did some good, but not enough, while the Alliance proved a sinkhole for stolen money and lost ideals. Meanwhile, plans for the proxy invasion of Cuba continued, and the Joint Chiefs assured McNamara, Kennedy's Secretary of Defense, that a "small invasion force" of 1,200–1,500 men could effect regime change.

Lee Harvey Oswald continued to be a one-man "peace corps" of his own, working in the radio factory and attending parties and dances—including one at the Palace of Culture in Minsk, on March 17, where he met Marina Prusakova, the attractive niece of a colonel in the MVD (the domestic police). Lee and Marina saw each other again at a dance a week later. They began dating.

President Kennedy appointed a friend, Grant Stockdale, as Ambassador to Ireland. On March 23, he overrode the Joint Chiefs, who were pushing for a war against communists in Laos. At a news conference, the president said that the U.S. "strongly and unreservedly" supported "the goal of a neutral and independent Laos." Five days later, he announced a major nuclear weapons buildup. The Navy's force of Polaris submarines would grow from six to 29. Instead of 96 atomic missiles, America's undersea fleet would now carry 464. There was to be a doubling of ICBMs—von Braun's department—from 300 to 600 Minuteman nukes. And the B-52 bomber fleet, on 15 minutes' ground alert, was to be increased by 50 percent. Since he knew that U.S. nuclear forces greatly outnumbered the Russian ones, it's hard to understand why Kennedy chose a course of action so wasteful, and provocative. Perhaps, having defied them over Laos, he wanted to conciliate the Joint Chiefs and NATO Commander General Lauris Norstad, an ardent nuclear-war-fighter, by giving them a $2.4 billion budget increase.

Jack Kennedy felt more comfortable around Colonel Ed Lansdale, an Army man who had received a certain notoriety for practicing "counterinsurgency" warfare in the Philippines. In theory this meant fighting guerrillas on their own turf, using their own methods. In practice it usually involved murdering dark-skinned people, herding them into concentration camps, or both. But Kennedy, like Lee Oswald, was a fan of Ian Fleming's James Bond books, whose secret agent hero was "licensed to kill, with gun, hand or knife." Espionage and guerrilla-style warfare appealed to him, and—if the alternative was thermonuclear Armageddon—who could complain? Also, there were already two popular novels and two Hollywood movies based on Lansdale and his undercover exploits: *The Quiet American* and *The Ugly American*. Kennedy's fascination for covert ops was in tune with the times, and not entirely original. Eisenhower had authorized CIA's overthrow of presidents Árbenz in Guatemala, and Mosaddegh in Iran, seven years previously. CIA had been lucky on both occasions, and was banking on good luck again.

On March 25, Martin Luther King was told by a Kennedy aide, Kenneth O'Donnell, that "the present international situation" made a meeting with the president impossible. Dr. King was viewed in establishment circles as "controversial," possibly a dangerous radical. But Robert Kennedy extended an offer to meet King, provided it was done in secret.

On April 4, at a meeting to discuss the Cuban invasion, the president asked those present if they approved of it. All were in favor—including Rusk, McNamara, Dulles and Bissell—with the exception of Senator William Fulbright of Arkansas, who called the plan immoral. The same day, immigration agents seized a high-ranking *mafioso*, Carlos Marcello, when he showed up for a scheduled meeting at the New Orleans Immigration Department. On the direct orders of the Attorney General, Marcello—who was in the country illegally—was handcuffed, driven to the airport, and flown on a government jet to Guatemala, where he was dumped. On April 12, a Russian, Yuri Gagarin, made history as the first human being to orbit the Earth, in space. On Earth, Allen Dulles and his deputies, Charles Cabell and Richard Bissell, briefed the president on the state of the Cuban resistance. The CIA men assured him that they possessed an undercover army of 2,500 Cubans who would support the invasion, plus a further 20,000 sympathizers, and that within days a quarter of the island's population would rise up against Castro. A CIA paper reported as many as 7,000 armed insurgents were in place and ready for action. Thus briefed, Kennedy went along with the plan. Enamored of his dashing Colonel Lansdale, the president also allocated 19 million dollars for the creation of a "counterinsurgency" force, 3,000 strong: the Green Berets.

On April 15, Lee Oswald proposed marriage to Marina Prusakova. In the "April 1–30" entry in his "historic diary," Oswald described the romantic process thus:

"We are going steady and I decide I must have her, she puts me off, so on April 15th I propose, she accepts."

That's it? Lee Harvey Oswald was trying to get out of Russia. He had other girlfriends. Why marry one, even one as bright and pretty as Marina, when he was in a hurry to depart? Did marrying into the family of an MVD colonel help him? Edward J. Epstein, who uncovered the photograph of Oswald and John Wayne, suspected that Oswald and Prusakova were both Russian spies. He considered their "courtship" entirely implausible, most of it taking place while Oswald was in the hospital for an ear disorder, and having his adenoids removed.[4]

Let us suppose that Oswald betrayed American secrets on arrival in Moscow. His debriefing might have occurred during the weeklong hospitalization which followed his "suicide attempt." If Oswald became a Russian spy—or remained an American spy whom the Russians thought they had "turned"—this second hospital stay might be a cover, used by the KGB to brief the youngsters on their mission. Marina still seems an unlikely KGB agent. She was even younger than Lee, and very "girly." Her behavior in the United States would be passive and unfocused. And only a very purposeful and dedicated secret agent would have two babies just to maintain her "cover story." Lee, on the other hand, demonstrated scant affection for Marina, and repeatedly abandoned his new family. By marrying, the mysterious ex-Marine complicated his already complex situation; did someone instruct him to marry Marina and move her to the United States?

(Marina may have known a great deal more about Lee and his activities than she admitted. In conversation with another Russian exile in Dallas, Katya Ford, Marina said her husband had defected after working at a trade exposition in Moscow. What caused Marina to confuse Robert Webster's cover story with Lee Oswald's? Did she meet Webster? She had his Leningrad apartment building listed in her address book, under someone else's name. Had Marina been instructed, by her uncle in the MVD, or by his colleagues at the KGB, to "keep an eye" on more than one defector?)

The invasion of Cuba began the same day as Oswald delivered his romantic proposal—April 15—with a bombing raid by CIA planes based at Puerto Cabezas, Nicaragua. The raid was meant to knock out the Cuban air force, but it destroyed only five of 36 military aircraft. Cuban intelligence had advance knowledge of the attack—plans had been leaked to various U.S. newspapers—and the expeditionary force of anti-Castro mercenaries was quickly trapped, and forced back to the beaches where it had landed, in the Bay of Pigs. President Kennedy had been assured repeatedly that there would be no need for U.S. military support, that the expeditionary force was self-sufficient and would triumph with the help of numerous in-country sympathizers. Now CIA and the Joint Chiefs had an update for him: the expedition was doomed, and would be annihilated unless Kennedy authorized military backup immediately.

To his great credit, Kennedy refused to budge. He authorized no further support of any kind to the expatriate invasion force, most of whom surrendered. One hundred and fourteen Cuban mercenaries and as many as 4,000 islanders died in the fighting. It was, of course, a propaganda coup for Castro and the Revolution (also a material and economic coup when they ransomed the prisoners back to the USA). It was a disaster for American sympathizers in Cuba, many of whom were rounded up and shot. Most of all, it was something Kennedy should not have agreed to in the first place: the fact that he "inherited" an illegal scheme dreamed up by Eisenhower and the CIA did not mean he had to go along with it. But Kennedy *chose* to support the Cuban invasion plan, based on the parameters Dulles and the Chiefs gave him. When their optimistic predictions proved inaccurate, he washed his hands and walked away. He was right, if late, to do so: the alternative was to commit the U.S. military to all-out war and an invasion of the island, disgracing the U.S. internationally, and causing many more deaths.

There's still debate as to whether the Kennedy brothers knew of the numerous CIA plots to murder Fidel Castro, his colleague Che Guevara, and his brother Raul. Some authors believe the Kennedys capable of great wickedness, including the alleged murder of Marilyn Monroe. Others have an entirely positive view of the brothers, claiming that Jack never approved the plots to assassinate Fidel, and that Bobby was horrified when he learned of them. I don't understand this debate. Jack Kennedy authorized the Bay of Pigs invasion. This was a military action, involving thousands of heavily armed men, preceded by a bombing raid. No matter how it turned out, one thing was certain: people were going to get killed.

Thousands would have to be slain before the invasion could be termed a "success." Jack Kennedy knew this: *he had signed off on it.*

Like other presidents—including those awarded Nobel Peace Prizes—Jack Kennedy was willing to see people killed for a political "gain." (It made it easier if the people were brown, and in a foreign country, but I can't remember any president who *didn't* sign off on some sort of large-scale killing activity during the course of his administration. Hiring mercenaries or the mafia to do the killing adds repugnance to the process, but the result is the same.) Why, then, would Kennedy *not* approve the assassination of a single individual, or several individuals, to achieve the same result? Only if a head of state is in some way different from a *campesino* or a schoolteacher can his or her killing be considered uniquely wrong. You or I might think any premeditated murder is unacceptable. Politicians view things differently. Kennedy had hired a Republican technocrat from the Ford Motor Company to run the Pentagon. Both men saw things in terms of cost-benefit analysis. Was it not more rational to kill one, two or three people, rather than ten thousand, and achieve the same goal?

Kennedy never gave up on regime change in Cuba. Furious at the bad intelligence he'd received, he decided to fire the top men at CIA—Dulles, Cabell, Bissell—after a decent interval, and to make changes at the Pentagon. But he drew closer to Lansdale, whose "black ops" seemed—in their imaginations—more likely to succeed. As the FPCC organized demonstrations to protest the invasion, party politics demanded the president's attention; he flew to Chicago to attend a "thank you" dinner for Mayor Richard Daley. Kennedy's own detachment of Secret Service agents would be supplemented by the Chicago office, which employed one of the first black agents, Abraham Bolden. While other Secret Service men received high-profile assignments, Bolden was told to guard a restroom in the basement.

I have a vision of Bolden as the Army sergeant played by Keenan Wynn in Stanley Kubrick's film *Dr. Strangelove*. Just as Sgt. "Bat" Guano protects the property of the Coca-Cola company to the best of his ability, so I picture Bolden searching the restroom and surrounding area, securing the perimeter, standing at his post, ready for anything, convinced nothing will happen. Then Kennedy decides to take a leak, and pursued by the mayor, a senator, a congressman, and the press, he's directed to Abraham's bathroom. Bolden takes up the story:

"Are you a Secret Service agent or one of Mayor Daley's finest?" he asked, causing the mayor to chuckle lightly.

Collecting myself, I replied, "I'm a Secret Service agent, Mr. President."

"He's assigned to the Chicago office," a more senior agent offered. "His name is Abraham Bolden."

Kennedy nodded slightly in acknowledgement and continued on in his crisp Boston accent. "Has there ever been a Negro agent on the Secret Service White House detail, Mr. Bolden?"

"Not to my knowledge, Mr. President."

"Would you like to be the first?" Kennedy asked, his eyes twinkling under the bright hotel lights...

"Yes sir, Mr. President."[4]

What a fine, theatrical moment! A cynic may say that this was Kennedy the politician, playing up before the crowd. But he *was doing the right thing*, too. And that's more important than theatrical instincts or political ability. Kennedy had tasked Vice President Johnson to deal with the civil rights issue. But he couldn't ignore it, and he didn't. This conversation with Bolden resulted in another high-profile black appointment.

On April 20, Kennedy gave Johnson a new mission: to come up with a space project where the Americans could "beat the Russians." Johnson, chair of Kennedy's National Space Council, asked Wernher von Braun for suggestions. Von Braun opined that the U.S. had "a sporting chance" of beating the Russians into orbit around the Moon, and "an excellent chance" of beating them to a manned Lunar landing. On April 22, Robert Kennedy met, as agreed, with Martin Luther King, at a private dining room in the Mayflower Hotel. He and his aides tried to push King to support voter registration, rather than more direct civil rights activism. Afterwards, Bobby walked Martin over to the White House, and Dr. King met the president "unofficially." Jack found Martin polite, intelligent, and to his liking. A few days later, Senator Thomas J. Dodd opened hearings on the FPCC. Among Dodd's witnesses was CBS reporter Richard Gibson, head of the New York chapter, who had already spilled the organization's secrets in a CIA honeytrap.

On April 30 Lee Oswald and Marina Prusakova were married. They had planned to marry on May 1—the Workers' Holiday—but presumably the public registry was closed on that day. Later in May another CBS journalist, Robert Taber, had a meeting in Havana, Cuba, with a Doctor Enrique Luaces and a "Lieutenant Harvey Oswald" who, he was told, was an arms expert. Taber was not only a reporter, he was also a "founding member" of the FPCC. Later he would claim that the Lieutenant and Lee Harvey Oswald were one and the same.[6]

On May 4, two buses filled with "freedom riders" left Washington, DC, with an itinerary of stops in Southern cities. The mission was the work of CORE—the Congress of Racial Equality—one of the more activist civil rights groups. Where bus stations were racially segregated, CORE's riders planned to demonstrate in favor of integration.

The same day, the president told a meeting of the National Security Council that "U.S. policy towards Cuba should aim at the downfall of Castro." So that was clear. But Kennedy was also beginning to weed out belligerent right-wingers within the military, starting with General Edwin Walker. Walker, whom Eisenhower had placed in command of an American division in Germany, had joined the John Birch Society, and, following the president's instructions, begun indoctrinating his men in anticommunist propaganda. Walker also condemned the New Deal, Eleanor Roosevelt, Adlai Stevenson, Harvard University, and *Mad* magazine. In April it had been reported that he was instructing his troops in how to vote—breaking Army regulations, federal laws, and the Hatch Act, which prohibits political activity by government employees. Kennedy relieved him of his command and transferred him to a desk job in Heidelberg, but Walker's right-wing networking continued undiminished. Among his supporters was General Lemnitzer, head of the Joint Chiefs.

On May 5, Abraham Bolden reported for duty at the White House. Bolden had already heard that the Secret Service agents surrounding the president were party boys who drank on the job. But what he found when he took up his post was even worse. Kennedy's alleged security detail was composed mainly of Southern racists. They hated blacks, hated Kennedy, and regularly abandoned their posts, leaving the president unprotected. Harvey Henderson, Bolden's line manager, was a heavy drinker who did his best to provoke his one black agent with torrents of racial abuse. Drinking on duty and abandoning one's post were grounds for instant dismissal, and Bolden made an official complaint. But he saw no change.[7]

On May 14, the freedom riders came under attack, in Anniston, Alabama, and again in Birmingham. The public safety commissioner, "Bull" Connor, gave police officers leave—for Mother's Day—and let the Ku Klux Klan know that they would have at least ten minutes before any police intervened. The Klan took full advantage of Connor's offer: a bus was burned; mobs attacked the riders. The first two busloads of beaten-up protesters, unable to leave Birmingham by road, flew out by plane. Then another bus arrived, with ten more CORE riders aboard. Connor arrested them, "for their own protection." A third wave of riders, arriving by train, boarded a bus bound for Montgomery. Again, local police failed to appear, and a white mob attacked the bus. FBI agents watched as riders, including Kennedy aide John Seigenthaler, were beaten with lead pipes and baseball bats.

Goaded into action, Attorney General Robert Kennedy dispatched 400 U.S. marshals and federal agents to protect the demonstrators. Back from a state visit to Canada, President Kennedy issued a written statement, in which he called the violence "a source of deepest concern to me," then implicitly blamed the freedom riders! "I would hope that any persons, whether a citizen of Alabama or a visitor there, would refrain from any action which would in any way tend to provoke further outbreaks." In Birmingham and Montgomery the violence had been indiscriminate: roving mobs of Klansmen beat up blacks who were not connected with the freedom riders. In Montgomery one such white mob set a black man on fire. Blacks in the south, according to Kennedy's tortured logic, were "provoking" whites by the unavoidable fact of their blackness. For the president to blame the victims for the violence was despicable.

Why was Jack Kennedy so weak on the civil rights front? On a symbolic level, placing blacks in visible positions, the president did well. But in terms of real progress, on the part of the poorest and most discriminated-against, his achievements were few. Did he lack empathy? Did he have a moral compass for foreign affairs, but not for domestic ones? Or did he overestimate the power of reactionaries in his own party—what we now call "blue dog" Democrats? It's hard to credit, in the iron grip of the twenty-first century, but at this moment in American history, all the up-and-coming political players—all the presidential material—were considered liberals. Richard Nixon was very liberal on domestic issues: Martin Luther King seriously considered supporting him. Nelson Rockefeller, Nixon's main Republican rival, was to the left of Nixon, domestically and in foreign affairs. Hubert Humphrey and Lyndon Johnson were liberals, too. Of the whole bunch, Jack Kennedy was probably the most conservative. By modern standards there wasn't a right-winger among them. So, lacking any political cover, the Kennedys were being pushed toward an active position on civil rights.

Not that Dr. King and his congregation knew this, trapped in the First Baptist Church in Montgomery, by a white riot 3,000 strong. Only one hundred U.S. marshals had made it through the mob; when they tried to put a cordon around the church, the rioters threw bricks and Molotov cocktails. The stained glass windows shattered and the marshals responded with tear gas. That evening, John Patterson, the governor of Alabama, sent in the National Guard. Kennedy was greatly relieved that he wouldn't have to commit federal troops. Patterson, a white supremacist, was an old ally from Kennedy's Congressional days. The two men were at loggerheads now, but Patterson's action enabled the president to lay low. But Kennedy was infuriated to learn of the FBI's spectator status at the riots. Next morning he called J. Edgar Hoover to complain. Arrests followed.

On Monday, May 20, Kennedy met with the National Advisory Council of the Peace Corps. It should have been a breeze, but on the Council were Harry Belafonte, the actor, Eugene Rostow, the dean of Yale law school, and Benjamin Mays, president of Moorhouse College. All of them criticized the president for failure to speak out against the racist violence. Belafonte, a skillful thespian, was subtle and deferential. Rostow was blunter and more outspoken, which pissed the president off. Afterwards, Kennedy exclaimed to an aide, "Doesn't he know I've done more for civil rights than any president in American history? How could any man have done more than I've done?"

Nowhere were Kennedy's good intentions more visibly coupled with his inattention than in his effort to integrate his all-white, all-male, mostly Southern Secret Service detail. After his thirty-day White House trial was over, Abraham Bolden asked to be returned to Illinois. He disliked the racist atmosphere of the president's detail, and preferred the Chicago counterfeiting squad. It's not recorded whether Kennedy noticed Bolden's absence; he didn't replace him with another black bodyguard.

On May 25, Lee Oswald wrote to the U.S. Embassy in Moscow, telling them that he had married, and that he wanted to bring his wife home with him.

The same day, Jack Kennedy addressed Congress in bellicose terms. He had recently been challenged, by one of his Republican rivals, for permitting a "fallout-shelter gap" to develop. Kennedy knew this was nonsense, and that the U.S.—which still enjoyed a massive nuclear advantage over the Russians—didn't need to build more fallout shelters. Nonetheless, he proposed tripling the Civil Defense budget. And he made another proposal, every bit as divorced from the demands of reality: that the U.S. land an astronaut on the Moon. Neither plan was popular with the public. "We choose to go to the Moon!" Kennedy insisted, and repeated, as if back on the campaign trail. "We choose to go to the Moon!" But the American people didn't. 58 percent of the electorate *opposed* spending $40 billion—$225 per person—on a manned Moon mission. Lyndon Johnson, on the other hand, was all in favor of it. As chair of the president's National Space Council, Johnson embarked on an ambitious plan to relocate half of NASA's space operations to a new command center, in his hometown of Houston, Texas.

On May 30, General Rafael Trujillo, the dictator of the Dominican Republic, was assassinated. Trujillo had begun his career as a U.S.-approved president-for-life, in the style of Somoza in Nicaragua or Saddam Hussein in Iraq. Trujillo called himself *El Benefactor*, and by 1961 owned most of the country. He had given refuge to Fulgencio Batista, when the Cuban dictator was forced to flee. But he'd also supported Castro's guerrillas, and the Americans wanted him gone. According to L. Gonzalez-Mata, who was briefly Trujillo's Chief of Security, the guns used in the assassination were supplied by a CIA agent, E. Howard Hunt. Another CIA agent, Frank Sturgis, claimed to have been in the Dominican Republic, meeting with the conspirators. (Hunt and Sturgis had both worked on the CIA's Guatemalan and Bay of Pigs projects.) The assassination was an ambush, with multiple rifles firing on Trujillo as he rode on the highway in a chauffeur-driven car. The murder had been approved by Eisenhower; it's hard to imagine that the new president wasn't briefed on it.

The news of Trujillo's killing reached Kennedy in Paris, where he was meeting with President DeGaulle. The two Roberts, Kennedy and McNamara, called Jack after midnight, urging him to send in the Marines and occupy the Dominican Republic. This he declined to do.

Kennedy and Khrushchev held a summit in Vienna on June 3. The Russian premier was prickly, bombastic and unpredictable. Kennedy's youth and charm availed him not at all. Both men were worried by atomic weapons, and keen to find a way to end the burgeoning arms race. But neither could convey this to the other. Their first meeting was utterly dispiriting, the second one worse. At odds over nuclear testing, Cuba, and Berlin, the only thing they could agree upon was that there was no sense in fighting about Laos as well. Kennedy also broached a subject which he thought might provide focus for Americans and Russians to cooperate: a joint, manned expedition to the Moon. But Khrushchev did not respond.

Returning to the U.S., Kennedy appointed General Curtis LeMay head of the Air Force, and hence one of the Joint Chiefs. LeMay made no secret of his loathing for the Russians, or for the Kennedys, whom, in an official history, he called "ruthless," "vindictive" and "the most egotistical people that I ever saw in my life." LeMay began briefing against the president, terrifying a senator's wife at a Georgetown dinner party by predicting nuclear war within the year. LeMay's off-hand announcement that Washington, New York, Los Angeles, Chicago, and all major Russian cities would be destroyed made it into the *Washington Post*. LeMay denied the story. A few days later, Kennedy created a new post, that of his military advisor. Snubbing the Joint Chiefs, the president brought General Maxwell Taylor out of retirement to fill it (Taylor had prepared a report—still classified—on the Bay of Pigs debacle, which apparently concluded that the invasion should have been canceled). Taylor, despite Kennedy's enthusiasm, was critical of the way things went in the White House:

> "As an old military type, I was accustomed to the support of a highly professional staff trained to prepare careful analyses of issues in advance of decisions and to take meticulous care of classified information. I was shocked at the disorderly and careless ways of the new White House staff... I found that I could walk into almost any office, request and receive a sheaf of top secret papers, and depart without signing a receipt..."[8]

Taylor remarked that things got done through the individual initiative of those who were assigned the tasks: presumably, those closest and most loyal to the president. But it also meant that Kennedy—even more distrustful of bureaucracies and committees than Ronald Reagan or Dick Cheney—was relying on individuals rather than a system set up to (slowly) achieve results. This might work well if the individual was Maxwell Taylor, or Lyndon Johnson, or his own brother, Robert. But a task in the hands of a less able subordinate, with no bureaucracy in place to back him up, could disappear into the wind.

On July 3, Agent John W. Fain of the Dallas FBI issued the first of several reports about Lee Harvey Oswald. This one, titled "Lee Harvey Oswald" and sub-headed "Internal Security – R," detailed Oswald's early history in Texas and Louisiana (there is no mention of any time spent in New York or Nebraska) and his more recent defection. Based mainly on interviews with Marguerite and Robert Oswald, it was copied to the Office of Naval Intelligence in New Orleans.[9]

Fain's report refers to two "Dallas Confidential Informants" whom he calls T-1 and T-2. T-2 advised Fain that Oswald had failed to show up at Albert Schweitzer College, while T-1 had inside knowledge about Oswald's Marine career. T-1 reported that Lee reenlisted in the U.S. Marine Corps Reserve the day he received his honorable discharge—a patriotic act for someone planning to betray his country. Fain had other confidential informants—T-3 and T-4—who told him that Oswald wasn't a member of the Communist Party in Fort Worth. Presumably T-3 and T-4 were infiltrators of that terrifying body. But who were T-1 and T-2?

On July 8, without obtaining permission from the authorities, Lee Oswald flew from Minsk to Moscow. He met with Consul Snyder. The next day, he called Marina, who followed him to Moscow and began filling out paperwork at the American Embassy: in addition to the return of his passport and a visa for her, the Oswalds would need permission from the Russian government in order to leave. On July 11, Oswald was interviewed by Boris Klosson, a political officer at the Embassy. Klosson (who does not appear in *Who's Who in CIA*) asked Oswald about his statement in 1959 that he would willingly make secret information available to the Russians. Oswald replied:

> "...he was never in fact subjected to any questioning or briefing by Soviet authorities concerning his life experiences

prior to entering the Soviet Union and never provided such
information to any Soviet organization. He stated he doubted
in fact he would have given such information if requested
despite his statements made at the Embassy."

From Norman Mailer's researches, we know that Oswald had a KGB
case officer and was under constant surveillance. The officer in
question denied actually contacting Lee. But how likely was that?
Presumably Klosson didn't believe him. But there is more. Oswald
continued:

> "OSWALD indicated some anxiety as to whether, should he
> return to the United States, he would face possible lengthy
> imprisonment for his act of remaining in the Soviet Union.
> OSWALD was told informally that the Embassy did not
> perceive, on the basis of the information in its possession, on
> what grounds he might be subject to conviction leading to
> punishment of such severity as he apparently had in mind."

This Oswald was no fool. He had declared himself a Marxist,
threatened to commit an act of treason, and defected to Russia.
Now he was seeking an assurance that he wouldn't face a long prison
sentence in the United States. His anxiety might suggest that he had
acted alone, out of youthful exuberance, and had only lately begun to
worry about the consequences. Or it could mean that he had started
to distrust his sponsors, and that, after two years of political theater,
he was looking for a third party's assurance that he was still okay.

In early July a crisis erupted over the status of Berlin, the former
capital of Germany. At the end of the War in Europe, Germany had
been occupied by the Russians in the east, and by the Americans
and their allies in the west. The Western powers also seized a
portion of Berlin, though the city was situated in the east. After
the War, Germany was divided into two nations, but the U.S. held
onto West Berlin. As the Cold War progressed, many East Germans
used Berlin as a route to the west, where higher living standards
and greater political freedoms were believed to pertain. To stem
this embarrassing exodus, the Russians and their East German
surrogates proposed to conclude a peace treaty and turn control of
all Berlin over to the east.

And what had this to do with us? Germany had been cut in two at the end of the Second World War, with an obvious goal: to punish the Germans and prevent a united Germany from ever threatening the world. Anyone could understand the logic of it. If the Russians wanted to impose extra-high levels of grayness and conformity on West Berlin, it mattered little to most Europeans, who had not yet forgotten what the Nazis did, or why that War had to be fought.

Nevertheless, thousands of miles away, in Washington, DC, a group of Americans—none of whom spoke German—were debating the fate of Germany, as if West Berlin were their property to keep or give away. On July 13, the National Security Council met, and Dean Rusk—secretary of state, as gray a bureaucrat as ever graced the Kremlin—opposed even negotiating with the Russians, quoting his even grayer mentor, Dean Acheson: "negotiation is harmful until the crisis is well developed; then it is useful only for propaganda purposes."

Russian insistence on a peace treaty was not unreasonable. Sixteen years had passed since the end of the War, and a treaty was overdue. Acheson pressed Kennedy to declare a national emergency, and add a further five billion dollars to the military budget. This the president refused to do. Worried that, in the absence of diplomacy, a nuclear war might break out between the U.S. and Russia, Kennedy requested "an analysis of the possible levels and implications of nuclear warfare and the possible gradations of our own nuclear response." The National Security Council met again on July 20 to discuss a report by General Hickey and his group, the Net Evaluation Subcommittee. Present were Kennedy, Rusk, Dulles, and the Joint Chiefs. But instead of a list of possible tactical nuclear responses in the context of the Berlin crisis, the Pentagon had revamped its plans for a Gaither-style "preemptive" strike against the Russians—a massive nuclear surprise attack which, the Chiefs assured the president, would be completely successful.

The Pentagon's preferred date for the surprise attack was December 1963. The president asked if the strike could be earlier, in December 1962, say. Allen Dulles responded that "the attack would be much less effective since there would be considerably fewer missiles involved." Everyone in the room knew that the "missile gap" entirely favored the Americans: at that moment the Russians had a grand total of four ICBMs in place, all on low alert in the same location, a test site called Plesetsk. In contrast, the U.S. had 185 ICBMs and over 3,400 deliverable nuclear bombs. Kennedy had just okayed a massive nuclear buildup, and the Joint Chiefs and CIA wanted to wait until it was complete, in 1963. That way, the devastation could be maximized.

Kennedy asked one more question: how long would "citizens" have to remain in shelters following the massive attack? "Two weeks" was the reply: clearly this was an optimistic reference to Americans who had taken shelter from the world-encircling radioactive fallout, rather than the thrice-fried Russians. According to Arthur Schlesinger, who was present, the president got up and walked out of the meeting. McGeorge Bundy, another aide, recalls Kennedy remarking, "And we call ourselves the human race." James K. Galbraith wrote that:

> "...the reasoning behind the fallout shelter program now begins to fall into place. As a civil defense measure against a Soviet nuclear attack, the flimsy cinderblock shelters Americans were told to build were absurd. But they could indeed protect those in them, for a couple of weeks, from radiation drifting thousands of miles after a U.S. preemptive strike on the Soviet Union. It is known that Kennedy later regretted this program."[10]

Today it's also known that even a "limited" atomic war would engulf the northern hemisphere in a devastating nuclear winter with fatal consequences for us all. But this was not the scientific consensus of 1961. Back then, experts spoke of "surviving" nuclear conflicts; perhaps without realizing it, Kennedy himself had stoked the fires of Armageddon by supporting the Civil Defense program.

On July 20, the Oswalds sent their paperwork to the Russian authorities, requesting two exit visas.

To intensify its pressure on the president, the Pentagon leaked to *Newsweek* its plans for a limited national emergency, a military buildup in Germany, and "some demonstration of U.S. intent to employ nuclear weapons." In response, on July 25, Kennedy made a bellicose TV address, claiming that "the freedom of human beings is at stake" in the former Nazi capital, and promising yet another military buildup. Additional defense appropriations of $3.25 billion were requested from Congress; draft calls were tripled; and 150,000 reservists were called to active duty. Meanwhile McNamara ordered an overhaul of the Pentagon's nuclear war-fighting strategy, the Single Integrated Operating Plan (SIOP), so that the president might have alternatives beyond all-out nuclear war, and that operational control of nuclear weapons would be in *his*, and not the Joint Chiefs', hands. General LeMay had asked for at least 2,400 Minuteman ICBMs, while General Powers of the Strategic Air Command wanted 10,000. After his review, McNamara imposed a limit of 1,000 Minutemen.

The Russians were clearly shaken by Kennedy's speech and this latest military buildup. Khrushchev was at that very moment engaged in arms control negotiations with the presidential envoy, John McCloy. On July 26, the Russian president told McCloy that "the United States had declared preliminary war on the Soviet Union. It had presented an ultimatum and clearly intended hostilities."

On August 1, two British/American tourists, Rita Naman and Monica Kramer, were approached in Moscow by a young man who spoke English with an American accent. The man's presence agitated their Intourist guide. Anthony Summers interviewed Naman, who told him that she met the American in two different cities in the course of a motoring holiday behind the "Iron Curtain." The CIA would later identify him as Lee Harvey Oswald.[11]

In Washington, at Jack Kennedy's suggestion, Senator Fulbright counterattacked against the military activists. On August 2, he denounced officers who disseminated conservative propaganda, declaring, "If the military is infected with the virus of right-wing radicalism, the danger is worthy of attention." Fulbright pointed to the French generals' recent *coup* attempt against de Gaulle "as an example of the ultimate danger." The media picked the story up, not least Drew Pearson, who described the situation in terms which recalled the fascist leanings of the duPont *coup* attempt against FDR: "Certain Pentagon brass-hats were lining up with industrial right-wingers to foment a sort of neo-fascism despite the fact they were wearing Uncle Sam's uniform."

On August 8, Lee Oswald, still in Minsk, wrote again to his Embassy in Moscow. This time he asked if he and Marina would be permitted to travel through Poland by train after leaving Minsk. This was not a question the Embassy could answer; it was a matter for the communist authorities. Then Lee got to what was perhaps his point: as he could not afford to fly from Moscow to New York

City, he stated his belief that he could catch a military flight to the U.S. from Berlin. This is a remarkable assumption. It suggests either: 1) great stupidity and naiveté on Oswald's part, given the reception a would-be traitor and defector might receive from active duty military personnel; or 2) confidence that—his mission accomplished—he would be flying home among friends. Whatever the case, the Embassy didn't offer Oswald an invitation to Berlin.[12]

A week later, Naman and Kramer arrived in Minsk. They took photos in the square before the impressive columns of the Palace of Culture. By a remarkable coincidence, the American whom they'd just met in Moscow was in Minsk as well, and they had their picture taken with him. Naman and Kramer were debriefed by CIA on their return to the U.S., and provided the Agency with a number of photographs. CIA later submitted two of these to the Warren Commission, identifying them as photos of Lee Oswald. "Officially," Oswald had returned to Minsk on July 14. So who was the person the tourists thought was Oswald in Moscow?[13]

On August 13, the East German military began building a wall to surround West Berlin. It was an ugly but effective piece of crisis resolution. At this point, Kennedy submitted once again to the disastrous counsel of Dean Acheson, and authorized a military incursion into East Germany. A battle group of 1,500 American troops raced down the *autobahn* from West Germany to West Berlin. Had there been a peace treaty, this would have been an invasion of a sovereign state, illegal under international law. The incursion served no purpose, descending into farce when a Stetson-clad Lyndon Johnson flew in to greet the invaders. But it was still immensely provocative: as Robert Kennedy later told a biographer, "We felt war was very possible, then."[14]

While vocally condemning Khrushchev and the communists, Kennedy forced the retirement of one of the Chiefs, Admiral Arleigh Burke. In September, he instructed McNamara to establish a police academy to train the Latin American militaries in counterinsurgency techniques. Liberals and sentimental leftists tend to blame their political opponents—Nixon, or George W. Bush—for all the Empire's ills. So it's worth remembering that a Democrat, Harry Truman, set up the CIA; that a Democrat, Jimmy Carter, authorized funding for the *contras* and the Muslim terrorists in Afghanistan; and that a Democrat, John F. Kennedy, promoted the notorious U.S. Army

School of the Americas, where so many killers, dictators and drug lords were to learn their trades.

Such *largesse* to the military failed to head off a near-rebellion by the Fourth U.S. Army Division, at Fort Sam Houston, Texas. There, in late September, the Army sponsored a two-day propaganda show, which drew thousands of attendees. On stage, uniformed military personnel denounced the president and the civil rights movement. Kennedy was accustomed to good relations with the press; now he learned that his popularity did not extend as far as Texas. At a White House lunch, the president was verbally abused by E.M. Dealey, publisher of the *Dallas Morning News*. Reading from a prepared statement, Dealey declared "We can annihilate Russia and should make that clear to the Soviet government... We need a man on horseback to lead this nation, and many people in Texas and the Southwest think you are riding Caroline's tricycle." Also in October, another right-wing General, Lucius Clay, provoked the Russians and the East Germans with a threat to "knock down" the Berlin Wall.

We have grown used to celebrity army men, to the glorification of military culture in films, sports and games, and to the regular appearance of paid pundits on FOX News. The military throw their weight around nowadays in a way that made many people uneasy back in the early 1960s. When Fletcher Knebel interviewed Kennedy's Navy Secretary, John Connally, at the Pentagon, Connally spoke of "the frustrations of his admirals, who bridled under the restraints of civilian leadership, and felt muzzled in their political expression." Connally, as Knebel understood him, seemed to be musing that possession of nuclear weapons might lead the United States to become a military dictatorship.

> "Knebel was struck with Connally's foreboding, especially with the sense of helplessness in a high government official. If that were widespread in the Pentagon, it was significant. The novelist appropriated the feelings and instilled them in the thoughts of his fictional president, Jordan Lyman, who became the target of a military coup in the book *Seven Days In May*."[15]

Seven Days In May, written by Knebel and Charles W. Bailey II, was a best-selling novel, and a feature film. It tells the story of a *coup* attempt by the U.S. Joint Chiefs, foiled by a loyal officer. Neither Connally nor Knebel were friends of Kennedy: both leaked the story of his Addison's disease, and Knebel worked the Catholic-unfit-to-be-president angle till he broke it. But Kennedy was generous to them when he was in the White House, giving Connally a job and Knebel unprecedented access.

On September 22, a group of 20 American "peace walkers" arrived in Minsk. They had begun their journey on the West Coast of the United States, and, thanks to the support of the influential pacifist A.J. Muste, they had been allowed to walk through Eastern Europe and Russia in support of peace. Contemporary accounts suggest their presence was seen as a big deal: the marchers opposed both American and Russian nuclear weapons policy, and loyal Russians and Byelorussians were not used to seeing antiwar banners, or being handed pamphlets which criticized the state. From a civil rights viewpoint, it was very significant. But Oswald's "historic diary" makes no mention of the peace walkers: another indication that it was fabricated later, by someone who wasn't there. On October 4, Lee wrote to the U.S. Embassy, asking the government to intervene in his emigration case. The Embassy replied a few days later, offering no assistance.

On October 9, the president paid a brief visit to Dallas. Landing at Love Field airport, he visited the ailing Speaker of the House, Sam Rayburn, at Baylor Hospital. Then he returned to Washington. On October 21, Roswell Gilpatric, Kennedy's deputy secretary of defense, revealed that the "missile gap" favored the Americans. In a speech designed to reassure conservatives and intimidate the Russians, Gilpatric disclosed that the United States had tens of thousands of nuclear delivery vehicles, and Russia only a handful. The strategy, if one can call it that, backfired: Khrushchev began talks with Castro about siting nuclear missiles in Cuba.

Marina being absent with her family, Lee Oswald spent his 22nd birthday at the opera. On October 24, Robert Webster, the other reluctant defector, again applied to the Russian authorities for an exit visa.

Kennedy was under increasing pressure to support the Diem regime, installed by Eisenhower in Vietnam. In mid-October he sent Maxwell Taylor, Walt Rostow, and Ed Lansdale to investigate the situation there. He also authorized the use of Agent Orange and other poisons to defoliate the jungle and destroy "enemy" crops. This chemical warfare would be waged via a secret program known first as Operation HADES, then as Operation RANCHHAND.[16]

The Russians gave the Americans nuclear nightmares with a series of provocative atomic tests: after exploding one 50-megaton bomb, they engaged in 50 further nuclear blasts over a two-month period. In November, Kennedy authorized Operation MONGOOSE, a large program of covert action, involving the Pentagon and CIA, "to undermine the Cuban government." MONGOOSE would be run by Bobby, with Lansdale as his chief of operations. MONGOOSE anticipated sabotage, destabilization, and bribery, and possibly another invasion of Cuba. There's no question that both Kennedy brothers enthusiastically supported MONGOOSE as a means of getting rid of Fidel Castro, yet the genteel debate as to whether they approved his murder still continues. On November 9, the president had a conversation with a journalist, Tad Szulc, in which the ethics of killing Castro supposedly came up. Dick Goodwin, Kennedy's Cuba specialist, was present when Kennedy asked Szulc, "What would you think if I ordered Castro to be assassinated?" Szulc said he was against the idea, and Kennedy replied, "I agree with you completely," adding that he was under intense pressure from officials within his government to order the hit.

Now this is a very fine story. Kennedy comes out of it well, and so does Szulc. But Szulc, who wrote for the *New York Times*, was one of those journalists who liked to be helpful to the CIA. He was at the White House to apply for a job; in just over a year he'd be proposing active measures to cultivate *coup* leaders in Cuba—a program CIA called AMTRUNK. It isn't clear that Szulc was one of the MOCKINGBIRDs, but his song was very similar. His brief conversation with Kennedy—overheard by a loyal aide—sounds like play-acting: the president seeking cover from an Agency-friendly journalist who would spread the word.[17]

Whatever he did or didn't do, Kennedy couldn't seem to please his generals. At November 15, at a National Security Council meeting, he expressed concern that the Chiefs' desire for action could land him in two simultaneous wars: one in Germany, and one in "French" Indochina. General Lemnitzer replied that a communist victory in Vietnam "would deal a severe blow to freedom and extend communism to a great portion of the world." He then urged simultaneous military strikes, in Cuba and Vietnam. Kennedy did not commit to this. He did authorize the dispatch to Vietnam of U.S. military "advisors"—who quickly rose to some 3,500 in number.

On November 16, Kennedy attacked the right in a speech at the University of Washington, in Seattle. Perhaps he'd learned something in this past year, as he observed to the students, "We must face the fact that the United States is neither omnipotent nor omniscient, that we are only 6 percent of the world's population, that we cannot impose our will on the other 94 percent, that we cannot fight every wrong or reverse each adversity, and that therefore there cannot be an American solution to every world problem." These were remarkable words—the kind we might hear today, very briefly, from Barbara Lee or Ralph Nader. If the president was sincere when he spoke them, they suggested at the very least the possibility of a less aggressive foreign policy.

The same day, Robert Kennedy's Justice Department contacted the Internal Revenue Service to enquire about the tax-exempt status of several right-wing groups, including the John Birch Society and the Christian Anti-Communist Crusade. This was the beginning of the Ideological Organizations Project (IOP)—a secret IRS program, initiated by the White House, to deprive certain right-wing organizations (and, later, two leftist groups including the FPCC) of an enormous financial advantage: the right to pay no tax.[18]

Two days later, the president journeyed to nut country: Los Angeles, a city more redneck then than it is today. At the Hollywood Palladium he gave a rousing speech against right-wing extremism. "They call for a 'man on horseback' because they do not trust the people. They find treason in our churches, in our highest court, and even in the treatment of our water." Kennedy mentioned no group or individual by name, but singled out "armed bands of civilian guerrillas"—which the *New York Times* said was a reference to a right-wing group known as the Minutemen—and "the discordant voices of extremism." As many as three thousand right-wingers gathered outside the building, chanting and singing in protest against his presence and his policies. Back in Washington, Kennedy worried about seeming too liberal; he transferred Dick Goodwin to the State Department and fired his most liberal foreign policy adviser, Chester Bowles, who had been an undersecretary of state. Then, on November 29, he finally replaced Dulles, Cabell and Bissell. His new CIA chief was John McCone, a Wall Street lawyer and Kennedy friend. In Latin America, the third military *coup* of the year occurred: in Ecuador, where the government of Velasco Ibarra was overthrown.

On November 23, Eisenhower gave Kennedy a hand when he declared, in a CBS interview, that it was "very bad practice" for a military officer to express opinions, on political or economic matters, which differed from the president's. "I believe the Army officer, Navy officer, Air officer should not be talking about political matters, particularly domestically, and never in the international field," he said. Of course, it was President Eisenhower who had instigated the military propaganda program in the first place, just as he had helped create the military-industrial complex which later troubled him. Presidents like to have things both ways. The *New York Times* took Eisenhower's comments as a reference to General Walker of Dallas, though they applied equally to the Joint Chiefs.

Around this time, someone claiming to be Lee Harvey Oswald showed up in New York, where he became a brief fixture in right-wing agitations, according to an ex-Marine called Steven Landesberg. Landesberg maintained various aliases and was the founder of a one-man New York branch of the NSRP. On December 25, Marina was called to the passport office in Minsk, and told that she and Lee would be granted exit visas.[19]

December saw stepped-up espionage against the Fair Play for Cuba Committee. The FBI's New York office prepared and mailed an anonymous leaflet "to selected FPCC members throughout the country for the purpose of disrupting FPCC and causing split between FPCC and Socialist Workers Party (SWP) supporters, which technique was very effective." And in mid-December, FBI director Hoover dropped a bombshell on the Kennedys. FBI agents had secretly taped a Chicago *mafioso*, Sam Giancana, claiming that the mafia had delivered the Chicago vote to Jack Kennedy, based on a deal it had made with Joe. In the light of Bobby's pursuit of the mafia as Attorney General, Giancana insisted that the mob had been betrayed. It was a destabilizing Christmas gift from Hoover, reminding the Kennedys of the informational power the domestic intelligence chief held. The Kennedys might have got rid of Dulles, but they would think twice, perhaps, before "retiring" their FBI Director.

On December 16, President Kennedy paid a weekend visit to Latin America. In Venezuela and Colombia he proved popular, though the crowds were smaller than anticipated. Seeking to put some energy into a moribund Alliance for Progress, Kennedy made a speech in Bogotá urging Latin America's industrialists and landowners "to admit past mistakes and to accept new responsibilities": in other words, pay better wages and accept some measure of land reform. This was unexceptionable stuff—the poor approved of it, the rich knew Kennedy would leave shortly and there would be no more talk of this. There was also a certain irony to his exhortation, for the richest landowners and industrialists in Latin America weren't Latin Americans at all. They were Jack Kennedy's colleagues from Capitol Hill: super-wealthy, old-money families like the Rockefellers, who were the biggest private landowners in Venezuela, and owned that country's oil industry; in addition to the largest oil, banking, agribusiness and mining businesses in Brazil.

Jack Kennedy wasn't calling upon some local *latifundistas* to reform themselves; he was telling his likely rival in the 1964 presidential race, Nelson Rockefeller, to get his ethical act together. This was great political theater. It was also fortuitous, since the president was out of the United States on a day when Dr. Martin Luther King and 150 other black people were arrested—for the crime of praying outside city hall—in Albany, Georgia.

A few days after Jack's return, his father suffered a massive stroke.

notes

1 Armstrong, "Harvey & Lee," *The Assassinations*, p. 114.
2 WH 17 CE No. 822, John W. Fain, FBI Report, *Lee Harvey Oswald, Internal Security* - R, p. 10.
3 Newman, *Oswald and The CIA*, pp. 241–243.
4 Epstein, *Legend*, pp. 135–138.
5 Abraham Bolden, *The Echo from Dealey Plaza*, Harmony Books, NY, 2008, p. 5.
6 Armstrong, "Harvey & Lee," *The Assassinations*, p. 114.

7   The Secret Service's tradition of drunken partying while on duty continues to this day. In April, 2012, several Secret Service agents were disciplined for drunkenness and misconduct with prostitutes during a presidential visit to Cartagena, Colombia. The Homeland Security inspector's report revealed that Secret Service agents also hired prostitutes while on duty in El Salvador, Panama, Romania, and China. Greg Seaby, "Investigation Revisits Secret Service Prostitution Scandal," CNN.com, Oct. 20, 2012.

8   Gary Wills, *The Kennedy Imprisonment*, p. 245, quoting General Taylor's "memoirs."

9   WH 17 CE No. 822, John W. Fain, FBI Report, "Lee Harvey Oswald, Internal Security – R."

10 James K. Galbraith, "Did the U.S. Military Plan a Nuclear First Strike for 1963?", *The American Prospect*, Vol. 5, No. 19, Sept. 21, 1994.

11 Anthony Summers, *Not In Your Lifetime*, Marlowe & Co, NY, 1998, pp. 142–3.

12 WH 17 CE No. 823, John W. Fain, FBI report, "Lee Harvey Oswald," p. 3.

13 Summers, *Not In Your Lifetime*, pp 142–5, WH 20 CE Nos. 474, 475, Kramer Exhibits 1 & 2 (the CIA photographs of Oswald with the tourists in Minsk). Naman and Kramer had been joined by a third woman, Marie Loretta Hyde, of Port Angeles, Washington, who claimed to have "become separated" from her tour group: Hyde was the maiden name of Oswald's future Dallas associate, Ruth Paine. WH 23, CE 1845, p. 522.

14 Hugh Sidey, *John F. Kennedy, President*, Atheneum, NY, 1964, p. 245.

15 James Reston Jr., *The Lone Star: the Life of John Connally*, Harper & Row, NY, 1989, pp. 208–209.

16 Ralph Stavins, *Washington Determines the Fate of Vietnam*, in Stavins, Barnet & Raskin, *Washington Plans an Aggressive War*, Vintage, NY, 1971, p. 71.

17 Lamar Waldron with Thom Hartmann, *Ultimate Sacrifice*, Carroll & Graf, NY, 2005, pp. 27, 110–112. Szulc posed as Fidel Castro's biographer (*Fidel, A Critical Portrait*), while plotting his ruin. He also penned a biography of E. Howard Hunt.

18 John A. Andrew, *Power to Destroy: the Political Uses of the IRS from Kennedy to Nixon*, Ivan R. Dee, Chicago, 2002, pp. 24–31.

19 Stan C. Weeber, "Stephen H. Landesberg and the Greenwich Village Hoax," *The Fourth Decade*, Vol. 2, No. 2, Jan. 1995, pp. 14–18; Carlton W. Sterling, "Stephen Landesberg: Another Media Cover-Up?", *The Fourth Decade*, Vol. 3, No. 6, Sept. 1996, pp. 26–30.

CHAPTER 5

ASIDE

★ ★ ★

POLITICAL VIOLENCE
in the United States

Yesterday, as I finished writing the previous chapter, a gunman shot an Arizona congresswoman in the head. He left her brain-damaged, and killed six other people, including a nine-year-old girl. The congresswoman, a Democrat, was one of a number "targeted" by a Republican, Sarah Palin, during the 2010 midterm elections. Palin's targeting was quite specific—a video map of the United States, superimposed with a dozen sets of cross-hairs: telescopic sights, such as you might see looking down the barrel of a hunting gun, or an assassin's rifle. Gabrielle Giffords had beaten her Republican challenger, Jesse Kelly, in the election, but she is out of office as of yesterday. A campaign event organized by Kelly was promoted thus: "Get on target for victory in November. Help remove Gabrielle Giffords from office. Shoot a fully automatic M-16 with Jesse Kelly."

Palin expressed immediate sympathy, via the touching medium of her Facebook page. Palin's aides would soon insist repeatedly that the gunsights over Gabrielle Giffords' name, and the "on target" machine-gun-shooting event, were never intended to incite violence. The gunman, young, white, and male, would be declared a lone assassin, mentally ill, of no particular political persuasion.

But the image of those cross-hairs and the slogan "on target" are not new: they bring us right back to the early 1960s, when extreme right-wing movements, often financed by business interests or by the CIA, flourished—and openly incited violence. Some of these (the ones CIA funded) were racial or nationalist in nature, such as Alpha 66 and DRE and the other anti-Castro Cuban gangs. Others (the ones funded by business, usually the oil men) were white, and racist in nature; many were offshoots of the American Liberty League. The League, which shut down after FDR won his second term, spawned a number of extreme right-wing and paramilitary groups. Among them were the John Birch Society, the NSRP, the American Nazi Party, and the Minutemen. These Minutemen were not to be confused with Wernher von Braun's nuclear missiles: instead, they were an organized, right-wing, paramilitary underground. Founded in St. Louis in June 1960 by Richard Lauchli and Robert DePugh, the Minutemen intended, like the survivalists of the 1980s, to be a partisan guerrilla force after the Russians took over the United States. DePugh, addressing the NSRP convention in Montgomery, Alabama, in 1962, spoke of the need for guerrilla warfare "in the event the U.S. government was taken over by communists." Like the Militia in the 1990s, the Minutemen also believed in violent action against Washington, DC, and its representatives. In the early 1960s the Minutemen put out a newsletter titled *On Target*—the letter "O" being a cross-hair gunsight.

> "See the old man on the corner where you buy your paper? He may have a silencer-equipped pistol under his coat. That extra fountain pen in the pocket of the insurance salesman that calls on you might be a cyanide-gas gun. What about your milkman? Arsenic works slow but sure. Your auto mechanic may stay up all night studying booby traps."

> "These patriots are not going to let you take their freedom away from them. They have learned the silent knife, the strangler's cord, the target rifle that hits sparrows at 200 yards. Only their leaders restrain them."

> "Traitors beware! Even now the cross-hairs are on the back of your necks…"

The above appeared on the cover of *On Target* shortly before Jack Kennedy's assassination. Inevitably, given their perhaps modest numbers, the Minutemen got into a membership fight with the Nazi Party and lost personnel to a new Los Angeles outfit, calling itself "the Real Minutemen." And the NSRP and the Klan likewise lost members to a new, more radical outfit, NACIREMA—"American" spelled backwards!—which also called itself the Dixie Clan. In April 1963, the Clan, a.k.a. the Congress of Freedom, Inc., held a meeting in New Orleans. According to a police detective who infiltrated the event, the organizers presented an elaborate plan to assassinate several industrialists and investment bankers. "Membership within the Congress of Freedom, Inc., contain high-ranking members of the Armed Forces that secretly belong to the organization," Detective Lochart F. Gracey reported.

Five days after President Kennedy was murdered, the head of the American Nazi Party, George Lincoln Rockwell, wrote to J. Edgar Hoover denouncing 27 right-wingers and segregationists who he felt could be involved in "violent acts of a nature to involve the security of the United States." Condemning force and violence in his opening paragraph, Rockwell continued:

> "Inevitably, however, such an extreme political movement [as the Nazi Party] attracts irresponsible and lunatic elements who are not welcome, but who force themselves upon the movement and are very hard to get rid of."

> "The assassination of the President was, I believe, the work of such a 'nut' over on the other side from us. As vile and evil as I believe our communist opponents to be, I do not think they would be stupid enough to have shot the President as part of their filthy plans."

Rockwell was later murdered by one of his own henchmen. Adrift for a decade, ex-Nazis, gun-runners and right-wing survivalists coalesced around the Militia movement. This culminated in the bombing of the Oklahoma City Federal Building in 1995. The Minutemen disappeared from view, resurfacing with the George W. Bush administration, in Arizona and Texas, as an armed militia and volunteer border patrol. In May 2009, a group of Minutemen invaded a home in Arivaca, Arizona. The unit was commanded by one Shawna Ford, who thought she was robbing a drug dealer so as to fund her militant, anti-immigrant group. When no drugs were found, the Minutemen shot the homeowner and his nine-year-old daughter dead.

The angry self-pity of these heavily armed paranoids has changed little in half a century: "Do not expect a big roundup of patriots," wrote Bobby LeRoy in *On Target* in summer of '63. "We will be picked up one by one for real or imaginary violations. You will have little or no warning when your time comes."

CHAPTER 6

1962

MORE CRISES, AND A CHANGE OF SCENE

★ ★ ★

Lee Harvey Oswald leaped into action in the new year. On January 2, he wrote to his mother, in Fort Worth, advising her that he and Marina would be in the U.S. in March. He exchanged letters with the U.S. Embassy. Given the many immigration hurdles still to be overcome, the Embassy proposed that Oswald and his wife travel separately. Oswald's reply was emphatic: "I certainly will not consider going to the U.S. alone for any reason, particularly since it appears my passport will be confiscated upon my arrival in the United States."

What made Oswald think this? The Embassy was going out of its way to help him: the Consul was considering his request—dated January 5—for a loan to cover the cost of his return. His mother wrote him, suggesting she reveal his financial plight to the newspapers, so as to raise funds. Oswald told her not to. From Marguerite's letters, Lee learned that the USMC had revoked his honorable discharge.

This incensed him, and from Minsk on January 30 (dating his letter 1961) he wrote to John Connally, to protest the reclassification of his discharge as "undesirable":

> Dear Sir,
>
> I wish to call your attention to a case about which you may have personal knowledge since you are a resident of Ft. Worth as I am. In November 1959 an event was well publicated [sic] in the Ft. Worth newspapers concerning a person who had gone to the Soviet Union to reside for a short time, (much in the same way E. Hemingway resided in Paris.)
>
> This person in answers to questions put to him by reporteds [sic] in Moscow criticized certain facets of american [sic] life. The story was blown up into another "turncoat" sensation, with the result that the navy department gave this person a belated dishonourable [sic] discharge,although he had received an honourable [sic] discharge after three years service on Sept. 11, 1959 at El Toro, marine corps base in California.
>
> These are the basic facts of my case.
>
> I have and always had the full sanction of the U.S. Embassy, Moscow USSR and hence the U.S. government. In as much as I am returning to the USA in this year with the aid of the US Embassy bring [sic] with me my family (since I married in the U.S.S.R.) I shall employ all means to right this gross mistake or injustice to a boni-fied [sic] U.S. citizen and ex-serviceman. The U.S. government has no charges or complaints against me. I ask you to look into this case and take the necessary steps to repair the damage done to me and my family. For information I would direct you to consult the American Embassy, Chikovski St, 19/21, Moscow, USSR
>
> Thank You
> Lee H. Oswald

This is a wonderful letter, solipsistic (he compares himself to Hemingway!) but very well composed. It has relatively few spelling mistakes compared to his alleged diary or his later writings (Lee Harvey Oswald's grammar was generally good). His claim to have "always had the full sanction of the U.S. Embassy... and hence the

U.S. government" is fascinating. It's been suggested that the letter was written, or tidied up, by someone other than Oswald; that might explain his twice spelling "honorable" with a 'u' in the manner of an Englishman.[1]

Unfortunately for Lee, the letter did no good. Connally had resigned as Navy Secretary, in order to run for Governor of Texas. He acknowledged receipt, and forwarded the letter to his successor, Fred Korth. The Navy advised Oswald that no change or correction to his status was warranted.

Meanwhile, at the second Punta del Este conference, the Kennedy administration leaned hard on the Latin American nations to banish Cuba from the Organization of American States. When the larger countries—Mexico, Venezuela, Argentina, and Brazil— refused to support him, the president was forced to rely on the votes of pro-American dictators such as Somoza of Nicaragua, Stroessner of Paraguay, and "Papa Doc" Duvalier of Haiti. Arthur Schlesinger, one of Kennedy's representatives at the conference, later described how he won Duvalier's support: "We finally yielded to blackmail and agreed to resume our aid to the airport at Port-au-Prince."[2]

On February 6, American Consul Joseph B. Norbury wrote to Oswald, "We are prepared to take your application for a loan." Around this time, Lee wrote an undated letter to John Tower, the Texas senator, claiming to be a U.S. citizen held in Russia against his will, and asking for assistance; Tower, wrongly advised by State that Oswald had renounced his citizenship, did not reply. Meanwhile Lee argued by mail with the Embassy over the amount of his loan— he wanted $800, they offered $500. In all this correspondence—with the exception of the politer letter to Tower—Oswald adopted an annoyed and entitled tone, as if an honorable discharge and an easy return to the U.S. were his by right.

On February 15, Marina and Lee's daughter was born in a Minsk hospital. They named her June Lee. In March, Oswald received his certificate of undesirable discharge; he began a correspondence with the USMC protesting their decision and insisting that his discharge be reviewed.

The year had begun well for Jack Kennedy. His new CIA director, John McCone, another right-wing, bellicose Republican, played well with Agency insiders and the military. There were no immediate crises, and the president thought he had dealt with the threat of inflation by brokering a series of no-pay-rise, no-price-rise deals with key industries, among them steel. January saw the resignation of his civil rights point man, Harris Wofford, who requested a transfer to the Peace Corps. In February, Air Force Colonel John Glenn was blasted into orbit by one of von Braun's rockets, becoming the first American in space. "If only he was a Negro!" Lyndon Johnson exclaimed as he and Kennedy watched the heroic mission on TV (unlike Laika, provision had been made to bring the Colonel back alive). Jackie Kennedy conducted a televised tour of the White House which was broadcast on Valentine's Day. On February 26, Robert Kennedy, frustrated that Lansdale's Cuban plans seemed to be going nowhere, told him to drop the anti-Castro efforts and concentrate on a three-month period of intelligence gathering. He had no idea that, only a week earlier, Lemnitzer and the Joint Chiefs had approached Lansdale with a plan—in the event that von Braun's rocket exploded—to blame Glenn's death on Cuban sabotage, and use this as a pretext for an immediate invasion of the island.

As the Kennedys backed away from a military solution to the "Cuba problem," the Pentagon pushed harder for one. In March, the Joint Chiefs approached McNamara and Kennedy with a plan which, if not as terrible in its implications as the Net Evaluation Subcommittee proposal for nuclear war, was equally immoral and even more illegal. This was Operation NORTHWOODS: a plan, backed by every one of the Joint Chiefs, to stage terrorist attacks against American civilians on U.S. soil, in order to justify an invasion of Cuba. One incident which the Chiefs proposed involved hijacking and shooting down American passenger airliners. Another involved faking an attack on the U.S. naval base at Guantanamo. Still another Pentagon proposal was for a wave of bombings, targeting civilians, in Washington, DC, and Miami, Florida. All these terrorist acts— sponsored and probably carried out by the U.S. military—were to be blamed on Castro. Just as an explosion aboard the U.S. battleship *Maine* had been used as an excuse to seize Cuba from Spain in 1898, the fake NORTHWOODS attacks would justify another Cuban war.

Operation NORTHWOODS was first revealed by James Bamford in *Body of Secrets*, one of three books he has written about the NSA. Bamford is patriotic and admires the U.S. military. At the same time, he has a one-word description of the Pentagon's NORTHWOODS plan: treason. Bamford refers to two contemporary U.S. politicians

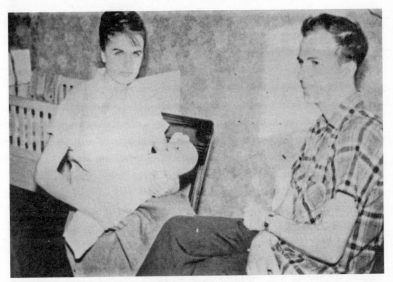

Fig. 2: Warren Commission Exhibit 2622: the Oswalds' baby photo?

who were considered "very cooperative" by NSA, in the sense that they asked no questions and worked actively to keep their colleagues in the dark about intelligence operations. They were Michigan congressman Gerald Ford and Georgia senator Richard Russell— future members of the Warren Commission.[3]

In the last sentence of his letter to McNamara, Lemnitzer made a power play: "It is recommended that this responsibility both for overt and covert military operations be assigned to the Joint Chiefs of Staff"—in other words, CIA, FBI and the White House would be kept out of the NORTHWOODS loop. The Chiefs wanted the military to have total responsibility for these acts of domestic terrorism. Lemnitzer presented the NORTHWOODS plan to McNamara on March 13. McNamara's response is not recorded. Lemnitzer met Kennedy on March 16. Kennedy's response to the proposal is not recorded. But he made it clear that he didn't intend to invade Cuba any time soon.

In March, Robert Webster received his Russian exit visa. And Landesberg, the one-man NSRP provocateur, caused a disturbance at a meeting of the American Jewish Congress in New York. He later told the FBI that Lee Harvey Oswald was present, taking photographs. But Oswald and Marina remained in Minsk, waiting for a raft of paperwork to arrive from the United States.

THE PRESIDENT AND THE PROVOCATEUR

Fig. 2 is a photograph, supposedly taken around this time, and found—according to the Warren Report—among the Oswalds' possessions. It is Commission Exhibit 2622. The version published by the Commission is too overexposed to reveal any detail. A darker print, from the National Archives, was obtained by researcher Jack White. It purports to show Marina, baby June, and Lee. The reader will not gaze long at the photo before concluding that several things are wrong with it. For a start, what is Marina holding? It's not a baby: it's too stiff, and its "eye" appears to be painted onto the photo where we might expect a baby's or a doll's cheek to be. Oswald's "leg" has a white rim, and appears to emerge not from his hip, but from his stomach. Marina casts a shadow on the wall, but not on the bed. Some items of furniture cast shadows; others do not. Behind Lee's head is something resembling a lamp, but it appears to be in motion, and two-dimensional.

Clearly the photo is a fake, or, to be more exact, a photomontage. Someone has gone to the trouble of trying to merge separate pictures of Lee and Marina holding a doll. But why? The matte-work (fake shadows, the lamp, Lee's mysterious leg) is bad, so my guess is that this was done by someone quite inexperienced in photomontage, for fun or practice. Did Lee do it himself? He was interested in photography, and would have access to a darkroom and photographic equipment when he returned to the States. We still know little about his time in Minsk; perhaps he had access to such tools there, too.[4]

In March, the IRS produced an internal memo listing right-wing groups to be investigated as part of the Ideological Organizations Project. Among them were the John Birch Society and two Dallas-based groups, the National Indignation Convention and the Life Line Foundation—a right-wing media network which included radio, television and a book club, funded by oil man H.L. Hunt.[5]

Meanwhile Dr. King, waiting to be sentenced for the crime of leading a protest in Albany, Georgia, criticized the administration's "cautious and defensive" civil rights strategy. "Its efforts have been directed towards limited accomplishments in a number of areas, affecting few individuals and altering old patterns only superficially," he wrote in a magazine article. "It is a melancholy fact that the Administration is aggressively driving only towards the limited goal of token integration." In Argentina, the military staged a *coup*. The president, Arturo Frondizi, had permitted the populist *Peronistas* to run for office in the general election. When they won ten governorships, the generals ousted the president, banned the *Peronistas* and the communist party, nullified the election results, and called for new elections in a year's time. Such things do not occur in Latin America without the input of the CIA. Whether Kennedy knew in advance is unclear; he withheld recognition of the puppet regime for a mere three weeks, and did nothing else to impede the generals. He soon had other troubles to contend with. In the absence of an immediate crisis, Jack Kennedy tended to womanize. He did so carelessly, knowing that the FBI surveilled him and kept files on his adventures. Then, on March 22, he took lunch with FBI director Hoover at the White House.

Jack Kennedy had not met with Hoover in more than a year. It was common knowledge that the FBI Director and the Attorney General did not get along. Drew Pearson, in a radio broadcast, had speculated that the Kennedys planned to fire Hoover, just as they had Dulles and his coterie. But Hoover didn't come to luncheon unprepared. He brought with him evidence that one of the president's girlfriends, Judith Campbell, was also sexually involved with two mafia bosses, Sam Giancana and John Roselli. According to Summers' biography, Hoover had a much larger file of evidence, detailing Kennedy's involvement with prostitutes and several other affairs. But—absent any communists or Nazis—it was the suggestion that the president shared a mistress with Italian *mafiosi* that would be most damaging, and both men knew it. (Hoover may have heard the news directly from Roselli: the FBI chief and the mobster were frequent guests at the Texas oil men's Del Charro resort.) Lunch lasted four hours, and Kennedy was in a foul mood when it was over. Hoover was not fired.[6]

Also on March 22, Richard Helms, who had replaced Wisner at CIA, sent a letter to the former Nazi spymaster, Reinhard Gehlen. It is so bizarre and gross that I shall simply reprint it without further comment[7]:

Dear General Gehlen

I wish to extend to you on the occasion of your sixtieth birthday my sincere congratulations. A real milestone has been reached and with my congratulations I send best wishes for your good health and continued success. I look back with great pleasure

on our meetings during the past years and the opportunity they afforded for us to renew our friendship and I trust the future will afford us similar occasions.
Cordially,
Richard Helms

On the same day as Kennedy and Hoover lunched and Helms sent the Nazi "general" birthday greetings, Lee Oswald fired off a letter of his own. It was addressed to R. McC. Tompkins, Brigadier General, USMC, Assistant Director of Personnel. Once again, Lee protested that he had received an "undiresable" [sic] discharge. In surprisingly legalistic terms, he wrote,

> "I have not violated Section 1544, Title 18, US code, therefore you have no legel [sic] or even moral right to reverse my honourable discharge from the USMC of Sept. 11, 1960... You may consider this letter a request by me for a full review of my case in the light of these facts, since by the time you recive [sic] this letter I shall have returned to the USA with my family, and shall be prepared to appear in person at a reasonable time and place in my area, before a reviewing board of officers."[8]

Supposedly, at this time, Oswald was a lone American among factory workers in Minsk, Byelorussia. He had a couple of English-speaking friends, but no access to books detailing the Marine Corps' internal procedures. There was no Internet in those days, and no long-distance phone. According to the Warren Report, Lee was a poorly educated Southern boy who joined the military as a teenager. Someone had to be helping him research his case and formulate his arguments on paper—someone who knew the USMC code, and who spelled "honorable" with a 'u,' like an Englishman. Who was Oswald's educated, knowledgeable helper?

In April, Jack Kennedy found a crisis suitable for his attention when U.S. Steel unilaterally raised its prices, having previously agreed to the president's anti-inflation policy. This was a serious test. No major corporation—or labor union—could be relied upon to hold the line on prices, or wages, if U.S. Steel was able to break its deal at will. Kennedy reacted boldly, in a way that many wish the president would treat corporate wrongdoers today: by publicly condemning the company and instructing government contractors and the Pentagon to seek alternative sources for their steel needs.

The president's doubts about invading Cuba were reinforced by an April 10 memo to CIA chief McCone, from Sherman Kent, chairman of CIA's Board of National Estimates. The Kent memo doubted the Joint Chiefs' guaranteed rapid victory; it predicted that initial resistance to an American invasion would melt away within a few days, but that "substantial numbers" of Castro's forces would survive the military assault and continue a guerrilla resistance. Establishment of a pro-U.S. government would be difficult due to urban terrorism and guerrilla warfare in the countryside. The U.S. would be drawn into a "prolonged" role as an occupation force, increasingly becoming a target for attacks, and a focus for general hostility, in Cuba and around the world. If this sounds like the aftermath of our later invasions of Iraq, and of Afghanistan, it may be because the results of invading a foreign country—even one ruled by a dictator—are predictable, in terms of increased violence, repression, damage to national prestige, and project failure. What is remarkable is not that Sherman Kent pointed out the flaw in the Pentagon's plans, but that Jack Kennedy read his report—*and paid attention*. Meanwhile Jack's pet project moved forward: on April 11, NSC memorandum number 144 assigned the highest priority to a manned Lunar landing —putting the Moon mission on the same footing as Atlas and Titan ICBMs, and Polaris and Minuteman missiles.

On April 12, Bobby Kennedy took the battle to the steel executives by sending FBI agents to their homes in the middle of the night. Suspecting U.S. Steel and Bethlehem Steel of illegal price-fixing, the Attorney General also had agents raid their offices. The raids and the threat of an IRS investigation worked. The other companies dropped their prices, and U.S. Steel chairman Roger Blough caved the following day. The Chamber of Commerce might be against him, but the public greatly approved of Kennedy's anti-corporate stand. The president had won, and while dealing with this crisis he still found time to meet with the Joint Chiefs, listen to them again propose an immediate military strike against Cuba, and turn them down.

Jack Kennedy was on a roll. Popular psychology might suggest this was because he hadn't spoken with his father in a quarter of a year. Old Joe's stroke had left him incapable of speech, and, inevitably, Jack was growing away from him. Saying no to people in positions of power came more easily. He cancelled Skybolt, though he also increased the military budget. He was briefed by John Kenneth Galbraith, his ambassador to India, who had just returned from Vietnam. Galbraith advised him that the U.S. should avoid the French trap, and get out. He also signed off on a new round of atmospheric nuclear tests, though he insisted, for political purposes, that they take place in the Pacific, rather than in Nevada. This way, the Russians' nuclear provocation was countered: nuclear blasts being seen as "bargaining chips" rather than agents of environmental degradation.

On May 8 Robert Webster appeared at the U.S. Embassy in Moscow to fill out his final paperwork. Though he had married while in Russia, he did not seek exit papers for his wife. A week later, he left for the United States.

The same day, in Washington, John Sherman Cooper, a Kentucky Republican, joined the Democratic Southern Caucus in opposition to a modest civil rights bill: an attempt to outlaw literacy tests as a voting requirement. The president had supported the legislation, without much passion. It was allowed to die when subjected to a mild Republican filibuster. On May 11, Jack Kennedy discussed economic policy with David Rockefeller, Nelson's brother. David had been Jack's first choice for treasury secretary, and Jack asked him to write a letter detailing his economic ideas. Not surprisingly, Rockefeller sent a proposal for reduced government spending and a cut in corporate income tax. Kennedy replied, disagreeing politely, and arranged to have their exchange published in *Life* magazine, to show voters he had good relations with business. But he did not, and, perceived as anti-business and weak on communism, he could no longer count on the support of Henry Luce's *Life, Fortune* or *Time*. Nelson Rockefeller, having just won reelection to the Senate, let it be known that he was confident he could beat Kennedy in '64 if he were the Republican candidate.

According to CIA counsel Lawrence Houston, on May 14 Robert Kennedy learned of the CIA/mafia plot to kill Fidel Castro. Houston told the Church Committee in 1975 that he and Sheffield Edwards —CIA's chief of security—advised Kennedy that the Agency needed to accommodate Giancana, the mafia boss, in certain ways because of their joint enterprise to murder the Cuban president. Kennedy acted as if this was the first he'd heard of the arrangement, and chastised the CIA men, who assured him that all CIA/mafia plots had been terminated (this was not true). Richard Bissell, who had initiated the plots in the Eisenhower administration, told the Church Committee he had briefed Bobby and Maxwell Taylor about the CIA/mafia connection in spring 1961, after the Bay of Pigs. But Taylor told the Committee that no such briefing had occurred.

So, was Bissell lying, to blacken the Kennedys' reputation? He had a reason to dislike them, having been fired by the president along with Dulles and Cabell. But consider his claim in the context of the Bay of Pigs, and of Operation MONGOOSE. Both were illegal, covert actions. Both financed the activities of violent criminals, at a cost of innocent human lives. Bobby Kennedy was *in charge of* Operation MONGOOSE. What did he think it did?

On May 17, Martin Luther King told a reporter, "I do not feel the president has given the leadership that the enormity of the problem demands." King had backed the voting rights campaign, only to see Kennedy ditch it. He and other black leaders reacted to White House inaction with alarm. Segregationists, like Russell and Cooper, reveled in it. Still, life for the president was not bad. On May 19, Jack celebrated his birthday ten days early, with a bash for 15,000 people at Madison Square Garden in New York. Marilyn Monroe sang "Happy Birthday, Mr. President." Kennedy came on stage to thank her for the "sweet, wholesome" song. The two were rumored to be having an affair, Jacqueline Kennedy being absent from the birthday party. Soon afterward, Jack also had a meeting with Edward Teller, the atom scientist who enjoyed the sobriquet "Father of the Hydrogen Bomb." Teller, head of the nuclear laboratory at Livermore, was another keen advocate of nuclear war-fighting. He wanted to congratulate the president on his strong Civil Defense commitment, and to impress on him the importance of further atmospheric nuclear testing. The meeting seems to have had the opposite effect: Kennedy worried increasingly about the health impact of nuclear fallout, and stopped promoting Civil Defense.

On May 24, the Oswalds visited the Embassy in Moscow. On June 1, Lee returned, and signed a promissory note for $435.71—money the Embassy was lending him. The government continued to be nice to Oswald, returning his passport, giving his wife and child immigrant visas, even lending him money to come home. It was as if his threats to betray military secrets, and the missing years in Minsk, had never occurred. The same day Marina was given a medical examination at the Embassy by an Air Force assistant attaché, Dr. Alexis Davison. Davison also met Lee and gave him the address of his mother, a conservative White Russian who lived in Atlanta, Georgia.

The Oswalds took a train from Moscow to Amsterdam the next day. They spent several days in Holland, departing for New York on June 6. Their ship docked at Hoboken, NJ, on June 13. Supposedly, no attempt was made to interview or debrief Oswald, a person of continuing interest to CIA, the FBI, and ONI, or his intelligence-connected Russian wife.[10]

Instead the Oswalds were met by one Spas T. Raikin, whom the Warren Report described as "a representative of the Travelers Aid Society, which had been contacted by the Department of State." Raikin was also the secretary-general of the "American Friends of the Anti-Bolshevik Bloc of Nations"—which sounds like another one-man fundraising operation, but was, according to Anthony Summers, an *émigré* group in direct touch with the FBI and U.S. military intelligence.[11]

Per Raikin, Oswald lied to him and claimed he had been a Marine guard at the Embassy in Moscow. Nevertheless, Raikin arranged accommodation for the Oswalds, and helped Lee contact his brother Robert, in Fort Worth. Robert was persuaded to wire Lee $200, so that Lee and family could fly to Texas at once, and live with him.

Robert Oswald noticed, on meeting Lee, Marina, and baby at the airport, that they had only two suitcases. As Summers points out, this is extremely strange. The Oswalds landed in New Jersey with *seven* suitcases; left New York with *five* cases; and showed up in Fort Worth with *two*. Where did the other cases go? And what was in them? Oswald was consistently tight-fisted, and would not have missed a chance to harass Delta Air Lines over several pieces of lost luggage. But there is no record of any such complaint. Why did the Oswalds fly to Texas in the first place? Money was tight, and trains and buses were a lot cheaper. Or, if money was no object, why didn't they take a nonstop flight? Robert Oswald paid for two expensive tickets, yet Lee and Marina chose to change planes in Atlanta, Georgia. The Oswalds had just met Captain Alexis Davison: Lee had, in his address book, the Atlanta address of Natasha Davison, the Captain's mother. Davison told the HSCA that the Oswalds never visited her. As Summers observes, "there never has been an adequate explanation for the Oswalds' travel home through Davison's home city of Atlanta, a route they had no known reason to take."[12]

Though the Warren Commission would choose to ignore it, Lee Harvey Oswald (or one of his avatars) had other business in Atlanta, as we shall see.

On June 26, Oswald applied for work with the Commercial Employment Agency in Fort Worth. He told them he had been in Moscow, working for the State Department. He proceeded to the FBI office for a meeting which had been scheduled with Special Agents John Fain and Tom Carter. According to Fain's report, Oswald burst into the office unannounced, exclaiming, "Here I am, what do you want me to talk about?" Fain said Oswald acted in a cocky and aggressive way, and refused to take a polygraph.

> During most of the interview, Oswald exhibited an impatient and arrogant attitude. Oswald finally stated that Soviet officials had asked him upon his arrival why he had come to Russia. Oswald stated that he told them, "I came because I wanted to." Oswald added that he went to Russia to "see the country."[13]

This was all rubbish. Presumably Fain knew it was rubbish, as he had filed reports on Oswald, and interviewed Marguerite, while Lee was still in Russia[14]—when the Director was concerned that Oswald was being impersonated by an impostor. We can approach Fain's report in two ways: 1) that it was a truthful account of the FBI man's interview with the young James Dean, ending in a stalemate and generating no useful intelligence, or 2) that it was bogus, to conceal the content of their real meeting.

Neither man was stupid, and both had better things to discuss than the anodyne, inaccurate blather in Fain's account. So I'd assume 2) to be the case. If it was, what did Oswald and Fain really talk about, at his first official meeting with the FBI?

By going to Russia, Oswald had established a reputation as a leftist, a communist, and an extremist. If he were also an intelligence agent, whether for CIA, or for ONI, this made him a person of interest and potential value to the FBI as well. The FBI was running surveillance-on-steroids of the FPCC and SWP: Oswald's rap sheet was ready-made to infiltrate either organization. Also, Oswald spoke

Russian. If he made appropriate contacts, he might be able to identify local Russian-speaking espionage agents, should there be any. John Newman remarks that it is "amazing" that CIA was not furnished with Agent Fain's report, devoid of intelligence though it was.[15]

Perhaps it's less amazing if the FBI was in the process of recruiting Oswald as its own informant.

(After the assassination, Allan Sweatt—Chief Criminal Deputy Sheriff of Dallas County—told a Houston journalist that Lee had been an FBI informant. Sweatt claimed that "Oswald was being paid $200 a month as an informant in connection with their subversive investigations" and gave the "alleged informant number assigned to Oswald by the FBI as S172." The Warren Commission, aware of Sweatt's accusation, ignored it.)[16]

In June, President Kennedy signed a National Security Directive authorizing U.S. counterinsurgency actions in Ecuador, Colombia, Guatemala and Venezuela. Around this time he approved CIA activities aimed at destabilizing the Brazilian government. He also paid a state visit to Mexico, riding with President Lopez Mateos in an open limo through the streets of the capital. Lopez Mateos acted receptive to Kennedy's promotion of the Alliance for Progress, but was disinclined to break relations with Cuba. In July a U.S. hydrogen bomb was exploded above the atmosphere, creating an artificial extension of the Van Allen belts, in an attempt "to disrupt the magnetosphere." The scientific need for this was unclear. In Peru, a military *coup* took place, courtesy of General Juan Velasco Alvarado. For once, Kennedy reacted with disapproval, canceling military assistance and civilian aid, as this was a *golpe* from the left, with certain socialist consequences. Otherwise, his support for Latin American military takeovers was unwavering. Domestically, Congress offered the president some defeats. His allocation of Civil Defense funds was reduced from $695 million to $80 million, and his medical insurance bill—an early attempt at creating Medicare for elderly taxpayers—failed by four votes in the Senate. A taping system was installed in the White House. On July 10, Martin Luther King and Ralph Abernathy were sentenced to 45 days in jail or a $176 fine for protesting in Albany, Georgia. They chose jail; the mayor paid their fines, anonymously, two days later, in the hope that they'd leave town. Instead, King vowed to remain and continue fighting for civil rights.

The same day—July 10—Agent Fain filed a confidential, 15-page report titled *Lee Harvey Oswald* with the Dallas FBI office. Copies also went to the ONI in New Orleans and to the Immigration Service in Dallas. The report referenced Fain's interview with Marguerite Oswald and his more recent interviews with Mrs. Robert Oswald, and with Lee himself. Fain recounted Oswald's time in Russia based on documents from the U.S. Embassy: he reported on Lee's attempts to get his "dishonorable" discharge reversed, and on the letter Lee had sent to the Embassy—dated August 8, 1961—in which he made his remarkable proposal to fly home via military jet from Berlin.

On July 14, Lee, Marina and baby June moved into Marguerite Oswald's home on West Seventh Street in Fort Worth. Two days later, the Texas Employment Commission found Lee a job as a metal worker at the Leslie Welding company. Lee rented an apartment at 2703 Mercedes Avenue, moved Marina and the baby in, and renewed his correspondence with the Navy, demanding a review of his discharge. He also subscribed to the leftist magazine *The Worker*, sent an enquiry to the SWP, and ordered a Russian periodical, all from the Mercedes address—guaranteeing that his mail would be intercepted and probably opened by the Postal Inspection Service, since the SWP was watchlisted as a "subversive organization."

J. Robert Elliot was one of several white supremacists whom Jack Kennedy had appointed to the federal bench, as an offering to the right wing of his party. On July 21, Judge Elliot signed an injunction barring Dr. King, Ralph Abernathy, and other named protesters from protesting. Elliot ruled that black demonstrations infringed the civil rights of white Albany homeowners to equal protection by the police. King suspected that the Justice Department was behind the ruling. When Bobby Kennedy learned—from FBI wiretaps—that Martin was planning to defy Judge Elliot, he called him and urged him to obey the court order. Martin pointed out that higher moral issues were at stake, and Bobby, furious, yelled at him that no individual was above the law. This from an individual who ran Operation MONGOOSE and had authorized secret wiretaps on King and all his close associates! King didn't protest, but others did; arrests and waves of racist violence followed. On July 24, the Court of Appeals in Atlanta ruled Elliot's ban unconstitutional. Martin and many others were soon in jail again. Black leaders pressed Jack to make a statement, but he ducked out, making himself "unavailable for comment" as he celebrated Jackie's birthday at Hyannis Port. Only when Nelson Rockefeller intervened, demanding King be given federal protection and the Albany police investigated, did the president speak up, referring to the Albany crisis at his press conference on August 1.

"I find it wholly inexplicable why the city council of Albany will not sit down with the citizens of Albany, who may be Negroes, and attempt to secure them, in a peaceful way, their rights," Kennedy said. "The U.S. government is involved in sitting down at Geneva with the Soviet Union. I do not understand why the government of Albany... cannot do the same for U.S. citizens." How interesting that he used an analogy from foreign policy! But that was the policy which engaged him most. Still, Kennedy's words were much appreciated. Dr. King wired his thanks from jail. Segregationists, in particular Richard Russell, were outraged—even more so when the Albany City Commissioners sought an injunction banning all future protests, and the Justice Department opposed it. The Justice Department's amicus brief was serious symbolism; Martin was released two days later. However, his attempts at negotiation with the City Commissioners went nowhere. Albany remained segregated; racial tension remained high.

On August 16, the FBI came visiting in Fort Worth. Special Agents Fain and Arnold Brown sat in their car with Oswald for two hours. Fain's new report supposedly satisfied the Bureau that Lee was not a security risk, not violent, and not working in a sensitive industry. Unlike his first report, this one was forwarded to CIA, and Oswald's file was, according to the official record, placed in an inactive status. In her statement to the Warren Commission, Marina reported:

> "Lee said that the FBI had told him that in the event some Russians might visit him and would try to recruit him to work for them, he should notify the FBI agents."

This makes somewhat more sense than Fain's report. It might also explain why, if Oswald had been assigned some "deep cover" activity by the FBI, possibly involving Russian spies, his file was officially made "inactive."

The next day—August 17—Lee filed a change-of-address card with the post office, stating that his new address was 2703 Mercedes Avenue, Fort Worth.[17]

In August, the State Department reported to the president on the Alliance for Progress. It was not good news: the *Alianza*, one of his first initiatives, had so far achieved virtually nothing. Meanwhile the costs of the new Apollo Command Center in Houston—the Moon mission base—continued to escalate. While publicly committed to a Lunar landing, Kennedy was suffering private doubts. He wrote to his budget director, Dave Bell, "It seems to me the cost is excessive for this Center, and it does raise the question of the funding of the entire program."

The same month the Teamster boss, Jimmy Hoffa, discussed the possibility of assassinating Robert Kennedy, who had assembled a special "Get Hoffa Squad" within the Justice Department. Unaware that his trusted deputy, Ed Partin, was about to become a government informant, Hoffa proposed to him two ways of getting rid of the Attorney General: plastic explosives, or assassination by rifles when he was driving in an open car. Hoffa remarked that the best place to kill Bobby was in the South, where the murder could be blamed on white supremacists. On August 29, Jack Kennedy hosted a special White House screening of John Frankenheimer's new movie *The Manchurian Candidate*. The president had a reason for the screening, beyond the edgy excellence of the film. Fletcher Knebel had sent him a proof copy of the novel he had co-authored, *Seven Days in May*. Kennedy wanted Frankenheimer to make a movie based on the book.

This wasn't a great idea, but it may have been a necessary one. While Richard Condon's original novel *The Manchurian Candidate* was excellent material. Knebel's book was a potboiler, with dull characters and an uninteresting plot: one good Marine saves the day and the few rotten apples are simply removed from the Pentagon's barrel. But Kennedy wasn't interested in character detail or who was the better writer; he saw *Seven Days in May* as ammunition in a media war, part of a long-term process he had only just become involved in: reducing the power of the Pentagon, and restoring civilian control over the military and in particular over nuclear weapons. (This, of course, was the subject matter of another great film in production at that very moment: *Dr. Strangelove*.)

On August 31, Martin Luther King sent a telegram to the president, asking him to intervene in the Albany stalemate by making a national address. Nick Bryant wrote, "But with the intensity of the crisis already subsiding, the White House failed even to acknowledge King's request. Albany was finally quiet—the aim of administration policy from the outset."[18]

Baron George de Mohrenschildt had entered the United States in 1938. Though a Russian national, he became an American citizen without difficulty. In 1942, the State Department placed a "refusal" or "lookout" on his passport office file on the grounds that he was alleged to be a Nazi agent. The Baron traveled to Mexico the same year, and lived there for several months. Expelled by the Mexican government, he returned to the U.S. and attended the University of Texas. In 1957, he applied for a new passport, so as to visit Yugoslavia—a communist country. Despite his lookout notice, the Baron's application was approved. His employer was the American Co-operation Administration, a CIA front company. On his return, de Mohrenschildt was debriefed in Washington, and in Dallas, where he lived. His CIA liaison there was J. Walton Moore, a Domestic Contacts Division agent. From late 1960 till autumn 1961, the Baron and his wife, Jeanne, enjoyed a "walking tour" of Central America which took them to CIA bases in Guatemala and to the residence of the American Ambassador in Costa Rica. George took film of the trip, and screened it for Moore in Dallas. Moore raised the subject of a young American who had defected to Russia—Lee Harvey Oswald.[19]

George de Mohrenschildt was a busy man. Employed as a petroleum geologist by George Brown of Brown and Root, Lyndon Johnson's principal financial backer, the Baron was educated, urbane, multilingual, with a wide circle of friends. Most of them were, like him, very conservative. Some were Russian *émigrés*. All were anticommunist. Nevertheless, when Moore, or one of Moore's associates—perhaps a wealthy Russian named George Bouhe—suggested that he contact Lee Harvey Oswald, the Baron was happy to oblige.

De Mohrenschildt and Oswald met in September. In his testimony to the Warren Commission, George spoke contemptuously of Lee:

> "His mind was of a man with exceedingly poor background, who read rather advanced books, and did not understand even the words in them... how can you take seriously a person like that? You just laugh at him..."

A Warren Commission counsel asked de Mohrenschildt if he thought the government might entrust Oswald with any complex, high-pressure job.

"I never would believe that any government would be stupid enough to trust Lee with anything important... an unstable individual, mixed-up individual, uneducated individual, without background. What government would give him any confidential work? No government would. Even the government of Ghana would not give him any type of job."

But the questioner hadn't asked about Oswald doing *confidential* work for the government: de Mohrenschildt supplied that adjective in his reply. And after he gave his testimony, George began work on a long manuscript, entitled *I Am A Patsy! I Am A Patsy!* in which he described Lee Oswald in an entirely different way. This Lee is a compelling young man of firm convictions, a single-minded, self-made hero in the Ayn Rand mold. George marveled at Lee's "concentration, thought and toughness," and dismissed Marina, despite her sense of humor and melodious Russian, as mousy, with "bad teeths."

From their first meeting, despite the difference in their age, class, and politics, the two men acted like fast friends. Perhaps they were. Or perhaps they recognized each other as kindred spirits, in that neither man was what he seemed to be. If Oswald were a CIA agent, he would have a direct connection to the Domestic Contacts Division. Was de Mohrenschildt a cut-out, keeping Oswald at arm's length from J. Walton Moore and the Agency? The Baron's CIA contacts weren't limited to Moore. He was also "close friends" with Nicholas Anikeeff, a branch chief in CIA's Soviet Russia Division, based in Washington, DC. If de Mohrenschildt was acting on CIA's behalf—probing Oswald for real intelligence, or directing him to some end—then we should treat his "confessional" manuscript as *another* cover story, like his Warren Commission testimony.[20]

This Baron was a slippery customer. Yet his manuscript suggests that he was genuinely fond of the supposedly disgruntled, Marxist ex-Marine. (There is a homoerotic undertone to George's celebration of Lee, and dislike of Marina, which we will also encounter in Lee's activities in New Orleans. Poor Marina! To have been dragged into this narcissistic nest of expatriates by a bisexual spook, with no money, a small child, another baby on the way, and bad teeths cannot have been much of a joke.)

Both de Mohrenschildt and Marguerite Oswald commented on the frugality of the young couple's existence. Lee and Marina had no TV or stereo, almost nothing in the way of furniture, and very few clothes: her wool dresses did not work well in Texas. So the Russian community chipped in and gave them furniture, a crib, toys, and clothes, for which Marina was grateful, and which made Oswald mad. He criticized the expatriates for their politics and their bourgeois American lifestyles. Having complained in his "historic diary" of a lack of parties and things to spend his money on in Russia, Lee showed little interest in such pleasures at home. George considered the Oswalds' neighborhood a "gruesome Fort Worth slum" and wanted them to move to Dallas, where he and the other Russians resided.

On September 11, President Kennedy flew in Air Force One to Huntsville, Alabama, to meet Wernher von Braun. It was a photo opportunity for both men, and they were filmed together, tanned and smiling, in the back seat of the open-top presidential limo. Von Braun assured the president that NASA had figured out a way to land American astronauts on the Moon—and bring them back again. Two days later, in an interview, Kennedy was asked about the ongoing violence against black voter registration workers. The president responded in no uncertain terms:

> "I don't know any more outrageous action... than the burning of a church... To shoot, as we saw in the case of Mississippi, two young people who were involved in an effort to register people, to burn churches as a reprisal... I consider both cowardly, as well as outrageous."

Three days later, Ben Bradlee traveled to Newport, where Kennedy was vacationing. Kennedy had fallen out with the newsman over some unflattering remarks of Bradlee's in *Look* magazine. Now Bradlee came bearing gifts: an article he had written for *Newsweek*, with the help of the FBI. This addressed a rumor which had been current for some months: that Jack had been "secretly married to a two-time divorcée" prior to wedding Jackie. The mainstream press had thus far ignored the story, but right-wing publications like the NSRP's *Thunderbolt* were promoting it enthusiastically. Even if entirely untrue, such a rumor might create a damaging scandal, in the manner of the Obama "birth certificate" alarms. To deflect this, Bradlee had written his *Newsweek* article, profiling the "crackpot hate sheets" which were spreading the rumor. Kennedy read the piece at Hammersmith Farm, which, Bradlee later informed his readers, was "the Auchincloss summer mansion," and approved its publication. He then snubbed Bradlee by not inviting him to the yacht races.[21]

On September 22, Lee Oswald went to Montgomery Ward's department store in Fort Worth, and purchased a TV set. Since he had no credit record and no references, his brother Robert cosigned for the purchase. The television was delivered to their home on Mercedes Avenue. Lee, normally so scrupulous in these matters, made no payments on the set, valued at $127.40.

On September 28, 1962, an IRS field audit proposed the revocation of the Life Line Foundation's tax exemption. Such a move could prove very costly to H.L. Hunt. Millions of dollars' worth of tax deductions—oil revenue which went to his media network—might be disallowed by the IRS, and the oil man would lose millions more in anticipated revenue: unlike certain of Hunt's other businesses, Life Line was profitable. The foundation was given till January 31, 1963, to file a brief arguing against revocation of its tax exemption.

At the end of September came the civil rights crisis which the brothers had sought to avoid. A black student, James Meredith, had attempted to register as a student at the University of Mississippi. Because civil rights was not their priority, the Kennedys fumbled the matter badly: attempting to re-segregate U.S. troops, so as not to give offense to white racists, while a riot brewed. Meredith and a small force of federal marshals were repeatedly turned back by the University authorities and the Mississippi Highway Patrol. When Meredith was sneaked onto the campus, the federal marshals found themselves outnumbered and pinned down in and around the University administration building. A lynch mob, formed of students, Klansmen, and off-duty cops, burned cars and attacked journalists. All were spurred on by General Edwin Walker, who had resigned from his desk job in Heidelberg and returned home, to embark on a new career as a roving promoter of white supremacy and anticommunism. Now, wearing a cowboy hat and standing beneath the statue of a Confederate soldier, the General addressed the crowd. The *New York Times* quoted him thus:

> "This is Edwin A. Walker. I am in Mississippi beside Gov. Ross
> Barnett. I call for a national protest against the conspiracy
> from within. Rally to the cause of freedom in righteous

indignation, violent vocal protest, and bitter silence under the flag of Mississippi at the use of Federal troops. This today is a disgrace to the nation in 'dire peril,' a disgrace beyond the capacity of anyone except its enemies. This is the conspiracy of the crucifixion by anti-Christ conspirators of the Supreme Court in their denial of prayer and their betrayal of a nation."[22]

Not since the Civil War had a military officer, even a retiree, called for violent action against the federal government. Other sources reported his words differently. On October 3, an AP reporter, Van Savel, wrote that the General "took command of a group of students, climbed a Confederate statue, and told the crowd that Governor Ross Barnett had betrayed Mississippi." Could this be so? Walker and Barnett had been ardent allies up until this point. According to Van Savel, Walker, standing on the Confederate podium, declared,

"But don't let up now. You may lose this battle, but you will have been heard. This is a dangerous situation. You must be prepared for possible death. If you are not, go home now."

These were incendiary words. A UPI dispatch, dated September 30, described Walker as trying to calm the rioters, telling them "This is not the proper route to Cuba." But why would his audience care about Cuba? This mob of all-white "students," armed with baseball bats, rifles, and gasoline bombs, had a domestic agenda, not a foreign policy one.[23]

Armed racists poured into Oxford, Mississippi from as far away as California and Florida. In Walker's hometown—Dallas, Texas—one Ashland Frederic Burchwell was arrested with a .303 rifle, three automatic pistols, a revolver, a switchblade, and 3,000 rounds of ammunition in his car. He told police that he was on his way to Mississippi to assist General Walker. Burchwell said he worked for Walker; in his possession was the unlisted phone number of Robert Surrey, the General's principal aide.[24]

Dallas Confidential Informant T-1 (the same informant who had advised FBI Agent Fain about Lee Oswald's USMC career) reported that Burchwell had just attended a midnight meeting of Dallas right-wingers in the suburb of Pleasant Grove. According to T-1, "the purpose of the meeting was to convince various members that they should not [sic] go to Mississippi to assist former GENERAL WALKER." Burchwell, somehow, got the opposite impression. But Walker may not have been the only military man fomenting violence in Mississippi. According to Clive Webb, in *Rabble Rousers: The American Far Right in the Civil Rights Era*, Rear Admiral John Crommelin, another NSRP stalwart, was there as well:

> "Crommelin... resumed his involvement in political violence in September 1962 when he and a squad of NSRP foot soldiers became involved in the bloody conflict... at the University of Mississippi."[25]

The University of Mississippi blamed General Walker for the riot. Its official history, *The Meredith Case*, attributed the violence to armed racists under the General's command. L.L. Love, Dean of the Division of Student Personnel, wrote:

> "The campus was flooded with armed undesirables... A student managed to work his way into the Lyceum to tell me that General Walker was present and was a very active agitator. I reported this information immediately to every Justice Department official in the Lyceum and heard the information telephoned to the White House. I repeatedly urged the officials to take General Walker into custody—that by doing so they might break the back of the riot. I could get no response until I finally forced one. It was said that they 'did not have force enough.'"[26]

In the White House, Jack discussed *Seven Days in May* with his aide, Ted Sorensen. Kennedy told Sorensen he thought the dialogue very poor, but found the character of the treasonous general, "Gentleman Jim" Scott, compelling. By phone, he tried again to negotiate a solution with Mississippi's fanatical yet indecisive governor, Barnett. When this failed, the president prepared to make a televised address. As night fell, Barnett instructed the Highway Patrolmen, who had been guarding Meredith and the marshals, to withdraw. Hidden snipers opened fire on the Lyceum building, where the marshals were barricaded. Many were seriously injured. White rioters hurled bottles filled with acid through the windows. On TV,

Kennedy's speech flopped: relying on tortuous legal explanations, he showed no sympathy for Meredith, praised the Southern states, and insisted that "to the extent that there has been failure [of civil rights progress], the responsibility for that failure must be shared by us all, by every state, by every citizen."

Did the president really believe that Meredith and the marshals were as blameworthy as Barnett, Walker, and the snipers? One assumes not. Once again, Jack Kennedy was indulging—disastrously—his politician's yen to have things both ways, to appeal to both sides at the same time. This was impossible. To the victims of racist violence, he appeared uncaring and ambivalent. To the racists, he appeared weak. Then, news reached the White House that a journalist, Paul Guihard, had been shot dead outside the Lyceum. Concerned about the international reaction (Guihard was French), Kennedy finally ordered the 503rd Military Police Battalion to Oxford, to relieve the marshals. Now matters were in the hands of Army Secretary Cyrus Vance and Major General Creighton Abrams. Abrams would later be in charge of military actions in Vietnam; Vance, who would be President Carter's Secretary of Defense, was listed as an active intelligence agent by *Who's Who in CIA*. For whatever reason, both men fumbled their mission: to move the battalion 50 miles down the main highway from Memphis, Tennessee to Oxford, Mississippi. The Army blamed bad planning—caused by the Kennedys' desire for the troops to keep a low profile, and for there to be no black soldiers visible—for between three and five hours' delay.

When the military arrived, by air and road, they routed the rioters. But two men were dead, and 166 federal marshals had been wounded, some of them very seriously, by rocks, incendiary weapons, and sniper fire. James Meredith finally registered as a student, and attended his first class: Colonial American History. Bobby Kennedy had General Walker arrested and flown to a federal psychiatric prison in Springfield, Missouri for evaluation. His seizure was highly irregular, in the manner of the kidnapping and eviction of Carlos Marcello: there was no discussion of bail or even of the charges against him, though Bobby insisted Walker would be tried for insurrection. Yet this did not occur. Despite ample evidence, the Justice Department failed to pursue the case. When Walker's supporters began calling him "the United States' first political prisoner," the General was quickly released.[27]

The same month, Marcello, back in the U.S. despite the efforts of the Justice Department, predicted the death of President Kennedy: an assassination which he said would be staged so that a "nut" could be set up to take the blame. And Santos Trafficante, a gangster associate of Marcello and Hoffa, also advised police informants that "Kennedy's not going to make it to the election. He is going to be hit." In later years, both men would claim to have been involved in the assassination of the president. Such gangster talk—all of it reported to the appropriate authorities—certainly suggests prior knowledge or wishful thinking on the part of the *mafiosi* concerned. But it does not make them the authors of the crime.

On October 3, Dallas Confidential Informant T-1 identified a membership card found in the possession of Walker's henchman, Burchwell. He/she advised the FBI that the card identified him as part of a right-wing organization in Dallas. "According to Dallas T-1, this organization has no name," the FBI reported. "It at one time had a name but it was decided that if the organization had no name it could not be cited, and its members if asked if they belonged to an organization, they could deny membership in the organization since it had no name and, therefore, could not be identified as such... Dallas T-1 denied that there was any connection by [sic] this group and former Army Major General Edwin A. Walker, and denied that H.L. Hunt is a member, though stated he is a good patriot... Dallas T-1 further advised that one third of the membership of that organization are instructed to join 'liberal' organizations, such as the American Civil Liberties Union, and establish a reputation as 'liberals,' and thus be in a position to remain behind when and if the communists take over..." Confidential Informant T-1 declined to name any of the nameless organization's members. Given its stated purpose, was Burchwell's group the Minutemen?[28]

General Maxwell Taylor reported optimistically to Kennedy on prospects in Vietnam. The program of "strategic hamlets"—whereby Vietnamese villagers were rounded up and put in concentration camps—was proving a great success, he said. Kennedy had appointed Taylor for the same reason he hired Lansdale: he found them companionable and saner than the Joint Chiefs. But there are degrees of sanity. The Chiefs said nuke Russia in late '63; Taylor and Lansdale were confident that counterinsurgency was working on the ground, so long as the U.S. committed more men and spent more money. (But it did not work. The Vietnam War, which dragged on till 1975, proved that a counterinsurgency war *favored the insurgents, not the superpower*. These were the conclusions of a generation of U.S. military leaders, including General Colin Powell.)

Kennedy seemed to be growing more reticent in matters military. But he had little room to maneuver. Khrushchev had just rejected his proposals for a nuclear test ban treaty. Then, on October 14, a U-2 overflight revealed Russian nuclear missile sites under construction on the island of Cuba, and all hell broke loose again...

Lee and Marina fought with increasing frequency. Marguerite recalled one occasion where Lee gave Marina a black eye. The de Mohrenschildts reported several such attacks. Lee would become furious when Marina drank or smoked. According to George, teetotaler Lee stubbed a cigarette out on Marina's shoulder to punish her. Was this the same Lee Oswald who had been court-martialed for brawling in a bar? Encouraged by George, the Oswalds separated. Marina and June moved in with Russian-speaking friends. On October 8, Lee quit his job, telling the welding company he'd "accepted a better paying position." He moved to Dallas, leaving his television to be picked up by Montgomery Ward. He had made no payments and asked them to take it back, claiming it was "unsatisfactory."[29]

On October 11, the Employment Commission referred him to a graphics-arts company, Jaggers-Chiles-Stovall. The Baron's wife and daughter later recalled that it was George, not the Employment Commission, who found Lee the job. Either way, Oswald began work at JCS the very next day. He also filed a change-of-address card, listing his new address as Dallas P.O. Box 2915.

For most of the next month, where Lee lived is a mystery. He checked in at the YMCA in Dallas on October 15, and stayed four nights. Daytimes he showed up at JCS, a business which prepared newspaper ads and trade catalogues, but also did more specialized work. Among its clients was the U.S. Army Map Service, which required large-scale maps based on U-2 surveillance photographs. In theory, only employees with security clearances—the kind Oswald had had, in Japan—could work on the Army map jobs, but in practice the employees all worked together, in a small office. As Oswald prepared advertisements, his neighbor applied typescript to aerial photographs of Cuba.

Once again Oswald, notorious traitor and communist, was part of the intelligence data chain, working for a defense contractor at a crucial time. JCS's maps, crafted from U-2 data, were the evidence on which statesmen, politicians or generals would base decisions of peace or war.

Jack Kennedy saw the U-2 pictures on October 16. Almost at once, CIA began leaking information about the missiles to friendly journalists, in an attempt to force the president's hand. On October 19, he met with the Joint Chiefs, who were proactive as usual. Led by Air Force General LeMay, the Chiefs insisted on immediate military action to "take out" the missile sites. Kennedy asked LeMay to predict what the Russians would do if the U.S. bombed Cuba. "They'll do nothing," the General replied. Once again, the Chiefs were dogmatic and insubordinate. When Kennedy suggested a blockade instead of a bombardment, LeMay accused him of appeasement. Kennedy kept his temper and concluded the meeting. On October 22, the president met with Congressional leaders, who gave him similarly insane counsel. Senator Richard Russell, recorded by the White House taping system, advised Kennedy to attack Russian ships at sea with nuclear weapons.

> "The time is going to come, Mr. President, when we're going
> to have to take this step in Berlin and Korea and Washington,
> D.C., and Winder, Georgia, for the nuclear war…"

Even Senator William Fulbright, normally a voice of reason, counseled an invasion of the island.

> "I'm in favor, on the basis of this information, of an invasion,
> and an all-out one, and as quickly as possible. I would do
> nothing until you're ready to invade."

In a televised speech that evening, the president announced that he was willing to risk atomic war. "We will not prematurely or unnecessarily risk the costs of nuclear war," he told the public, "but neither will we shrink from that risk at any time it must be faced." Fortunately, the blockade—an act of war under international law—did not result in thermonuclear disaster. It gave Kennedy and Khrushchev time to reach an agreement from which both sides might gain. Not for the first time, the Pentagon had its estimates entirely wrong: there were not ten thousand Russian troops, but forty thousand, on the island. In addition to the long-range nuclear missiles on launchers aimed at the United States, the Russian commanders possessed almost one hundred tactical nuclear weapons which were to be used in the event of an American attack. Had Kennedy bombed the missile sites, and followed up with an invasion, nuclear war would have been inevitable.[30]

Instead, Armageddon was again put on hold. Russian ships bearing military gear turned back, and Khrushchev, cutting his partner Castro out of the deal, agreed to withdraw all atomic weapons from Cuba. In return, Kennedy promised to remove the "Jupiter" nuclear missiles which the U.S. had recently based in Turkey, and assured Khrushchev that the U.S. would not invade Cuba—essentially killing MONGOOSE. Arthur Schlesinger told author David Talbot that "We would've had nuclear war if Nixon had been president during the missile crisis. But Kennedy's war hero status allowed him to defy the Joint Chiefs. He dismissed them as a bunch of old men."[31]

But Robert Kennedy, in a secret meeting with Russian Ambassador Anatoly Dobrynin, told a different story:

> "The President is in a grave situation," [Dobrynin reported Kennedy as saying] "and he does not know how to get out of it. We are under very severe stress. In fact we are under pressure from our military to use force against Cuba... the President is appealing directly to Chairman Khrushchev for his help in liquidating this conflict. If the situation continues much longer, the President is not sure that the military will not overthrow him and seize power."[32]

I assume Dobrynin's report is true: he would hardly lie to his boss as to what the president's brother told him. Was Robert Kennedy telling the truth, or exaggerating, in order to get the Russians' attention? Daniel Ellsberg remarked on an atmosphere of "fury" within the Air Force over the Kennedy-Khrushchev deal. "There was virtually a *coup* atmosphere in Pentagon circles... The atmosphere was poisonous, poisonous."[33]

Khrushchev noted in his memoirs, about Kennedy: "For some time we had felt there was a danger that he might lose control of his military." This was certainly a motivating factor for the Russian leader to reach an agreement with his American counterpart.

In November, Kennedy issued Executive Order 11063, banning segregation in federally owned housing. This was an election promise, delivered almost two years late, and in the light of the events throughout the South it was an inadequate gesture. Perhaps the president made the order because he felt the alienation of certain Southern senators was now inevitable. Hubert Humphrey or Adlai Stevenson would have reached the same tipping point and "lost" the South much sooner. And Evelyn Lincoln, his secretary, felt that Kennedy had emerged from the Missile Crisis invigorated: "from the day that Khrushchev agreed to pull out the missiles, the president had an added ingredient of self-confidence. It seemed as though he had turned the corner and was now going up a different street. He relied more on his own staff and advisors than on the politicians."

On November 3, Oswald put down a deposit on Apartment 2, 604 Elspeth Street, a block from his previous digs. The family was reunited there a few days later. George de Mohrenschildt didn't approve of their new place, either. "It was on the ground floor of a dreary red-brick building, the atmosphere of the house and the neighbourhood [sic] conducive to suicide," he wrote. The Baron need not have worried. Lee and his family lasted one night together; next day, after a violent argument, Marina and June moved out.

Oswald subscribed to *New York Labor News* and *The Militant*. By mail, he applied for membership of the SWP (they turned him down). When Edward J. Epstein interviewed three of Oswald's former co-workers at JCS, they told him that during this time "Oswald was taught how to operate such highly specialized photographic equipment as distortion cameras, phototypesetters and Robertson vertical cameras. He was shown how to reproduce perfectly a pictorial display, then to reduce or distort it with optical lenses... Soon he became proficient in such techniques as line modifications, blowups, reverses and miniaturizations..."

So Oswald was learning the tricks of special effects photography. Epstein writes that he was also learning to forge documents, and that while at JCS Oswald created new identification papers for himself—a fake Selective Service card and a certificate of service in the USMC—in the name of A.J. Hidell.[34]

On November 18, the Oswalds got together again. On Thanksgiving Day, November 22, they rode the bus over to Fort Worth for dinner with Robert Oswald and his family. John Pic, Oswald's half-brother, was also there. He hadn't seen Lee in ten years. Robert had commented that Lee had changed physically during his absence, but John's reaction was even more pronounced. In his testimony to the Warren Commission, John said, "I would never have recognized him."

Brothers and sisters who disguise themselves, and pass unrecognized by siblings... this is the stuff of Shakespeare, of Elizabethan drama. Such things happen less frequently in real life. So what did John Pic mean when he said this?

Also in November, an unemployed con-man, William McEwan Duff, a.k.a. "Scotty" McDuff, showed up in Dallas. Duff, who not surprisingly had been born in Scotland, read about General Walker in the papers and paid a visit to Walker's house. There he passed himself off as a "batman," or professional valet, orderly, and personal aide. The General hired Scotty on the spot, and gave him his own room. His duties were to include cooking and driving for the General, though he was never paid.[35]

In November, the Kennedys watched movies in the White House. Ben Bradlee claimed to be shocked at the president's poor taste:

> "The President was determined to see a movie, even though Jackie said the choices were strictly limited. Jackie read off the list of what was available, and the President selected the one we had all unanimously voted against, a brutal sadistic little Western called *Lonely Are The Brave*. Kennedy watched, lying down on a bed placed in the front row, his head propped up on pillows."[36]

Bradlee's story is quoted by Gary Wills in *The Kennedy Imprisonment*. Both authors clearly mean it to show Kennedy as a selfish potentate. Perhaps he was. But his taste in movies seems impeccable. *Lonely Are The Brave* is a brilliant film, one of the last great Westerns, based on a novel by Ed Abbey, rarely brutal, sad/heroic rather than sadistic, with fine performances, a noble horse, and a spot-on script by Dalton Trumbo. There were no DVDs or VHS tapes in 1962, so Jackie was reading from a list of prints sent to them by the Hollywood studios. In such a context, *Lonely Are The Brave* was probably the best choice. (Nixon, it is said, watched *Patton* repeatedly, alone in the White House screening room.)[37]

On December 5, President Kennedy met again with the Joint Chiefs and his advisors to discuss the defense budget. All three branches of the military pushed for big nuclear increases: the Air Force wanted to accelerate and expand the Minuteman ICBM program *plus* a thousand air-launched ballistic missiles; the Navy felt the need for six more Polaris submarines, each equipped with up to 16 ICBMs; and the Army wanted money to build an untested "Nike-Zeus" antiballistic missile system. Maxwell Taylor, now head of the Joint Chiefs, sided with his colleagues: there were "too many imponderables," he said, to do anything but massively increase their nuclear advantage.

The president's science adviser, Jerome Weisner, spoke against an arms race, which he feared the United States would lose—unless its purpose was to bankrupt the Russian economy. Kennedy said he doubted this could be achieved, adding, "The space program is the one that's going to..." at which point the meeting erupted into laughter. Discussion as to the right yardstick for an adequate nuclear force was resumed; McNamara proposed acquiring "twice what any reasonable person would say is necessary." Both Weisner and Kennedy questioned why the Pentagon needed so many nuclear targets. Why were so many cities targeted with so many bombs? Why were so many civilian casualties intended?

"The only targets seem to me that really make any sense are at their missiles," Kennedy said. "That makes some sense to us. We should always suggest that... they assume that we'd fire at their cities if we have to, because that will deter them. But as a practical matter, if the deterrent fails and they attack, what we want to do is be firing at their missile sites. Beyond that, these targets don't seem to me to make much sense." While not overly grammatical (the president was recorded by hidden microphones in the Cabinet Room) his approach to nuclear war targeting had developed into something close to rational, signaling a break with the *actual* strategy of all-out nuclear attacks on Russian cities. Despite the good humor of the occasion, the gulf between the president and the Pentagon appeared to have widened.[38]

On December 7, Jack Kennedy made a three-hour tour of the underground nuclear command post near Omaha, Nebraska. He presented those present with a plaque honoring the Strategic Air Command, then flew to Los Alamos, where the nuclear bombs were designed, and to Albuquerque, where the weapons were built, to encourage all those involved. Four days later, at a ceremony at

Malstrom Air Force Base, Montana, the Minuteman ICBM was declared operational. Twenty of the new 54-foot rockets were now in place in underground silos, ready for launch on a few moments' notice. (The president did not attend this ceremony.)

On December 14 another black church, in Birmingham, was bombed. Three days later the president met with an invited list of black leaders, including Roy Wilkins, Martin Luther King, James Farmer, and Dorothy Height. Foreign, rather than domestic, issues were on Kennedy's agenda. He refused to impose sanctions on South Africa's apartheid regime, or on the Portuguese dictatorship. He expressed interest in a Marshall Plan for Africa, but rejected a civil rights bill for the United States. It was a long meeting—over three hours—and it did not go well. None of his guests felt Kennedy was prepared to act vigorously in support of civil rights; all believed more direct action was called for.

Kennedy, with other things on his mind, flew to Nassau for a three-day vacation/consultation with Prime Minister Harold Macmillan. The old Brit, conservative, courtly and relaxed, was probably Jack's favorite foreigner, and certainly his favorite politician. The president returned to the U.S. to engage in a piece of political theater as ill conceived as it was potentially catastrophic. At the Orange Bowl in Miami, on December 29, he addressed a gathering of veterans of the Bay of Pigs: Cuban exiles, most of them in uniform, many of them former prisoners who had been ransomed from the Castro government in exchange for money for medicines.

The president should not have been there at all. He'd made a deal with the Russians over Cuba. They had ignored their client, Castro. He had ignored the wishes of the anti-Castro Cubans in return. But Kennedy, as usual, wanted things both ways. The Russians didn't vote. The anti-Castro Cubans were a constituency which he thought he could keep on his side. So, when one of the *gusano* leaders gave him a flag—which the rebels had supposedly kept hidden during their imprisonment—the president replied, "Commander, I can assure you that this flag will be returned to this Brigade in a free Havana."

More than a thousand Cuban right-wingers leapt to their feet, applauding. There were cries of "freedom" and "war." As far as they were concerned, Kennedy had renewed his commitment to a military invasion.

notes

1 The letter is part of a CIA Document dated 01/25/64, Chronology of Oswald in the USSR, pp. 215-216; AARB / NARA record no. 104-10009-10078.

2 Arthur Schlesinger, Jr., *A Thousand Days: John F. Kennedy in the White House*, Fawcett, Greenwich, Conn., 1967, p. 717.

3 James Bamford, *Body of Secrets*, Anchor Books, NY, 2002, pp. 82–91, 103, 300–301.

4 Jack White, "A Most Curious Photo," *The Fourth Decade*, Vol. 1, No. 4, May 1994, p. 35; and "Curious Photo: A Follow-Up," *The Fourth Decade*, Vol. 1, No. 5, July 1994, pp. 36–38.

5 Andrew, *Power to Destroy*, p. 31.

6 Summers, *Official and Confidential*, pp. 333–337.

7 Nazi War Crimes Disclosure Act release, declassified by CIA 2001.

8 WH 17 CE No. 823, John W. Fain, FBI Report, "Lee Harvey Oswald," pp. 6–7.

9 Teller found Ronald Reagan more sympathetic when the California governor visited him at Livermore for a two-hour briefing in 1967. Unlike Kennedy, Reagan was inspired by Teller's vision, which now included "nuclear-pumped x-ray lasers in space." (David Hoffman, *The Dead Hand*, Doubleday 2009, p. 49.)

10 Mike Sylwester, "Why Didn't The Intelligence Community Interview Oswald About The Soviet Union?", *The Third Decade*, Vol. 9, No. 4, May 1993, pp. 1–4.

11 Summers, *Conspiracy*, p. 217.

12 Summers, *Conspiracy*, pp. 215–218. In May 1963, Captain Davison was accused of espionage by the Russians, and forced to leave the country. Penkovsky, Oleg, *The Penkovsky Papers*, Avon Books, NY, pp. 24, 360, 366.

13 Report of John W. Fain, Dallas FBI Office, July 10, 1962; NARA, JFK files, RIF 124-10010-10033; Newman, *Oswald and the CIA*, pp. 264–267.

14 Report of John W. Fain, Dallas FBI Office, May 12, 1960, p. 4; Newman, *Oswald and the CIA*, pp. 91–92.

15 Newman, *Oswald & The CIA*, p. 424.

16 Warren Commission Document 767—Summary of Secret Service Interview of Alonzo Hudkins—not published in either the Warren Report or the 26 Volumes of Evidence. FBI Agent Hosty, in his book *Assignment Oswald* (Arcade, NY, 1996, pp. 119-125), ascribed the story to D.A. Bill Alexander, and denied it.

17 WH 22 CE No. 1144, Secret Service Memorandum, *Chronology of Residences and Places of Employment for Lee Harvey Oswald*, p. 3.

18 Bryant, *The Bystander*, pp. 325–326.

19 De Mohrenschildt's story as to his relationship with CIA and Oswald constantly changed; he told the Warren Commission that he sought CIA's permission to meet Oswald; he told author Edward J. Epstein that Moore encouraged him to do so. Summers, *Not In Your Lifetime*, pp. 155–6; Epstein, *Legend*, p. 314. Carl Oglesby wrote, in *The Yankee and Cowboy War* (Sheed, Andrews & McMeel, 1976, p. 106) that de Mohrenschildt was "an officer of the World War II Gehlen-Vlassov operation." If so, he may have been gone to work for CIA along with the rest of the Gehlen *org*.

20 Newman, *Oswald and The CIA*, pp. 278–279; Tom Bower, in *The Red Web, MI-6 and The KGB Master Coup*, (Aurum Press, London, 1989, p. 159), writes that Anikeeff was a Gehlen *org* case officer.

21 Benjamin C. Bradlee, *Conversations With Kennedy*, Norton, NY, 1975, pp. 114–7.

22 *New York Times*, Sept. 30, 1962.

23 John Stormer, *None Dare Call It Treason*, Liberty Bell, Missouri, 1964, pp. 152–153.

24 FBI file, Record Number: 124-10321-10034, Subject: "Unnamed Organization of Dallas, Texas, Patriots".

25 Webb, *Rabble Rousers*, p. 127. The source for this is unclear. Webb cites William Doyle's history of the riot, *An American Insurrection* (Doubleday, New York, 2001), but Doyle does not mention Crommelin.

26 *The University of Mississippi & The Meredith Case*, University of Mississippi, November 1962, p. 25.

27 Forcing political dissidents to undergo psychiatric treatment was a crime of which the Russians used to be accused. But the U.S. government also incarcerated Americans in psychiatric hospitals—often the Federal Prison Medical Center at Springfield—for what seemed like political reasons: among them, General Walker, Abraham Bolden, Philip Graham, Steven Landesberg, Richard Case Nagell, Richard Pavlick, and at least one witness in the Billie Sol Estes case, Mary Kimbrough Jones.

28 FBI file, Record Number: 124-10321-10034, Subject: "Unnamed Organization of Dallas, Texas, Patriots".

29 WH 22 CE No. 1167, p. 252.

30 Robert Norris and Hans Kristensen, *The Cuban Missile Crisis: A Nuclear Order of Battle, October and November 1962*, Bulletin of the Atomic Scientists, October 12, 2012.

31 David Talbot, *Brothers: The Hidden History of The Kennedy Years*, Free Press, NY, 2007, p. 171.

32 Nikita Khrushchev, *Khrushchev Remembers*, Little, Brown, Boston, 1970, pp. 497–98.

33 Talbot, *Brothers*, pp. 172–3.

34 Edward J. Epstein, *Legend*, p. 194. Oswald's use of the name "Hidell"—whether as his alias, someone else's alias, or an imaginary friend—remains unclear and open to speculation. See Prof. Rose's articles "In The Name of A. Hidell," *The Third Decade*, Vol. 5, No. 4, May 1989, pp. 5–9, and "Hidell Again," *The Third Decade*, Vol. 5, No. 5, July 1989, pp. 10–12.

35 WH 26, CE No. 2981, FBI Report on William McEwan Duff.

36 Bradlee, *Conversations With Kennedy*, p. 128.

37 The film's producer, Edward Lewis, went on to produce *Seven Days In May* and the remarkable film *Seconds*. David Miller, director of *Lonely Are The Brave*, later made *Executive Action*, also produced by Ed Lewis: the first dramatic feature film about the Kennedy assassination. The script, by Trumbo, depicts a right-wing oil man (Burt Lancaster) and a CIA chief (Robert Ryan) conspiring to set up a crossfire in Dealey Plaza.

38 David Coleman, "Camelot's Nuclear Conscience", *Bulletin of Atomic Scientists*, May–June 2006, pp. 40–45.

CHAPTER 7

1963

YEAR OF THE PATSY

★ ★ ★

He enters the third year of his presidency. It is a four-year job, in theory. But Jack Kennedy knows that fourth year will be given up almost entirely to campaigning for re-election. At best, barring new, insane crises dreamed up by right-wing army men, or by the CIA, he has less than a year in which to progress his agenda. Which is what? He remains optimistic about some form of nuclear arms agreement. Berlin is quiet. Both sides have promised to leave Cuba alone. Health care reform remains a priority. He continues to backpedal on civil rights, perhaps because he sees them simply as one piece of a political chess game, rather than the game-changing event. Increasingly close to Bobby, he has not spoken with his father in a year.

In his State of the Union address, the president announced a big tax cut. Others advised against it, but he was convinced his proposal was a vote-winner. Individual tax rates would be lowered between 20 and 90 percent. Corporate rates would drop by five percent. To balance the cuts, various allowances would also be reduced, including the oil producers' depletion allowance—a tax break worth some 27.5 percent. This was not welcomed by the oil men. Meanwhile, his efforts to introduce Medicare and to reform education foundered. Despite pressure from Bobby and Dr. King, he refused to introduce a voting rights bill, or civil rights legislation.

Yet it was not an uphill struggle. Jack Kennedy continued to charm the media, and he took a keen interest in a Hollywood movie entitled *PT-109*, the story of his World War II adventures. The president vetoed Raoul Walsh as director (the film was directed by a TV hack), and chose Cliff Robertson to play the young Jack Kennedy. In doing so, he overruled the first lady, who preferred Warren Beatty for the role.

On January 14, Lee Oswald enrolled in a typing course at the Crozier Technical School in Dallas. He wrote several times to the Washington Book Store, which had probably been recommended to him by the Russian Embassy, subscribed to various communist magazines and requested other literature. He gave his return address as Box 2915, Dallas. As perhaps was his intention, this drew attention to Oswald and his mailbox, and the Post Office asked him to fill out Form 2153-X, instructing them to "always" deliver foreign propaganda mailings. He did, adding the comment, "I protest this intimidation."

Next day, John Connally took office as Governor of Texas. It had been a long campaign. General Walker had stood against him in the Democratic primary—he came last—and Connally had faced more serious opposition from a Democrat-turned-Republican, Jack Cox. But Texans traditionally voted Democrat and, for the next two years at least, the state would be in their hands.

At the end of the month, Lee Oswald made the last two payments on his State Department loan. He had already repaid the $200 lent him by his brother Robert. How had he managed this? Oswald had been in and out of work, all of it low-waged. He was renting apartments and hotel rooms, and feeding three people. That Lee repaid some $650 in loans so quickly speaks well of him. It also suggests that he had some income beyond his "official" earnings of a buck and a quarter an hour. Where did he get it?

Thomas Dodd was a freshman Democratic senator from Connecticut. He had been an FBI agent and one of the star American prosecutors of Nazi politicians at Nuremberg. An early CIA ally, he positioned himself to the right of Kennedy on foreign policy. Dodd made himself the hammer of the FPCC; he also railed against narcotics traffickers and juvenile crime. The latter interest led him to chair the Senate's Subcommittee to Investigate Juvenile Delinquency. One of the Subcommittee's concerns was the availability of firearms via mail order, and the likelihood that guns were making it into the wrong hands. In January, Senator Dodd held hearings into the unrestricted delivery of weapons via the U.S. mails. He named two companies involved in these illegal practices: Klein's Sporting Goods, of Chicago, and Seaport Traders, of Los Angeles (both were under investigation by the ATF's predecessor agency, the ATTD, which probably gave Dodd the tip).

On January 27, Lee ordered a .38 caliber Smith & Wesson revolver by mail, from Seaport Traders, of Los Angeles, using the alias A.J. Hidell. The gun cost $29.95.

Using a false name to acquire a firearm by interstate mail was a crime. In fact it was several crimes, conviction for any one of which could send Oswald to jail. And Oswald lived in Texas. He could walk into any gun store or pawn shop and buy a used revolver for 20 dollars without showing an ID. If he needed a gun, why didn't he go get one? Why incriminate himself—or "Hidell"—in this showy, time-consuming way? "Oswald was mad," the Warren Commission apologists will say, and that is one explanation. Another explanation is that the FBI informant was also working for Dodd's Senate Subcommittee, or the ATTD, ordering guns from suspect stores under a false name as part of their investigation—or that he *thought* he was.

Since his return from Russia, Oswald had acted bizarrely. According to his "historic diary," he had grown bored with the lack of opportunities for fun, and to spend money, in Russia. Yet when he came home, he acted more ascetic than a monk. He'd wanted guarantees he wouldn't be prosecuted for anything, and he wanted his honorable discharge reinstated. He maintained an ongoing correspondence with the Marines about getting this done. Yet, simultaneously, he ordered guns across state lines under a false name, and made contact with leftists and communists, via the U.S. mail.

Did Oswald, having completed an intelligence mission in Russia, find himself cut loose by the Marine Corps or CIA? Was he then picked up by another agency, as an infiltrator of political organizations? Such an assignment would account for Oswald's two new interests:

illegally ordering guns, and joining leftist groups. And it would explain why he kept up a correspondence with the Marine Corps, requesting the return of his good name.

Two days later, the Subcommittee opened its hearings into the mail-order traffic in guns. As Senator Dodd explained, it was already buying and tracking firearms through the mail. Such undercover evidentiary purchases continue to this day. In the aftermath of the 2011 Tucson massacre, New York mayor Michael Bloomberg sent a team of undercover agents to a gun show in Phoenix, AZ. The agents videotaped several transactions in which they illegally purchased firearms: like the Dodd Subcommittee, their mission used provocateurs to demonstrate how easy it is to break the law and acquire guns.

In January, Tad Szulc proposed a program to identify disgruntled Cuban officers who might be used to recruit higher-up military officials in a *coup* attempt. Szulc's idea was approved and the program given a name: AMTRUNK. That same month, Philip Graham, the *Washington Post* publisher and key figure in the MOCKINGBIRD program, suffered a nervous breakdown. Graham had left his wife and moved with a mistress to Phoenix. There he'd begun to complain to friends about the Agency and its influence on journalists. He attended a conference of journalists where, apparently drunk, he seized the microphone and began ranting about the president's sexual activities. Graham named one of Kennedy's current girlfriends, Mary Meyer, and identified her as the sister of a CIA agent, Cord Meyer, and the sister-in-law of Ben Bradlee. Even as Graham was speaking, a friendly journalist called the White House and spoke to the president. Kennedy called Katherine Graham, whose family owned the *Post*, and she offered to help rein her husband in. Phil Graham's assistant, James Truitt, took the phone and asked the president to send Phil's doctor to Phoenix on a military jet. An Air Force jet was duly dispatched with Graham's physician on board. The doctor, Leslie Farber, gave Graham a heavy dose of sedatives and the prostrate journalist was spirited away. His wife obtained a court order committing him to a psychiatric hospital. A "nervous breakdown," together with alcoholism, was the official explanation for his behavior.

On February 8, the Ba'ath Party, funded by CIA, took power in Iraq via a *coup*. The Agency assisted in the ensuing massacre of suspected communists, providing the Ba'athists—among them, one Saddam Hussein—with lists of "leftist" names.

On February 13 the Oswalds dined with the de Mohrenschildts. On February 17, Marina wrote to the Russian Embassy in Washington: at Lee's insistence she requested a visa to return home with baby June. On February 22, the two couples attended a party at the home of other friends. As Oswald expounded Marxist dogma to the conservative crowd, the Baron introduced Marina to Ruth Paine. According to de Mohrenschildt, he and Ruth had not met prior to this evening—yet Ruth was to become, almost immediately, a key part of Lee and Marina's life, or what little remained of it. In his manuscript, George wrote:

> "Thus began a friendship between these two women, a friendship which lasted till the days of assassination. Ruth Payne [sic] has done more for Marina and June than any other person, yet, for some reason Marina refused to see her after Lee's death."[1]

In that second sentence, the Baron certainly planted some seeds of doubt about Ruth Paine and her motives. Ruth was a member of a wealthy Quaker family, married to a research engineer, Michael Paine. Michael was related to the Forbes and Cabot families; from his grandmother, he had recently inherited a $269,000 trust fund. Yet the two lived modestly. Michael, like Lee, was having trouble with his wife; like Lee, he espoused left-wing views, held a security clearance, and moved in right-wing circles.[2]

Ruth's interest in Marina was, according to the official story, a desire to practice her Russian language skills. But Ruth was already proficient in Russian, knew some of the White Russians who lived in Dallas, and had a personal Russian tutor, Dorothy Gravitis. In spite of this, she began visiting Marina frequently.

After the assassination, Ruth Paine gave the Warren Commissioners her opinion of Lee Harvey Oswald:

> "I thought that he was not very intelligent. I saw as far as I could see that he had no particular contacts. He was not a person I would have hired for a job of any sort, no more than I would have let him borrow my car."

Unintelligent and unemployable: that was the way the Baron described Lee to the Warren Commissioners. But as to his having no particular contacts? Lee Harvey Oswald had quite excellent contacts, given his circumstances, among them Ruth Paine and George de Mohrenschildt, who, though they said they despised him, acted as Oswald's babysitters, drove him to dinner and appointments, gave him driving lessons, found him jobs, and arranged accommodations for his wife and child.

The Warren Commission ordered what it considered a thorough investigation of the Paines, and found them innocent of any connection to the assassination. But, as with its investigation of Jack Ruby, the FBI simply provided a mass of disorganized information about the couple, most of which had no bearing on the case. Thereafter, official bodies set up to enlighten us about the assassination, such as the HSCA and the ARRB, have steered clear of the Paines. This seems strange. Right when their only friend in Dallas, George de Mohrenschildt, was about to leave the country, Lee and Marina were befriended by two other rich, eccentric, politically ambiguous individuals. Michael Paine claimed to be a pacifist, yet he had served in the artillery in Korea, and worked for Bell Helicopter—a manufacturer of military aircraft—where a senior colleague was the Nazi rocketeer Walter Dornberger. Ruth Paine's "official" profile is that of a Quaker woman devoted to the principles of liberalism and the ACLU. In fact, her political activities prior to the assassination seem to have been limited to attempts at East-West student exchanges. Her sister, Sylvia Hoke, was employed by CIA with top secret clearance. After the assassination, Ruth tried to become involved in the civil rights movement, only to be rejected by the local black community. In the 1980s, she traveled to Nicaragua where she documented the activities of American solidarity workers. Carol Hewitt and colleagues write,

> "Her activities, such as popping up at peace marches and making calls to contact black leaders in the Dallas community, are consistent with the 'casual informant' classification. These are individuals who are not on any agency's payroll, but who will gladly identify participants in a rally or leaders of social/political movements."[3]

There are also individuals who are paid, as government agents, to infiltrate those social/political movements, report on their member-ships, and derail them. In 2009, it emerged that a British policeman, Mark Kennedy, had joined several green protest groups. He grew his hair long, pretended to be an activist, and slept with members of the groups. Kennedy organized and paid for protests which the authori-ties then claimed were illegal. He was given a false passport by the British police, and a budget that enabled him to visit 22 countries as a professional protester. The same year the British authorities also infiltrated "Plane Stupid"— a campaign against the expansion of an airport—and placed undercover infiltrators in anti-racist and Muslim groups. All were later exposed by suspicious group members.[4]

In the United States, the FBI has a history of paying informants and *agents provocateurs* to spy on suspected terrorist and dissident groups. In the decade following the 9/11 atrocities, the FBI developed a massive network of domestic spies to infiltrate Muslim groups: of 508 federal terrorism cases, 48 percent were targeted by an FBI informant, and 10 percent of defendants were "lured in" by an agent who led the plot.[5]

From the 1950s through to the 1970s, the FBI's COINTELPRO operation monitored and sabotaged leftist and civil rights organizations. In this light, Lee Oswald, done with his "defector" phase, was looking less like a "casual informant" and more like a full-time political *agent provocateur*. Like Mark Kennedy, he would shortly attempt to penetrate a number of different groups—on both sides of the political divide.

On March 2, the Oswalds moved again, to 214 West Neely Street in Dallas. A few days later, according to the Warren Report, Oswald went on a photography mission to the home of General Walker. The Report says Oswald had decided to kill Walker; since the "historic" Oswald didn't know how to drive, this involved him riding several buses to and from Walker's house at 4011 Turtle Creek (seven and a half miles away), carrying a rifle.

On March 12, Ruth came to visit Marina at the Neely Street apartment. And "A. Hidell" mail-ordered another gun: a rifle this time, to be delivered to P.O. Box 2915, Dallas, from Klein's Sporting Goods in Chicago. (The Commission says that Oswald did this; presumably, their handwriting experts identified the order form—signed by "Hidell"—as the work of Oswald. Klein's Sporting Goods was the other company which had been singled out by the Dodd Subcommittee. Oswald, after his arrest in Dallas, denied ordering this gun.)

The same month Nelson Rockefeller put Kennedy on the defensive. A reporter asked him to comment on Rockefeller's assertion that he had been "appointing segregationist judges to the federal bench in the South." It was a tough question, because Rockefeller was right. Unlike Eisenhower, who had appointed surprisingly liberal Southerners to the bench, Kennedy had nominated virulent racists, including Robert Elliot of Georgia, E. Gordon West of Louisiana, and W. Harold Cox of Mississippi, whose appointment the previous president's Justice Department had blocked. Kennedy replied, quite weakly, that his *and* Eisenhower's record in appointing judges was "very creditable." Perhaps, but *his* was not.

From March 18–20, the president attended a Conference of Presidents of Central American Republics in San Jose, Costa Rica. It was his seventh official trip outside the United States and one hopes there was some swimming or yachting in the offing, because nothing of note took place. Jack schmoozed with Somozas; Castro was condemned; the *Alianza* was promoted. The dictators smiled, nodded, and looked forward to more money, soon.

Klein's shipped a rifle with a telescopic scope, fully assembled, to "A. Hidell" via parcel post on March 20. It arrived at Lee Harvey Oswald's post office box on March 25. The pistol turned up in Dallas the same day. Did Lee collect the guns himself? There is no evidence that he did. According to the Warren Report, when Lee gave up his mailbox on May 14, 1963, the list of persons authorized to receive mail there was destroyed. Presumably "Hidell" was on that list. Were others? How many people were authorized to pick up mail there? This is unknown. Postal Inspector Harry D. Holmes of the Dallas Post Office told the Warren Commission that identification was not required of people picking up packages. Holmes also said that postal regulations required the destruction of the list of boxholders when the box was closed; in fact, the regulations mandated retaining the entire application, including the list of persons authorized to receive mail, for two years afterwards.

As authors Ray and Mary La Fontaine point out, postal regulations also mandated the retention of firearms delivery records for *four years* after delivery. Since no such record was ever produced, and it appears to have vanished from post office files, there's no way of knowing who signed for the rifle. Still more mysteriously, the FBI—in its thorough investigation of these events for the Warren Commission—could not discover where Oswald got his bullets from. Presumably ammo for his revolver was easy to come by, but the Italian rifle he had ordered required 6.5mm cartridges, which were uncommon. Independent research has established that there were only *two* local suppliers: gun shop owners John Brinegar and John Thomas Masen. Both denied selling Oswald any ammo. Masen, a Minuteman and associate of General Walker, was being investigated by the ATTD as a suspected gunrunner.[6]

On March 26, at the recommendation of Special Agent James Hosty, the FBI reopened their file on Oswald. This was done, according to FBI records, "because of Oswald's newly opened subscription to the Communist newspaper" *The Worker*. But when Oswald had previously subscribed to *The Worker*—in October 1962—the FBI had closed his file.[7]

Did Oswald mail-order the guns on the instructions of the ATTD, or Dodd Committee? Did he use the "Hidell" name so as to incriminate some leftist group, perhaps the FPCC, by association? Or did Oswald, would-be lone assassin, acquire the guns to murder General Walker? (If so, again the question: why not buy them locally, and anonymously?) Supposedly, he next made use of both firearms to permanently incriminate himself as a leftist, and a man of violence. On March 31, according to the Warren Report, Oswald posed for two photographs—taken by Marina—behind the house on Neely Street.[8]

These "backyard photos" depict Lee dressed all in black (or a dark color—they are monochrome) with a holstered revolver on his hip. In one hand he holds a rifle, in the other some reading material.

Fig. 3: Warren Commission documents CE-133 A and B, plus "C"—a non-Commission document.

In both pictures he stands at an odd angle, as if his right leg were shorter than his left, and he has a 10-degree list to starboard. If you try to stand at this angle, you will fall over.

There is much else that is not right with these "historic" photos. Oswald, when shown them by the Dallas police, said they were fakes: he told Captain Will Fritz that he knew something about photography and that his face had been pasted onto pictures he'd never seen before. Oswald was, according to most sources, 5'9" in height. If the individual in the photographs is assumed to be this height, then his rifle is roughly 43" long. If Oswald was 5'11", then the rifle is even longer: 44". But the Mannlicher-Carcano rifle which "Hidell" purchased, and which allegedly killed the president, is only 38" in length. Similarly, the communist newspapers Oswald is holding do not scale to the actual sizes of the papers in question, *The Militant* and *The Worker* both being smaller than the folded newspapers Oswald is holding.

As the years went by, more backyard prints appeared. In 1976 a third picture of Oswald in the same place was given to the HSCA by the widow of a Dallas policeman, Roscoe White. It features the same props but "Oswald" is standing a little straighter and holding them differently. The HCSA treated the three photographs as genuine, something they are clearly *not*. Researchers proved this decades ago by making three photo transparencies in which the head was scaled to the same size, then lining the three pictures up around the individual's face. This simple test proves Oswald right. The photos are fakes because Oswald's face is *exactly the same* in each of the three photos. Even though the individual's posture and position have changed, the face is identical. The shadow beneath the nose is unchanged.

The HSCA dealt with this problem by denying it outright. "There is no support for the statement that Oswald's head is identical in each of the backyard pictures. If anything, the photographs showed a marked variation in facial expression. For example, in CE 133-A Oswald is smiling, whereas in CE 133-B he appears to be frowning."[9]

What do you think?

In 1993, researchers discovered two more "backyard photos": one of a plainclothes Dallas detective, Bobby Brown, holding a gun and newspapers in the same location, the other of the backyard, minus detective Brown, with a hole cut in it to fit Oswald's profile. These photos were taken at a different time of year, perhaps during a Secret

Service reenactment on November 29, 1963. Brown told author Gary Savage that he also made the cutout, at the request of the Secret Service, a few days after the assassination. But why? And—since the cutout is of the *third* "backyard photo"—why did the Dallas police and/or the Secret Service keep the third photo a secret from the Warren Commission?[10]

Marina Oswald first testified to taking only one picture of her husband in the backyard that afternoon. She later amended her testimony, stating she had taken two photos. The HSCA didn't ask her about the third photo. Why?

On April 2, Ruth Paine invited the Oswalds over for dinner. Michael picked

Fig. 4: Backyard "cutout" from the DPD.

their guests up in his car, and drove them home after. This was particularly nice of him, as he and Ruth had parted company some weeks previously, in order to live separate lives.

On April 3, "Bull" Connor, in charge of public safety in Birmingham, Alabama, became internationally famous for setting dogs and fire hoses on black civil rights demonstrators. On April 4, 5 and 6 the Congress of Freedom, Inc., held its annual meeting at the Fontainebleau Motel-Hotel in New Orleans, Louisiana. The Congress was infiltrated by Miami police detective Lochart F. Gracey, who reported to his superiors that "there were in attendance high-ranking industrialists, bankers, insurance executives, men and women generally that have access to great amounts of money." According to detective Gracey, the participants feared that President Kennedy was about to turn the government of the United States over to the United Nations. They spoke openly of political assassination, and by the end of the Congress had drawn up a list of prominent individuals who should be killed. Jewish bankers and financiers were first on the list, which also included Juan Trippe, head of Pan Am, Henry Ford II, General Lucius Clay, and John McCloy, whom Gracey (or the would-be assassins) mistakenly identified as "head of CIA."

Gracey remarked that, unlike traditional conventioneers, the attendees did not drink in the bars or raise hell. "It appeared... that they were there strictly on business." Among those present were "the Dixie Clan of Georgia... which was represented by Harry Jack Brown of Chattanooga, Tennessee. The Dixie Clan of Georgia is an underground organization that... is being directed by J.A. Milteer, a past candidate for the governorship of Georgia... The Dixie Clan, which is an offshoot of hard-core membership of the KKK, John Birch, White Citizens Council and other groups, are pushing for this [program of] assassination." There seems to have been little or no follow-up to Gracey's report. Violent right-wing conspirators were not rounded up, but Milteer was kept under police surveillance.[11]

Perhaps of greater concern is Gracey's observation that "Membership within the Congress of Freedom, Inc. contain high-ranking members of the Armed Forces that secretly belong to the organization. One or two of these members have been brought to your attention in previous reports submitted to your office." So the Miami police were infiltrating right-wing extremist groups with ties to the U.S. military, just as Lee Harvey Oswald began stalking General Walker.

Did Oswald believe he was investigating right-wing groups? Special Agent James Hosty, the FBI man who reopened Oswald's file, told author Mary La Fontaine that looking into gun violations was part of his activities, which entailed "the investigation of mostly right-wing subversives, like Minutemen." Hosty was a close friend and bridge partner of Robert Surrey, General Walker's aide. Surrey— as a 1965 FBI monograph would reveal—led a secret group of about 30 American Nazi Party members, holding weekly meetings at his Dallas home. This ominous coincidence led researcher Jerry Rose to note: "it is possible that Surrey, as much as Walker, was the target of Oswald's surveillance."[12]

Such surveillance was already underway by the ATTD and Senator Dodd's Subcommittee, who had singled out the American Nazi Party for its mail-order purchases of firearms. (As the ATTD was not an independent agency, but part of the IRS, this firearms investigation may have resulted from the Kennedy brothers' IOP—their project to investigate the tax status and activities of radical political groups.)[13]

April 6 was Oswald's last day at Jaggers-Chiles-Stovall. He had been fired, officially for ineptitude, though he'd made no secret to his supervisors of his resurgent Marxism. Around this date, General Walker returned to Dallas, following a "Night Ride" tour of supporters on the West Coast. Rose speculates that Walker and

Surrey, newly aware how negatively perceived they were, conceived a plan to make the general appear not a violent extremist, but a *victim* of violent extremism. According to Rose's theory, Walker tasked Surrey and associates to fake an attack on him: something that could be blamed on the political left. The next evening, according to Surrey, "two white men in a 1963 Ford" parked in the alley behind the general's house. They were dressed in suits, Surrey said, "walking up to the property line and smoking, and looking the place over." They left, but Surrey said that two men showed up again on April 8, peering in the windows. (Scotty Duff, having fought with some of Walker's volunteers, was no longer on the premises.)

The same day, April 8, Oswald was dropped from his typing class for failing to appear. Two nights later, someone with a rifle took a shot at Walker. The general was seated at his desk, writing. The window frame deflected the bullet and it missed him. Two cars were seen speeding away.

According to Marina's testimony, Lee left their home between six and seven, to attend, she thought, his typing class. "When he came back, I asked him what happened... he told me not to ask him any questions. He only told me he had shot at General Edwin Walker." A dozen years later, she told the HSCA that Oswald had turned the radio on and scanned the stations, trying to learn if he had killed Walker or not.

Marina was the only witness to this. No one saw him there; no one else heard his confession; to others, Oswald denied being involved. And, as Marina pointed out to researchers, she only repeated what her husband said to her; even if Oswald said it, that doesn't make it true. The "historic" Oswald, we are told, couldn't drive and had no accomplices. He had to take several buses to the crime scene, carrying his camera and his rifle. Since two cars and at least two men were involved in the stakeout and the reported attack, the "loner" Oswald depicted by the Warren Commission cannot have been involved.

A note, written in Russian, which Oswald allegedly left for Marina, and which Ruth Paine gave to the FBI, reads as follows:

> (1) This is the key to the mailbox which is located in the main post office in the city on Ervay Street. This is the same street where the drugstore, in which you always waited is located. You will find the mailbox in the post office which is located 4 blocks

from the drugstore on that street. I paid for the box last month so don't worry about it.

(2) Send the information as to what has happened to me to the Embassy and include newspaper clippings (should there be anything about me in the newspapers). I believe that the Embassy will come quickly to your assistance upon learning everything.

(3) I paid the house rent on the second so don't worry about it.

(4) Recently I also paid for water and gas.

(5) The money from work will possibly be coming. The money will be sent to our post office box. Go to the bank and cash the check.

(6) You can either throw out or give my clothing etc. away. Do not keep these. However I prefer you hold on to my personal papers (military, civil etc.)

(7) Certain of my documents are in the small blue valise.

(8) The address book can be found on my table in the study should you need same.

(9) We have friends here. The Red Cross also will help you. [Red Cross in English].

(10) I left you as much money as I could, $60 on the second of the month. You and the baby can live for another two months using $10 per week.

(11) If I am alive and taken prisoner, the city jail is located at the end of the bridge through which we always passed on going to the city (right in the beginning of the city after crossing the bridge).

That is the note in its entirety. It is unsigned and undated. It does *not* mention General Walker. Its author was clearly planning something newsworthy and dangerous, in Dallas, which might get Lee killed or arrested. But what, and when?

The document portrays a selfish, narcissistic individual: "You and the baby can live for another two months using $10 per week" indeed! But did Lee Oswald write it? It's translated from (apparently grammatical) Russian, so this is not the occasionally dyslexic

Southern English with which we are familiar. Marina says Lee wrote the note and left it for her, but none of her testimony, given under duress, would hold up in a court. So what remains to connect Lee Harvey Oswald with this incriminating document? The evidence of an FBI handwriting expert?

According to George de Mohrenschildt, when he next saw Oswald he teased him about being the would-be assassin, asking, "How could you miss?" In response, Lee denied taking a shot at the General. Since the Warren Report accused Oswald of trying to kill Walker, that case has been treated as closed. But he was never charged with that crime, and the Dallas police chief, Jesse Curry, later remarked, "We had absolutely no evidence to connect him to the case." Walker initially fingered a different suspect: Scotty Duff. And the incident was quickly overshadowed, on April 11, by the news that an American nuclear submarine, the U.S.S. *Thresher*, had sunk off the coast of Greenland with 167 men aboard.

On Good Friday, April 12, Martin Luther King and many others were arrested for "demonstrating without a permit" in Birmingham, Alabama. King, held in solitary confinement, began writing his famous "Letter From A Birmingham Jail." Coretta King telephoned the White House and received calls from Bobby and the president, both of whom assured her that the FBI was checking on her husband, and that he was all right. Otherwise, in Washington, progress on civil rights was slow. Robert Kennedy fought with Vice President Johnson over it. The Justice Department, he said, had filed 42 lawsuits in support of black voting rights, whereas Johnson's Committee on Equal Employment Opportunity was dragging its feet. Bobby Kennedy, 37, was not discreet when he got agitated; Johnson, 54, a hard-fighting senior politician, did not appreciate being dressed down by one so young and privileged. It's also ironic that the Attorney General, who was technically J. Edgar Hoover's boss, should pick on Johnson for a lack of progress in civil rights: the FBI was illegally wiretapping and actively harassing King and other civil rights leaders, and assisting violent white racists. But after two years in the White House, there was little love left between the brothers and Johnson, if there had been any to begin with. Rumors that Jack was planning to drop Lyndon in 1964 had been circulating for almost a year.

President Kennedy's secretary, Evelyn Lincoln, noticed the estrangement: "Sometimes Mr. Johnson was brought into negotiations and other times he wasn't... I never heard anyone say, 'Let's exclude Lyndon,' but the fact is that his name appeared less and less on the lists of those who were invited to crucial White House policy and planning meetings."[14]

This was unfortunate. Johnson might have been villainous and vain but he was an excellent politician. If anyone could hold fractious Southern Democrats together it was this man. But the break was probably inevitable, since Lyndon faced bigger problems than his relationship with the Kennedys. Two major political scandals were looming, each involving a close associate of his: Billie Sol Estes and Bobby Baker. Estes was a Texas conman and longtime friend of Johnson who had scammed millions of dollars' worth of "agricultural subsidies." An enquiry into Estes was proceeding slowly through the Senate, but as yet it had not reached Johnson. Years later, Estes' attorney—seeking immunity from prosecution for his client—would claim that Estes and Johnson had been involved in no less than nine murders, including that of President Kennedy. Such immunity was not granted, and Estes' claims were never officially pursued.

The Bobby Baker scandal was more immediately threatening. Baker, a Senate staffer and the vice president's *protégé*, ran a motel and club where he provided bribes and sex for Washington politicians. Several Congressional committees were investigating him and other Texas lobbyists, while Bobby Kennedy's Justice Department was pursuing Baker for tax evasion and fraud. Even as Johnson carried out his civil rights and NASA duties, both enquiries must have preoccupied him.

On April 12, Lee Oswald filed for unemployment benefits in Dallas. On April 18, the DPD picked up Scotty Duff and grilled him about the Walker shooting; after he passed a polygraph test they let him go. The same day, Oswald mailed a letter to the Fair Play for Cuba Committee. In the last few weeks Lee had done several things that guaranteed he would be put on several lists: corresponding with the Russian embassy, ordering communist books and propaganda, writing to the SWP and the Communist Party. This new letter to the FPCC's national office drew him further into the investigatory realm of Senator Thomas Dodd.

The FPCC was already thoroughly surveilled and subverted. Senator Eastland's committee had investigated it, and published its report that month: *Castro's Network in the United States (Fair Play for Cuba Committee)*. Now, giving his post office box as his address, the Marxist ex-Marine asked the Committee for a favor.

> Dear Sirs:
> I do not like to ask for something for nothing but I am unemployed. Since I am unemployed, I stood yesterday for the first time in my life with a placare [sic] around my neck passing out fair play for Cuba pamplets [sic] ect... [sic] I only had 15 or so. In 40 minutes they were all gone. I was cursed as well as praised by some. My home-made placare said HANDS OFF CUBA! VIVA FIDEL!
> I now ask for 40 to 50 more of the fine, basic pamplets.
> Sincerely
> Lee H. Oswald

What "pamplets" were these? Oswald's letter soon found its way into the hands of the FBI, with an annotation—"sent 4/19"—in the margin. So he was quickly resupplied (amazingly quickly, if the date is correct). But with what? Most authors assume the "pamplet" was *The Crime Against Cuba*, a 20-page tract criticizing U.S. foreign policy, written by Corliss Lamont. Lamont was a wealthy leftist, and professor of philosophy at Columbia University in New York. Since the 1930s he had served on the board of directors of the ACLU. When he was called before Senator McCarthy's Committee in 1953, the ACLU had dropped him, and Lamont joined a smaller, more radical group, the Emergency Civil Liberties Committee, becoming its vice president.[15]

Oswald was later found in possession of *The Crime Against Cuba*, so assuming this was the "pamplet", where did he get it? The tract was published in 1961, while Oswald was in Russia. It was now out of print. Author James DiEugenio contacted Lamont, who showed him a purchase order for a 45-copy order *from the CIA*, dated June 28. CIA received first-edition copies; the pamphlet was in its fourth edition by the end of the year. Oswald's copy was a first edition, too.[16]

Did Oswald really demonstrate in Dallas, as he claimed, with a homemade placard around his neck? After the assassination, a Dallas cop, W.R. Finegan, wrote to Chief Curry that "in the late spring or summer of 1963" he saw a man, wearing a "Viva Fidel" sign on his back, handing out literature. When Finegan's superior,

Sgt. D.V. Harkness, showed up, the demonstrator disappeared into a department store.

If Finegan's story is true, then the lone demonstrator—not reported at the time, nor seen again—may have been Oswald. But why his sudden interest in Cuba? In the Marines, Oswald and a buddy, Nelson Delgado, had discussed joining Castro's guerrillas. But they didn't. And the individual who learned Russian and moved to Minsk had seemed largely indifferent to the Cuban revolution. Now, everything changed.

On April 19, the de Mohrenschildts left Dallas, bound for New York, Philadelphia, DC, and ultimately Haiti. A few days later, some blocks from Ruth Paine's house in Irving, Texas, two men bartered a .30 caliber Springfield rifle for auto repairs. The mechanic, Robert Taylor, was convinced that one of the men, who drove a 1959 Chevrolet, was Oswald. The Warren Commission ignored Taylor's statements; their Oswald had no accomplices, and couldn't drive.

On April 20, Dr. King was released from jail, and a white mailman, William Moore, engaged in a "freedom walk," was shot dead by unknown assailants on an Alabama highway. On April 22, in Washington, DC, a scientist named Adele Edisen had dinner with Dr. Jose Rivera, who claimed to be a science administrator in the National Institutes of Health. Rivera said a number of strange things which had nothing to do with the professional matters that had brought them together. While they waited to be seated at Blackie's House of Beef, they discussed a city they both knew: Dallas, Texas. According to Edisen, Rivera recommended that she visit a nightclub there called the Carousel, and that she should get to know Lee Harvey Oswald, who had lived in Russia, had a Russian wife, and would soon be moving to New Orleans.

The next day Rivera took Edisen on a sightseeing tour of the capital. During their drive, Rivera made vague threats to the president and his wife, and disparaging remarks about black people and the civil rights movement. The two ate dinner at the Marriot Motor Hotel, and Rivera again brought up the subject of Oswald: "Write down this name: Lee Harvey Oswald. Tell him to kill the chief." According to Edisen,

> "Rivera seemed agitated and excited. He began talking strangely about 'it' happening. 'Here,' he said, 'I'll show you

where it will happen.' He began to draw a rectangle. 'This is the room, with windows over here. And this'—he drew an 'X' next to the rectangle—'is where it will happen. It will be on the fifth floor. There'll be some men up there.'"

"I had no idea what he was talking about. Rivera was almost incoherent and very agitated... 'Oswald,' I was told by Rivera, 'was not what he seems.' 'We're going to send him over to the library to read about great assassinations in history.' 'After it's over, he'll call Abt to defend him.' 'After it's over, someone will kill him. They'll say his best friend killed him.' 'After it happens, the President's best friend will commit suicide. He'll jump out of a window because of his grief.'... 'When does the Shriners' Circus come to New Orleans? Oh, I remember, in November. It will happen after the Shriners' Circus comes to New Orleans.' 'After it's over, the men will be out of the country.' 'Remember, the first time it happens won't be real.'"[17]

Edisen says she called the number Rivera gave her, and after several attempts spoke to Oswald. She asked him if he knew Dr. Rivera, and he said he didn't. So she didn't pass on the message. If her strange tale is true, then Rivera was admitting in advance to participating in a plot to murder President Kennedy and pin the crime on Oswald. After the assassination, Edisen says she made a report to the FBI and to Special Agent J. Calvin Rice of the New Orleans Secret Service, and gave them the note with Oswald's phone number and Rivera's message. No report of the interview exists. Copies *do* exist of letters Edisen and her attorney, Jack Peebles, wrote to the Church Committee (in 1976) and the HSCA (in 1977), reporting her conversations with Rivera; in 1998 she testified before the ARRB. And Dr. Rivera himself was real: Anthony DiMaggio III, a biology professor at Loyola University in New Orleans, confirmed that he had replaced Rivera there in 1960, and that Rivera had gone on to work for the National Institutes of Health at Bethesda, Maryland. Rivera was a naturalized citizen, born either in Peru or Puerto Rico—government documents give him different birthplaces and birth dates. He possessed SECRET clearance at the U.S. Army chemical lab at Fort Detrick, Maryland, and TOP SECRET clearance at the Naval Biological Laboratory at Berkeley, California.[18]

According to Marina, two weeks after the Walker shooting—that is, around April 24, 1963—she prevented Lee from making an attempt on the life of former vice president Richard Nixon. In her FBI statement of February 25, 1964, Marina accused her husband of dressing in a suit and tie, packing a pistol, and stating, "Nixon is coming and I'm going to take a look." Marina claimed she foiled the attempt by trapping Oswald in the bathroom. But Nixon was not present in Dallas during this period.[19]

Also on April 24, Ruth Paine dropped by the Oswalds, only to discover they were leaving town. The de Mohrenschildts had pulled up stakes, and now the Oswalds were moving too, to New Orleans. According to Ruth's testimony, it was all a complete surprise. The family was packed and its few belongings fit into her car, so she drove them to the bus station. There, according to Ruth, she persuaded Lee to let June and Marina—who was three months pregnant—stay with her. He left alone for New Orleans; Ruth and the rest of his family went back to Irving. Fortunately, Ruth and Michael had recently separated, otherwise Ruth could never have accommodated Marina and June, plus her own two children, in her two-bedroom home.

Oswald arrived in New Orleans with two duffel bags. Supposedly, one of them contained his pistol and his disassembled rifle. He stayed with his aunt and uncle, Lilian and Charles "Dutz" Murret, who had cared for him when he was a baby. Dutz was, among other things, a bookmaker, and this has encouraged some to see a mafia link to Lee's activities in New Orleans. But it's also possible that Lilian and Dutz were something genuine in this sea of weirdos: kind relatives, possibly appalled by Marguerite's child-rearing practices, trying to look out for their nephew.

One of these Murrets, however, had an adventurous history which paralleled Lee's: Marilyn Dorothea, his cousin. Marilyn, a former reservations agent with Braniff Airlines, had left on a round-the-world adventure around the time Lee's international travels began. Marilyn visited England, France, Belgium, Holland, Germany, Hawaii, Hong Kong, Australia, New Zealand, Thailand, Japan, India, and Pakistan. She renewed her passport at the U.S. Embassy in Tokyo in 1960, and at the U.S. Embassy in Karachi in 1962, and seems to have returned to New Orleans around the time Lee showed up at her parents'. Interviewed by the FBI after the assassination, Marilyn said she had financed her three-year trip by working as a grade-school teacher; denied being a communist; and reported being "detained" for 12 hours in East Berlin, a revelation her interviewer did not pursue.

A separate FBI report suggested Marilyn Murret might be linked with the "communist 'apparatus' of Professor Harold Isaacs at the Massachusetts Institute of Technology." Isaacs worked for the Center for International Studies at M.I.T. According to David Wise, "the M.I.T. Center, which was set up with CIA money in 1950, has adopted many of the practices in effect at the CIA headquarters in Virginia. An armed guard watches over the door and the participating academicians must show badges on entering and leaving."[20]

If he worked for an academic branch of CIA, it's unlikely Prof. Isaacs was a genuine communist. So what was his relationship with Oswald's well-traveled cousin?

On May 2, Senator Thomas Kuchel, a moderate Republican, accused right-wing extremists of spreading rumors that African troops were being trained in Georgia, in preparation for a United Nations *coup d'état* in Washington, DC. On May 4, 18 months after separating from his wife, Nelson Rockefeller married "Happy" Murphy, a recent *divorcée*. A well-publicized honeymoon, on Nelson's ranch in Venezuela, followed. This tended to suggest Rockefeller was a billionaire playboy, which was true, and to undermine his support among mainstream Republicans. On May 6, a group of "prominent American citizens" including Edward Teller and Admiral Arleigh Burke—whom Kennedy had forced into retirement—announced the formation of a new Committee for a Free Cuba, dedicated to Castro's overthrow.

Meanwhile, civil rights demonstrators in Birmingham were being clubbed, fire-hosed, and attacked by police dogs. Hundreds of blacks were arrested, many of them children. Representative Adam Clayton Powell, Jr., predicted a massive race riot in Washington, DC, unless civil rights issues were addressed. Clarence Jones, Martin Luther King's lawyer and speechwriter, struggled to find bail money for the children and students who had been arrested and jailed by "Bull" Connor's peace officers. He got it from an unexpected source: Nelson Rockefeller, who had been contacted by Harry Belafonte. Rockefeller met Jones at one of his New York banks, on a Saturday, and gave him $100,000 in cash to make bail for the young people. Rockefeller got no mileage from his generosity, and the details remained secret until Jones told the story, 48 years later.[21]

In Washington, Democratic congressman Wayne Hays publicly urged an investigation of H.L. Hunt and his media network's tax status. A fellow congressman, Wright Patman, proposed that right-wing organizations such as Life Line be "listed as subversive by the Attorney General." Kennedy, trying to get his tax breaks passed while simultaneously leaning on his allies in Canada and Europe to accept a new, nuclear-armed alliance against the Russians, hoped to ride the racial turmoil out. This proved impossible. As the situation worsened, the president would again be forced to send federal troops against the police and sheriffs of a Southern city. On May 6 he issued a National Security Action Memo, NSAM 239, which reminded the heads of his national security apparatus—the Joint Chiefs, CIA director, Secretary of State, Secretary of Defense, and others— that "I have in no way changed my views as to the desirability of a test ban treaty or the value of our proposals on general and complete disarmament." In the absence of complete disarmament, the president asked for proposals for partial disarmament which the United States could make when the 18-nation Disarmament Committee met in Geneva.

Once again, Jack Kennedy was trying to have it both ways: threatening the Russians with a new, atomic alliance while simultaneously proposing reductions in—or the elimination of— both countries' nuclear arsenals. Yet Khrushchev understood him better now. The two men wanted to ratchet down the levels of international tension, and to lessen the nuclear threat. Both had to contend with big, influential military establishments. To threaten and cajole simultaneously is not the best negotiating strategy, but it may have been the only one available.

In Haiti, a fraudulent election was followed by civil unrest. The United States protested at the "harassment" of American officials in Port-au-Prince, and U.S. Navy ships gathered just outside Haitian waters. "Papa Doc" Duvalier, president and dictator, responded to threats of an impending rebellion by placing Haiti under martial law. He had reason to be worried. Haiti is half of an island, the other half being the Dominican Republic; Trujillo, Dominican president and dictator, had been killed with CIA assistance less than two years previously.

Would the Americans really plot a coup against "Papa Doc"? The dictator had supported Kennedy's anti-Cuba policy. Yet they disliked him, and his old supporters at CIA were gone. It was also rumored that the Americans wanted Haiti "stabilized" as the base for a new invasion of Cuba. On May 7, Dorethe Matlack, Assistant Director of the Army Chief of Staff for Intelligence in Washington, DC, set up a meeting between CIA, George de Mohrenschildt, and a Haitian banker, Clemard Charles. This was apparently of some importance to the Department of Defense, since Mrs. Matlack made hotel reservations for Charles and the de Mohrenschildts. Charles was believed to be intimate with "Papa Doc": according to Matlack, he acted "frantic and frightened" and urged that U.S. Marines invade Haiti and overthrow Duvalier: she said that de Morenschildt "dominated" Charles throughout the exchange. Matlick considered the meeting of no informational value, but was "disturbed" by de Mohrenschildt's presence and discussed it with her FBI liaison. She told the HSCA that she never heard what action, if any, the FBI took about de Mohrenschildt.

The Murrets told the FBI that Lee stayed with them in New Orleans for "a few days to a week"—leaving his whereabouts for the next seven to ten days unaccounted for. On May 10, Oswald moved into a new apartment, at 4905 Magazine Street, and started a new job as a maintenance man at the Reily Coffee Company. Once again, this was a strange place for a radical defector to find work. The company was owned by two brothers, Eustis and William Reily. Eustis was one of the backers of INCA, the Information Council on the Americas, a right-wing propaganda outfit associated with CIA, and William was a supporter of the Crusade to Free Cuba Committee. According to a CIA memo dated January 31, 1964, "this firm [Reily's] was of interest as of April 1949," and was assigned an Agency number: EE-334.[22]

Whether Oswald ever worked at Reily's is open to question. Some of his paychecks appear to have been fabricated later; so it remains possible that his "job" at the Coffee Company was a cover for other activities. In any case, he spent little time there. In 1981, author Michael Kurtz interviewed Hunter C. Leake, who claimed to have been second-in-command at the New Orleans CIA station. Leake apparently told Kurtz that CIA had brought Oswald to New Orleans and used him as a courier, and that he, Leake, had paid Oswald out of CIA funds. Case closed, smoking gun discovered, if this is true. But is it? Leake apparently died in 1981. He worked for the New Orleans CIA office; it is not clear that he was its deputy station chief. And, given the sensational nature of Leake's story, why didn't Kurtz air these revelations when he gave evidence to the ARRB?[23]

On May 11, Ruth Paine drove Marina and June to New Orleans. They moved in with Lee, and Ruth stayed for a couple of days, returning to Dallas on May 14—a round trip of more than a thousand miles.

A plan for the desegregation of Birmingham was announced, but on May 11 three bombs exploded—all targeting Martin Luther King and his family. Two went off at the home of A.D. King, his brother, miraculously killing no one; a third exploded at the Gaston Motel, where Dr. King and Ralph Abernathy had met 30 minutes before. Thousands of blacks rioted, the Klan fled, and the police lost control of the city for most of the night. It was the first urban riot of the 1960s and it greatly alarmed all sectors of the establishment. For the elite and the media, blacks might have been despised or pitied, but they were invariably treated as objects rather than subjects: they were not expected to arm themselves with guns, loot stores and burn police cars...

Concerned about a new phenomenon, "black violence," Kennedy sent troops to Birmingham, and ordered the federalization of the Alabama National Guard. But he left control of the Guard in the hands of Alabama governor George Wallace, a racist Democrat, sending him a telegram: "I trust that we can count on your constructive cooperation." In Washington, Senator Fulbright criticized the OAS for showing "apathy" over the Haitian crisis; Fulbright warned of a possible communist takeover there. In an effort to promote a test ban treaty, Kennedy canceled three scheduled Nevada nuclear tests.

On May 18, the president made a one-day tour of Alabama and Tennessee. He was enthusiastically greeted by black leaders, traveled by motorcade to Vanderbilt University, made a less-timid reference to civil rights, then flew with Governor Wallace to Redstone Arsenal for another photo session with Wernher von Braun. At Redstone, Kennedy's principal concern was not to be photographed with Wallace. Five days later, at a news conference, the president denied claims by Republicans that the United States might give the Guantanamo Bay naval base back to Cuba. "It has never been considered," Kennedy told reporters. The same day, the vice president gave a strong speech in favor of civil rights to the Capitol Press Club, in Washington. Johnson was far more vocal than Kennedy in his support of black demonstrators. He said, quite simply, that there was no "moral justification" for asking them to be more patient.

On May 22, Lee Oswald visited his local library in New Orleans. He borrowed a book, *Portrait of a Revolutionary: Mao Tse Tung* by Robert Payne.[24]

On May 24, Fidel Castro left Moscow after a monthlong Russian tour; President Kennedy traveled to New York, to attend an "informal, fund-raising birthday party" for 600 guests at the Waldorf-Astoria.

On May 26, Lee Harvey Oswald wrote again to the FPCC, enclosing five dollars.

> Dear Sirs
> I am requesting formal membership in your Organization.
> In the past I have received from you pamplets ect., both both bought by me and given to me by you. Now that I live in New Orleans I have been thinking about starting a small office at my own expense for the purpose of forming a FPCC branch here in New Orleans. Could you give me a charter?
> Also I would like information on buying pamplets ect. in large lots, as well as blank FPCC applications ect. Also, a picture of Fidel, suitable for framing would be a welcome touch.
> Offices down here rent for $30 a month and if I had a steady flow of literature I would be glad to take the expense. Of course I work and could not supervise the office at all times but I'm sure I could get some volunteers to do it. Could you add some advice or recommendations? I am not saying this project would be a roaring success, <u>but I am willing to try</u>. An office, literature, and getting people to know you are the fundementles [sic] of the FPCC as far as I can see so here's hoping to hear from you.
> Yours respectfully
> Lee H Oswald

Without waiting for a reply, Lee ordered up 1,000 handbills from a printer opposite the Coffee Company. *"HANDS OF CUBA!"* the handbills said, *"Join the Fair Play for Cuba Committee—New Orleans Charter Member Branch—Free Literature, Lectures."* Below the word *"LOCATION"* was a blank space. At the bottom, *"EVERYONE WELCOME!"*

What was this all about? Oswald hadn't received an answer, and didn't have an office or a "charter." What *was* this "charter" anyway, that he seemed so anxious to obtain? An authentic activist would just get busy. Lee mentioned volunteers but there is no evidence that he *ever* tried to recruit anyone to the communist or Castro cause (other than idle banter when he was in the Marines). Nor did he join a communist group, or attend any communist meetings. The Warren Commission decided he had no accomplices. So he just laid a paper trail.

On May 28, via his attorney, General Walker hired a former Oklahoma City cop, Cliff Roberts, to shadow Scotty Duff in Dallas. Roberts quickly located Duff, and moved into his apartment building. "After several drinking sprees with the subject," Roberts reported, "the conversation got around to the attempted assassination of General Walker." Duff denied involvement, but offered to kill the General for $5,000.[25]

V.T. Lee replied to Oswald the next day—May 29—with a three-page letter and an FPCC membership card. He advised Oswald not to rent an office: "at least not one that will be easily identifyable [sic] to the lunatic fringe in your community." He told him to get a post office box, and access to a mimeograph machine. He doubted that there were many potential members in the New Orleans area, but said a charter was possible, if enough people joined. "A good typewriter is essential and above all people that will carry out the million and one mechanical functions necessary to make it a going operation."

Who was V.T. Lee? Vincent Lee, National Director of the FPCC, was, like Lee Oswald, a former military man. He had the same capacity to write a decent letter, minus a few spelling mistakes. He showed a tendency to exaggerate (the FPCC might have had scores of functions, but not a million) and to self-pity: "These may sound like small things to you, but I can assure you that we have gone through thi [sic] a thousand and more time [sic] the length and breadth of the country and have learned a great deal over the last three years through some bitter experience." Shut up, already, Vincent! Genuine activists, whom I have known, tend to be cheerful and determined. They have made their commitment, know the odds are stacked against them, and have nothing to gain by whining. Provocateurs and government infiltrators, on the other hand, constantly complain and complicate things.[26]

Is it possible that the FPCC was entirely bogus, like the "revolutionary underground" in Harry Harrison's novel *Bill, The*

Galactic Hero, where all the plotters are revealed to be government spies? If so, this was quite a *coup* for the Americans—to have set up a fake support group to entrap unwary leftists, *and* to have got Castro to pay for it! On the other hand, V.T. Lee doesn't seem to have enjoyed Lee Oswald's easy access to funds: when he advised using someone else's mimeograph to produce cheap flyers, Oswald walked into a print shop and ordered an offset litho job—the most expensive way of doing it.

At some point during May, a New Orleans attorney, Dean Andrews, had a visit from Lee. Oswald wanted to know what could be done about his discharge from the Marines, which Andrews called "a yellow paper discharge." The lawyer told him he would have to advance the funds to transcribe his records at the Adjutant General's office. Oswald was accompanied "by some gay kids... Mexicanos," according to Andrews. Lee returned to the lawyer's office three or four times subsequently, enquiring about his discharge, his status as a citizen, and his wife's status. The "gay kids" did not return.

On May 29, Robert Kennedy and Lyndon Johnson clashed over civil rights issues. Arriving late to a meeting of Johnson's CEEO committee, the Attorney General laid into those present over the federal government's continued failure to hire blacks. Johnson responded that without school integration, blacks would inevitably lose out on the job market. "It may be, Mr. Attorney General," he added, "that deliberate speed is not enough." Kennedy stormed out. The next day, the vice president gave a tremendous speech at Gettysburg attacking gradualism and half-measures. "The backbone of white resistance is not going to be broken," Johnson thundered, "until the segregationists realize that the total moral force of the United States is arrayed against them... It is empty to pretend that the solution to the dilemmas of the present rests on the hands of a clock. The solution is in our own hands." As Nick Bryant observed, it was the speech the president should have made.[27]

The day after the vice president made his speech, Kennedy invited him to discuss civil rights legislation. Lyndon, the chief architect of the 1957 and 1960 Civil Rights Acts, professed ignorance of the Kennedys' intentions. But he urged them, if they put forward a new civil rights bill, *to really fight for it*. Johnson requested another brief, private meeting with the president afterwards, to discuss how to force such a bill on the Southern Democrats. In domestic politics,

Lyndon Johnson was the strongest member of Kennedy's team: if anyone could forge a consensus on Capitol Hill it was Lyndon. But Ken O'Donnell turned down his request for a 15-minute meeting. Deeply disappointed, Johnson harangued Ted Sorensen on the importance of moral leadership, insisting that the president start making major speeches on civil rights, pulling no punches, if he wanted to get his legislation passed. Sorensen passed the message on to Kennedy.

On May 31, after a month of demonstrations and riots, J. Edgar Hoover warned the Attorney General that Dr. King and a coterie of "communist spies" planned a new wave of protests. Hoover insisted that King "would like to see so much pressure on the president that he will have to sign an Executive Order making segregation unconstitutional." If only it had been so… King had no such delusions as to his power; and Kennedy was no more likely to make segregation unconstitutional than later presidents were, by Executive Order, to make the Equal Rights Amendment law. Nevertheless Martin and other civil rights leaders were planning a mass demonstration: the FBI recorded King telling an adviser, Stanley Levison, that "the threat itself may so frighten the president that he would have to do something."

On June 1, Lee Oswald borrowed two more library books: *The Berlin Wall*, by Dan and David Heller, and *the Huey Long Murder Case* by Herman B. Deutsch.

On June 2, the de Mohrenschildts arrived in Haiti. The Baron later told the Warren Commission that he had a contract with the Haitian government to conduct a geological survey of the island. de Mohrenschildt set up a corporation, the Haitian Holding Co., with Clemard Charles as one of his partners. On June 3, the United States resumed "normal diplomatic business" with the Haitian government. The same day, Pope John XIII died, and Oswald opened a post office box—Number 30061—in New Orleans, designating "Hidell" and Marina as additional mail recipients.

On June 3, a second Oklahoma City cop, William Keester, arrived in Dallas to assist with General Walker's sting; Keester was "to pose as the party for the money connection" in the ongoing entrapment of Duff. Cliff Roberts, Keester and Duff discussed murdering General Walker, and the investigators agreed to pay him $5,000. Roberts tape-recorded their conversations as they drove through Walker's neighborhood "and plans were discussed for the actual assassination, the escape route, the weapon to be used, and method in which the subject Duff would leave the country after the assassination."

In 1989, the author Jim Marrs unearthed a piece of economic history which researchers had previously ignored: President Kennedy's Executive Order 11,110, dated June 4th. Via this document, the president gave the Treasury Secretary the right to print money—a power which previously resided only with the Federal Reserve. The Executive Order called for the issuance of more than four billion dollars' worth of United States notes (Marrs still owns a $5 "United States Note" issued in 1963, but writes that most were withdrawn after the assassination).[28]

Per Marrs, the Federal Reserve loans the paper money it prints to the U.S. government *at interest*. So E.O. 11,110 was more provocative to powerful interests than Kennedy's showdown with U.S. Steel, or his threat to trim the oil depletion allowance. By printing money directly, the president was cutting into the income stream of some of the richest banks—and bankers—in the country. According to *Black's Law Dictionary*, the Federal Reserve System is a "network of twelve central banks to which most national banks belong." Each Federal Reserve Bank is a private corporation owned by commercial banks in its region. Since the financial crash of 2008 many smaller banks and financial institutions have been folded into three super-banks, Chase, Wells Fargo, and Bank of America, which are considered by politicians as "too big to fail." All three continue to profit from the arcane practice of loaning banknotes to the state.

E.O. 11,110 is still in effect. But no other president used it: Johnson, Nixon, Ford, Carter, Reagan, Clinton, the Bushes and Obama all preferred to pay interest on Federal Reserve notes.

Also on June 4, Lee Oswald returned to Jones Printing, paid off his balance, and picked up his handbill order. On June 8, he acquired a rubber stamp kit. At some point around this date he wrote again to V.T. Lee of the FPCC: a four-page, handwritten letter in which he told Lee that he'd taken P.O. Box 30061, but otherwise ignored his advice entirely:

> Against your advice, I have decided to take an office from the very beginning. I apologise from [sic] the circular.
>
> I had jumped the gun on the charter business but I don't think its too important, you may think the circular is too provocative,

but I want it too [sic] attract attention, even if its the attention
of the lunatic fringe. I had 2000 of them run off.

Oswald enclosed a copy of his "circular." V.T. Lee later testified that
he gave up on his new recruit at this point. One doubts that Oswald
cared much. And where was this office he wrote about?

In Dallas, next day, Cliff Roberts played the tape, which
incriminated him, Keester and Duff in a murder plot, to General
Walker. On June 6, Walker discussed it with his attorney, Clyde Watts,
and contacted the police. On June 7, Keester and Roberts played
their tape for Lieutenant Cunningham and other DPD detectives,
who said they would take over the investigation. Scotty Duff,
meanwhile, called the FBI office in Dallas to report the incident,
and spoke to Agent Hosty.

The Warren Commission made no effort to pursue the Duff/
Keester/Roberts murder conspiracy, despite several provocative
police reports. A DPD report dated May 1, 1964, titled *Edwin A.
Walker Group (2)* and submitted by Detective L.D. Stringfellow,
described Walker's organization as "an extremist group" which
included among its affiliates William M. Duff, Cliff Roberts, and
William Keester. So, more than a year after the shooting, the DPD
viewed all three as members of Walker's circle. This suggests that
Rose's theory of a fake attack, instigated by Walker, and carried
out by Duff and company, is probably correct. On December 10, 1963,
a Dallas restaurateur, Joe Loria, advised the FBI that he had seen
Duff and Oswald together. Duff denied knowing Oswald, but, in an
interview with Secret Service agent James R. Cantrell, he alleged
that Jack Ruby, the Dallas nightclub owner, visited the General's
home on three occasions. Duff offered Robert Surrey as a possible
witness to Ruby's visits. Mysteriously, the FBI believed Duff when
he said he didn't know Oswald, but described him as a "pathological
liar" in the context of his Ruby/Walker claims.[29]

Meanwhile the situation in Haiti worsened, as did events in
South Vietnam, where the military regime opened fire on Buddhist
priests. In the South, civil rights protesters continued to come
under attack. Whether or not the protestors fought back, white-
owned newspapers began describing these incidents as "race riots."
In far-off Honolulu, Hawaii, John Kennedy addressed the National
Conference of Mayors, urging them to end local segregation and

integrate their workforces. It was a well-meaning speech, full of good words, with none of the moral fire and excitement of Johnson's Gettysburg address. The same day, the American Jewish Congress criticized the president's lack of action on civil rights, Dr. King said that the administration had "substituted an inadequate approach for a miserable one," and Kennedy sold the TV rights to his book, *Profiles in Courage.*

Next day, June 10, Jack Kennedy made a commencement address at the American University in Washington which some consider the greatest speech of his presidency. It's become known as his Peace Speech. In it, the man who had advocated a massive nuclear buildup and a fallout shelter in every plot, seemed to have undergone a profound change.

> "Today the expenditure of billions of dollars every year on weapons acquired for the purpose of making sure we never need them is essential to the keeping of peace. But surely the acquisition of such idle stockpiles—which can only destroy and never create—is not the only, much less the most efficient, means of assuring peace. I speak of peace, therefore, as the necessary, rational end of rational men…"

Kennedy insisted that peace was achievable, a practical possibility. He insisted that Russian fears about the Americans' intentions were unfounded:

> "It is discouraging to read a recent, authoritative Soviet text on military strategy and find, on page after page, wholly baseless and incredible claims, such as an allegation that American imperialist circles are preparing to unleash different types of war, that there is a very real threat of a preventive war being unleashed by American imperialists against the Soviet Union."

But there was indeed such a threat! The Joint Chiefs had repeatedly proposed a surprise nuclear attack on the Russians, with December 1963 as their preferred deadline. Kennedy had rejected it, so perhaps this was his way of telling the Russians what he had done. His speech made it clear he understood that any nuclear war between the two countries would be disastrous:

> "It is an ironic but accurate fact that the two strongest powers are the two in the most danger of devastation. All we have built, all we have worked for, would be destroyed in the first 24 hours."

Kennedy announced the installation of a direct telephone line between Moscow and Washington, to facilitate communication in times of crisis. He said that the Russians, the Americans and the British would soon begin talks, in Moscow, on a comprehensive test ban treaty. And he declared an American moratorium on atmospheric nuclear tests, as long as the other nuclear powers did likewise.

> "No government or social system is so evil that its people must be considered as lacking in virtue... In the final analysis, our most basic common link is that we all inhabit this small planet. We all breathe the same air. We all cherish our children's futures. And we are all mortal."

Kennedy ended the speech by insisting that the United States "as the world knows" would never start a war. The world knew nothing of the kind. The United States frequently provoked civil wars or wars between states, in the service of some political or economic interest. What were the Bay of Pigs invasion or Operation MONGOOSE if not acts of war against Cuba? What of his own threats to engage in nuclear warfare, over Berlin and the Cuban missiles? No matter. Kennedy's Peace Speech was aimed not at popular opinion in client states, but at Chairman Khrushchev, in support of a nuclear test ban. If you listen to a recording of the speech, its importance may elude you. He delivers it in a monotone, without passion, and ends it abruptly—as if he wasn't entirely familiar with the text, and misjudged the finish. Despite its flat delivery, the content is striking: common-sensical, far-sighted and sane, it may indeed be the most important speech Jack Kennedy made.

On June 11, Governor Wallace bowed to national opinion, a hundred National Guardsmen, and a General, and gave up his attempt to physically prevent two blacks, Vivian Malone and James Hood, from enrolling in the University of Alabama. Troops were withdrawn from the campus of Ole Miss, where a second black student was now enrolled. Pleased that the Alabama events had been managed well, and ended without bloodshed, Kennedy himself contacted the heads of the three networks, to request airtime for a speech that evening at 8 p.m. His decision to do this shocked his aides, who felt a TV speech was unnecessary. But Kennedy's instincts told him it was time to lead, at last, on civil rights with an address to the nation. The job of writing the speech—in six hours—fell to Ted Sorensen, the author of his inaugural address and the "Peace Speech." Burke Marshall and Robert Kennedy also worked on the draft, as did—at Bobby's request—a black activist, Louis Martin. They used some of Lyndon's arguments, in particular that the nation did not discriminate against minorities when it sent soldiers to West Berlin, or Vietnam.

At eight o'clock, Jack Kennedy addressed the nation. As with the Peace Speech, the words are wonderful. At last, he spoke at length on the subject of civil rights, saying this was "a moral issue... as old as the scriptures and as clear as the American Constitution." He promised new legislation, and "a great change." It was the speech black leaders—and the black community—had been waiting for. Four hours later, an assassin shot NAACP organizer Medgar Evers dead outside his home in Jackson, Mississippi. Mass protests followed; these were violently suppressed. Byron de la Beckwith, a NSRP member, would be tried three times for the crime—acquitted twice— and finally convicted in 1994, more than 30 years after the murder.

The Russians launched a woman cosmonaut, Valentina V. Tereshkova, into space on June 16. A NASA spokesman confessed there were no plans, at present, to include women on American space missions.

The same day, Lee Harvey Oswald stood on the docks in New Orleans, handing out his FPCC circulars. As targets for his propaganda, he chose sailors from an aircraft carrier, the U.S.S. *Wasp*; again, this was an unlikely milieu for a serious leftist agitator. The handbills which Oswald gave out were stamped "A.J. Hidell P.O. Box 30061 New Orleans, LA." The address was wrong: Oswald had transposed the last two digits, from 16 to 61. Yet he made no attempt to correct the mistake on subsequent occasions. CIA made a similar mistake with many of their Oswald documents, filing them under "Oswald, Harvey Lee." It is an interesting coincidence, since it meant that a request for documents about "Oswald, Lee Harvey" could be ignored, and that the owner of Box 30061 wouldn't be bothered by genuine Cuban sympathizers.[30]

On June 14, Admiral George C. Burkley received formal orders assigning him the duty of "physician to the President of the United States." Burkley had been performing this function for some months, having weaned Kennedy off amphetamines, prescribed by Dr. Max Jacobson (the legendary "Dr. Feelgood"), and steroids, prescribed by Dr. Janet Travell. Now, thanks to a regimen of physical therapy and daily workouts, the president's health had begun to improve. The same day, the Secret Service interviewed Dr. Stanley Drennan, of North Hollywood, California. Drennan, an NSRP activist, had been fingered by various informants, including a Captain Robert Kenneth Brown. Brown claimed to have been a guest in Drennan's home, where he heard the doctor declare, "what the organization needed was a group of young men to get rid of Kennedy, the Cabinet, and all members of the Americans for Democratic Action and maybe 10,000 other people." Brown at first assumed the NSRP man was a crackpot, "however, as Drennan continued the conversation, he gained the impression that Drennan may have been propositioning him on this matter."[31]

On June 17, Lee Oswald was back at the Napoleon Avenue library, borrowing two more volumes about communism, and a philosophy book. On June 19, Medgar Evers was buried with full military honors—he was a World War II veteran—in Washington, DC. Jack asked Bobby to attend the funeral on his behalf. The government feared a riot, but there was none. After the funeral, the president invited Evers' widow and children to the White House.

On June 22, black leaders told President Kennedy that mass demonstrations would continue until the civil rights issue was resolved. The president's response was woefully off-track: once again he was guided by political considerations. First, Bobby leaned on Martin Luther King to break with two of his closest associates, Stanley Levison and Hunter Pitts O'Dell. The Attorney General insisted he had solid proof, based on the latest technology, that Levison was a paid communist agent. King refused to believe this, and so Jack Kennedy took him out into the Rose Garden and picked up the refrain: O'Dell was the sixth-ranking communist in the United States, he said, and Levison was above that—fifth highest, and O'Dell's boss, or "handler." King still didn't believe any of it, but he realized that the brothers were serious: they trusted J. Edgar Hoover's evidence, or said they did, and they were clearly afraid of

Hoover. King wondered if the White House itself had been bugged by the FBI director, and if that was why the president had brought him outside for their whispered talk. Any communist "linkage" could bring King down, the brothers kept insisting. Jack asked Martin if he was following the Profumo story, an English political scandal linked to call girls and Russian spies. Martin said he was. "If they shoot you down, they'll shoot us down, too," the president told him. "So we're asking you to be careful."

Dr. King followed the Kennedys' advice and distanced himself from two key advisers and fundraisers. Both men understood: they were Martin's closest white friends. Ironic that the Catholic president—himself a victim of sectarian prejudice—should instruct the black man to dump the Catholic and the Jew! Kennedy left that evening for a European tour. In his absence, Senator Richard Russell accused him of encouraging black radicalism.

At the library on June 24, Lee Oswald checked out a James Bond novel, *Thunderball*. He also applied for a new passport. On his application form, he indicated a desire to visit England, France, Germany, Holland, Russia, Finland, Italy, and Poland. At a time when most applicants waited several days to receive their passports, Lee received his within 24 hours.

In Germany on June 26, the president made his famous *"Ich bin ein Berliner"* speech, in which he declared himself to be a jelly donut. Regardless, his words were much appreciated by the West Berliners. Kennedy flew on to Ireland, and the next day he visited his cousins in Dunganstown, County Wexford, establishing a tradition among American presidents who thereafter would not fail to visit real or imagined Irish roots. On June 28, the president rode in a motorcade through Cork; the crowd was massive, rapt. Photographs of the parade show four Secret Service agents riding *on the same limo as the president*, for his protection.

In New Orleans, Lee was back at the library, borrowing a science fiction novel: Arthur C. Clarke's *A Fall of Moondust*. In Washington, Henry Cabot Lodge joined the Kennedy administration as ambassador to South Vietnam. Kennedy clearly believed in keeping his enemies within the tent, but it was another case of bipartisanship triumphing over common sense, as Lodge was a hawkish Republican, and a wealthy political rival. On June 30, the *New York Times* reported that "the Administration may order the first substantial cutback in the production of nuclear weapons. High officials believe that the United States' arsenal of tens of thousands of nuclear weapons is sufficient to meet its military needs."

On July 1, Marina Oswald wrote to the Russian Embassy again, asking to return to Russia. Lee added a letter of his own, requesting that Marina's request be approved on a rush basis, and that his request to return be considered separately. Oswald underlined the word "separately." He then repaired to the library, where he checked out *Portrait of a President*, William Manchester's book about John F. Kennedy.

The president's European tour progressed. He met NATO officials and Italian politicians, in Rome. On July 2, he met the new pope, Paul VI. Staff members impressed upon reporters that the president did not kneel or kiss the pontiff's ring, but shook his hand instead. In an East German sports arena, Khrushchev proposed an East-West nonaggression pact, to be signed simultaneously with a nuclear test ban. This would pose a problem for Kennedy, who, despite the noble promise of his Peace Speech, was still trying to beef up NATO with a nuclear-armed, multinational fleet.

Kennedy returned to Washington the next day. This had been his eighth, and longest, foreign trip as president. It was his last one, too. In total, President Kennedy visited somewhat more than a dozen countries, in North America, Europe and the Caribbean. By today's standards this is minimal: Bill Clinton, in two terms, made 133 separate country visits, and George W. Bush made 47. Of course, Kennedy traveled domestically, particularly when campaigning. But it indicates that presidents spent more time in the office back in those days.

While Air Force One was still in the air, J. Edgar Hoover met with Robert Kennedy. The FBI Director advised the Attorney General that his brother had been sleeping with a suspected communist spy. The alleged agent, a 27-year-old call girl named Ellen Rometsch, had fled East Germany in 1955. Acting on the assumption that all "defectors" are really spies, Hoover naturally deduced that Rometsch must be one. There was no evidence of her spying on her clients, or passing secrets to the enemy. More threatening was Hoover's knowledge that Bobby Baker was Rometsch's pimp. The press was traditionally tolerant of presidential womanizing, but a scandal linking Jack to Baker's prostitutes might be too tempting to pass up. Ignorant of the Rometsch business, the papers focused their readers' attention on an ideological split between the Russian communists and their Chinese counterparts. Chairman Khrushchev declared that only "madmen" could think of waging war against the capitalist countries to achieve world communism—a rejection of Beijing's official position. On July 4, he sent President Kennedy and the American people "warm congratulations," while his ministers continued to link a test ban treaty to an East-West nonaggression pact. Thousands of Republicans flooded Washington for a national rally to draft Senator Barry Goldwater, an extreme right-winger and potential nuclear war-fighter, as president.

At some point that summer, Lee Oswald based himself in the Newman Building at 544 Camp Street, in New Orleans. This was a strange location for his FCPP branch. The principal tenant in the building was Guy Banister, who had opened a detective agency there the previous year. A retired Naval Intelligence officer, Banister was the former SAIC of the Chicago FBI office. As an assistant police superintendent, he had set up the New Orleans Police Department Division of Intelligence Affairs—a red-hunting, anti-subversion unit. Now, using the Newman Building as his HQ, he maintained an ever-expanding dossier of leftists and subversives, and published a racist newsletter, the *Louisiana Intelligence Digest*. Banister was a right-wing multitasker: a Bircher, a Minuteman, and one of the top officials in the NSRP—which was the name the American Nazi Party went by in New Orleans.

Also based at 544 Camp Street was the Cuban Revolutionary Council (CRC), an anti-Castro front group created by E. Howard Hunt of CIA. According to Hunt's son, St. John, his father frequented the Camp Street office when in New Orleans, and may have met Lee Oswald there. Banister's secretary, Delphine Roberts, told the HCSA "she saw Oswald in Banister's office on several occasions, the first being when he was interviewed for a job during the summer of 1963." And Banister's brother, Ross, testified that they had discussed Oswald's handing out FPCC literature. For what job was Oswald interviewed?

The Marxist ex-Marine had again gravitated into right-wing circles. After infiltrating the White Russians of Dallas, spying on General Walker's compound, liaising with the FBI, and finding jobs with two CIA-connected companies, Lee was now based at the dead center of right-wing craziness in New Orleans. How did he gain entry to such circles? Had Banister, with his ONI and FBI connections, been advised to expect him?

Consuela "Connie" Martin had an office next to Banister's. She told Michael Kurtz that she did translation work for Banister, and that she saw Oswald in Banister's office on at least six occasions. Oswald gave her documents to translate into Spanish, including his *Hands off Cuba!* circulars. Kurtz himself saw Oswald and Banister together twice: first when they visited the campus of Louisiana State University, where Banister made a speech condemning racial integration, and again in the restaurant in the Newman Building.[32]

FBI agent Hosty, it will be recalled, said that he was assigned to investigate "mostly right-wing subversives, like Minutemen." So, what was Oswald? A leftist subversive, pretending to be a reactionary? A right-wing activist, at home in the Newman Building, laying traps for unsuspecting leftists? A CIA courier, sharing their offices and translation services? Or an undercover op, part of a covert infiltration of the Minutemen, or the American Nazi Party?[33]

Visiting the library on July 6, Oswald borrowed *One Day In The Life of Ivan Denisovich*, Solzhenitsyn's famous novel set in a Soviet prison camp, and C.S. Forester's *Hornblower and The Hotspur*, a seafaring adventure. On July 8, the United States froze Cuban bank deposits worth $33 million. The State Department said this would prevent Castro from using U.S. banks to finance subversion. Two days later, at a meeting chaired by Robert Kennedy, the NSC discussed the progress of CIA sabotage against Cuba. Back at the library, Lee borrowed two more books: *Russia Under Khrushchev* and *The Hugo Winners*, a science fiction anthology. Next day the U.S. asked Britain to ban Cuban aircraft from landing on Grand Cayman Island, claiming that "15 to 20 potential subversive agents" had transferred between planes there. President Kennedy, via personal mediation, managed to avert a national rail strike.

On July 11, Ruth Paine wrote to Marina Oswald, inviting her and baby June to live with her. Marina declined the invitation. In Ecuador, a military *coup* overthrew President Carlos Arosemena: the army *junta* banned the communist party, canceled elections, imposed censorship, and vowed to eradicate "pro-Castro terrorist bands."

In Washington, Southern senators railed against Kennedy's civil rights legislation, which Governor Bartlett of Mississippi called part of a "world communist conspiracy to divide and conquer" the USA. Senator Russell Long of Louisiana opposed a Kennedy plan to cut off Federal funds to segregated cities: "I expect to fight that proposition until hell freezes over. Then I propose to start fighting on the ice."

On July 15, Lee Oswald borrowed Jack Kennedy's book *Profiles In Courage*. On July 18, he checked out *Five Spy Novels*, an anthology. The same day, Libero Riccardelli, another defector who had returned from Russia, was debriefed by the CIA. On July 19, Oswald was fired from the Reily Coffee Company. He told Adrian Alba, who managed a garage next door, that he was going to work for NASA, adding, "I have found my pot of gold at the end of the rainbow." As usual with Oswald's haunts, this was no ordinary garage: Alba had a contract to look after unmarked cars belonging to the FBI and Secret Service. He told the Warren Commission and the HSCA that he saw an FBI man give Oswald "a good-sized envelope, a white envelope." The Warren Report ignored Alba's testimony; the HSCA said it found no evidence to corroborate it.[34]

Meanwhile, Oswald—or someone resembling him—showed up at a demonstration by peace activists in Scranton, Pennsylvania. A local preacher, Irwin Tucker, told the police that he had encountered Oswald passing out leaflets, and argued with him about Cuba. The Scranton peace demonstrations lasted from July 22 to July 25.[35]

On July 25, in Moscow, U.S. and Russian negotiators initialed the Limited Test Ban Treaty, and its text was given to the press. Averell Harriman, the principal U.S. negotiator, reported that Khrushchev seemed very happy. The Chinese were furious, calling the treaty "a big fraud to fool the people of the world." The treaty permitted underground nuclear testing, but otherwise the Russians and the Americans committed themselves to a moratorium. This was seen as a step forward, although a tough sell in the United States, where public opinion—molded by many years of "missile gaps"—was strongly against disarmament. (The treaty was officially signed on August 5.) In reality, the treaty's value was questionable: the Americans and the Russians continued to explode nuclear weapons underground, and much of the ensuing radiation filtered upward and entered the atmosphere.

That same day the Marine Corps wrote to Lee Harvey Oswald, informing him that there would be no change in the status of his discharge. Next day, July 26, some visitor to the Atomic Energy

Museum at Oak Ridge, Tennessee, wrote in the guest registry book: *Lee H. Oswald, USSR, Dallas Road, Dallas, Texas.* And Confidential Informant NO [New Orleans] T-1 advised the FBI that Oswald had taken P.O. Box 30061 on June 3. The Warren Commission decided the Oak Ridge signature was a forgery. But who forged it? Who, in Tennessee, knew Lee Oswald, on that day? Meanwhile, Confidential Informant NO T-1 has never been identified. Who was NO T-1? Was it the same person as Dallas T-1? Was it Oswald?

On the evening of July 26, President Kennedy spoke on television from the Oval Office. His subject was the Limited Test Ban Treaty. Kennedy described "the worlds of communism and free choice" as having been caught up for 18 years in a "vicious circle of conflicting ideology and interest... Yesterday a shaft of light cut into the darkness." He insisted that the U.S. had been resolute against aggression, most recently in Berlin and Cuba. "This treaty is not the millennium... But it is an important first step, a step towards peace, a step towards reason, a step away from war." He then flew to the family home at Hyannis Port, where Averell Harriman would join him—bearing a huge jar of caviar from Khrushchev.

On July 27, Oswald and Marina traveled, with his aunt and uncle, to Mobile, Alabama, where another cousin, Eugene, was studying to be a priest. Eugene Murret had invited him to speak at the Jesuit House of Studies, and Lee gave a speech to the trainee priests entitled "Contemporary Russia and the Practice of Communism There." He said the best thing about Russia was the state-provided health care, and the best thing about the U.S. was its material prosperity. Claiming he was still a Marxist, Lee said he did not like "the widespread lack of material goods" which the Russians had to endure.

According to several sources, Oswald made trips to Baton Rouge during the summer of 1963. There, Oswald accompanied Kent Courtney - a friend of Guy Banister, who led the New Orleans White Citizens Council and Louisiana John Birch Society. He was also the co-author of a book, sold by the Birchers, entitled *The Case of General Edwin A. Walker*. Revilo Oliver, one of his associates, told the Warren Commission of a further Oswald-Courtney connection: Oswald had applied to work for Courtney's newspaper, *The Independent American*. Most of Oswald's time in Louisiana remains "officially" unaccounted for. His dubious Reily job allowed him plenty of free time.[36]

An even more intriguing allegation of Oswald's attempts to penetrate right-wing groups was made by author Patsy Sims, who heard from a Ku Klux Klan source that the Imperial Wizard of the Klan, James Venable, was visited by Lee Oswald, in Atlanta, Georgia. Sims asked Venable directly if this was so, and Venable said it was. The Klan leader told her he was "fairly sure" that Oswald was trying to acquire the names of his right-wing associates, in the summer of 1963.[37]

Officially, Lee Harvey Oswald never went to Atlanta, except for that stopover between New York and Fort Worth, where his bags disappeared. Yet George de Mohrenschildt, in his manuscript, referred to Oswald's potentially suspicious activities "in Atlanta, New Orleans and Mexico City." Lee's officially "missing time" in New Orleans make trips to Atlanta, or Baton Rouge, or even Scranton, entirely possible.

In Washington, Edward Teller visited the Foreign Relations Committee to oppose the Test Ban Treaty. He told the senators "The signing was a mistake. If you ratify the treaty you will have committed an enormously greater mistake." On July 31, the FBI raided a vacation cottage north of Lake Pontchartrain, Louisiana, and seized more than a ton of dynamite, 20 bomb casings, and napalm material, apparently stockpiled for anti-Castro terrorist activities. Eleven men were arrested at a nearby exile training camp, some of them Cubans associated with the CIA-created MDC (*Movimiento Democratico Cristiano*) and DRE (*Directorio Revolucionario Estudantil*). One of the arrestees was a white arms dealer: the cofounder of the Minutemen, Richard Lauchli, Jr. No prosecutions resulted: the Minuteman and his Cuban customers were "temporarily detained" but soon released. The bust marks a rare FBI action against the DRE—an organization in which Lee Oswald was about to take an interest.

The same day, Oswald wrote to Texas Governor John Connally, asking to have his undesirable discharge reversed. Then he went to the library and borrowed *Nine Tomorrows* (short science fiction stories by Isaac Asimov), and F.R. Cowell's *Everyday Life In Ancient Rome*. And Scotty Duff left Dallas for Oklahoma City, Oklahoma, where he enlisted in the U.S. Army. (Duff was kicked out of the Army in 1964, on the grounds of "fraudulent enlistment," at which point General Walker's lawyer, Clyde Watts, found him a place to live in Oklahoma City, and a job selling lawnmowers. It appears that Walker's people wanted to keep Duff out of Dallas.)[38]

On August 1, Lee Oswald wrote again to the FPCC in New York:

> Dear Mr Lee
> In regards to my efforts to start a branch office in New Orleans. I rented an office as I planned and was promptly closed three days later for some obscure reasons by the renters, they said something about remodeling ect [sic]. I'm sure you understand. After that I worked out of a post office box and by using street demonstrations and some circular work have substained [sic] a great deal of interest but no new members.
> Through the efforts of some Cuban-exial [sic] "gusanos" a street demonstration was attacked and we were officially cautioned by police. This incident robbed me of what support I had leaving me alone. Nevertheless thousands of circulars were distributed and many, many pamplets [sic] which your office supplied.
> We also managed to picket the fleet when it came in and I was surprised at the number of officers who were interested in our literature. I continue to receive through my post office box inquiries and questions which I shall endeavor to keep answering to the best of my ability.
> Thank you,
> Lee H Oswald.

This is an interesting letter, partially for the flat-out lies it contains, but mainly for its ability to predict the future. There is no evidence that Oswald rented an office anywhere, though he certainly operated out of the Newman Building. Oswald wrote that "we" picketed the fleet, but witnesses said he was alone. It was unlikely that Oswald received many FPCC enquiries via his post office box since he had printed the wrong box number on his "circulars." Most surprising is his report of being attacked by Cuban exiles and the police arriving. This was a true account… only it hadn't happened yet.

Four days later, on August 5, Oswald walked into a clothing store owned by Carlos Bringuier, a Cuban exile. Bringuier was—as he later told the FBI—the only member of the DRE in New Orleans: a bit like Oswald, who was the FPCC's one and only member there. The FBI believed the FPCC was funded by the Cubans; the DRE had been created and covertly funded by the CIA. Nationally, like all CIA anti-Castro organizations, it had been penetrated by Cuban intelligence. But the lone DRE New Orleans member was no Castro agent.

Bringuier was talking to a customer about the situation in his country. Oswald listened for a while, then spoke up. According to Bringuier:

> "He told me that he was against Castro and that he was against communism. He told me—he asked me first for some English literature against Castro, and I gave him some copies of the Cuban report printed by the Cuban Student Directorate.
>
> "After that, Oswald told me that he had been in the Marine Corps and that he had training in guerrilla warfare and that he was willing to train Cubans to fight against Castro. Even more, he told me that he was willing to go himself to fight Castro. That was on August 5."

Bringuier said he rejected Oswald's offer, explaining that his duties were propaganda and information, not military recruiting. But Oswald promised to return, with a book as a present. He also offered Bringuier money. Distrusting Oswald, Bringuier declined. He later told the Warren Commission, "When Oswald came to me on August 5 I had inside myself the feeling, well, maybe this is from the FBI, or maybe this is a Communist, because the FBI already had told me that maybe they will infiltrate my organization."

It would have been difficult for the FBI to infiltrate Bringuier's one-man organization. Yet here was Oswald, suddenly a soldier of fortune and anti-Castro gun for hire, offering to help out the DRE. Once again, Lee was nosing around right-wing circles. A backfiring propaganda bonanza, at the expense of the FPCC, was about to result.

Oswald went to the library and checked out another science fiction collection: *The Expert Dreamers*, edited by Frederic Pohl. He returned to Bringuier's store the next day with a copy of his *Guidebook for Marines*. Bringuier was out, so Oswald left the book with his brother-in-law. In the same block as the clothing store was a bar, *La Habana*. The bar owner, Orest Peña, saw Oswald and a Latino man there in the early hours of the morning a few days later. In 1975, Peña told CBS News that he had seen Oswald frequently, in the company of an FBI agent, Warren de Brueys.

On the same day, August 6, a rebel force led by General Leon Cantave entered Haiti from the Dominican Republic. It was quickly routed. On August 7, Phil Graham committed suicide, and Jacqueline Kennedy went into labor prematurely. Her baby, Patrick, died two days later of an incurable lung ailment. The family was devastated.

As the Kennedys grieved, Lee Oswald stood on Canal Street in New Orleans, holding a placard reading *VIVA FIDEL!* The spot he had chosen to hand out his circulars was close to Bringuier's store. It wasn't long before Carlos showed up, with a couple of friends. The Cubans did a lot of shouting and threatened to punch him. Oswald lowered his hands and invited Carlos to hit him. Instead, the Cubans grabbed Lee's circulars and scattered them. Then the police showed up. All four were arrested.

Orest Peña posted bail for Carlos; Oswald spent the night in jail. He told the police that he had been born in Cuba, and that his branch of the FPCC had 35 members. Police lieutenant Frances Martello testified that Oswald "seemed to have set them up, so to speak, to create an incident, but when the incident occurred he remained absolutely peaceful and gentle." Sergeant Horace Austin said that Oswald "appeared as though he is being used by those people and is very uninformed."

Next morning—August 10—Oswald asked for a meeting with an FBI agent. Why would a Marxist in 1963 request an interview with the national intelligence agency? The equivalent in modern Britain would be if a Muslim, detained for attending a demonstration, and suspected of political activity, requested a private consultation with MI5. No genuine protester would likely do such a thing. But a fake activist—an *agent provocateur*—might well seek a discreet meeting with the agency that he was working for.

Warren Commission counsel Stern addressed this issue when FBI agent John Quigley testified about his meeting with Oswald:

Stern: Is there any possibility that he was trying to give the New Orleans police the idea that he was working with the FBI?

Quigley: Not to my knowledge, sir; no.

Stern: None of his conduct went in that direction?

Quigley: No; he certainly, to my knowledge, never advised the New Orleans police of this. As a matter of fact, he, during

the course of the interview with Lt. Martello, made a flat
statement that he would like to talk to an FBI agent, which
is not an unusual situation. Frequently persons who are in
custody of local authorities would like to talk to the FBI.

Really? As Sylvia Meagher wrote, "this is surprising intelligence,
and, with all deference to Quigley, one would wish to see some
statistics on the frequency of such requests."[39]

Agent Quigley had already made enquiries about Oswald—at
the Office of Naval Intelligence—in April 1961. Now he responded
promptly to Lee's request—this was a Saturday morning—and
the two met privately for 90 minutes. It may be significant that
FBI agent Quigley in New Orleans, like FBI agent Fain in Dallas,
was thoroughly briefed about Oswald prior to their meeting—even
though it occurred, supposedly, by chance. Quigley's report suggests
Oswald said nothing of value, while lying about a number of things
(such as Marina's maiden name, and his 35 imaginary followers).

Among Oswald's possessions were two FPCC membership cards,
one countersigned by "V.L. Lee," the other by "A.J. Hidell." According
to Quigley, Oswald said that "Hidell" asked him to distribute the
literature, for no payment. Dean Andrews saw him handing out his
circulars and recalled his client saying he was "being paid $25 per
day for the job." The police kept some of Oswald's circulars, stamped
FPCC — 544 CAMP ST — NEW ORLEANS, LA. This was the Newman
Building.

Oswald called his cousin Joyce, who refused to bail him out. At
5:20 p.m. he was paroled by one A. Heckman, a Jury Commissioner,
State of Louisiana, Orleans Parish, New Orleans. It has also been
reported that he was bailed out by Emile Bruneau, a shady friend
of his uncle with connections to organized crime and to Guy
Banister. Either way, Lee returned to court on August 12, only to find
newspapermen and television cameras awaiting him. He sat on the
"colored" side of the courtroom, pled guilty to a charge of disturbing
the peace, and was fined $10. The Cubans pleaded innocent, and the
charges against them were dropped. They went on making a fuss,
demanding to be interviewed, eclipsing the more modest Oswald.
But the *Times-Picayune* covered the story in detail. The same day,
at the library, Lee borrowed another science fiction anthology. His
interest in nonfiction books appeared to have expired.

Defense Secretary McNamara addressed the Senate Foreign Relations Committee on August 13. He told them that, the president's Peace Speech notwithstanding, the Kennedy administration still planned a long-term nuclear buildup. The U.S. currently possessed over 500 ICBMs, while the Russians had increased their stockpile to around 75. McNamara assured the Senators that American missile numbers would be more than 1,700 by 1966. Even this wasn't enough for the Pentagon, which demanded more underground testing, a readiness to resume atmospheric testing on short notice, and the maintenance of its nuclear labs. Afraid that the Joint Chiefs might sabotage the Test Ban Treaty in the Senate, Kennedy agreed to all their terms.[40]

On August 16, Oswald and another man (19–20 years old, six feet tall, slender build, dark hair, olive complexion) went to the International Trade Mart in New Orleans. Together with three or four others, whom Oswald had supposedly hired at two dollars a head, they handed out his FPCC literature. This time the "circulars" were stamped with his name and home address, 4907 Magazine Street. A local TV station, WDSU-TV, came and filmed the event. Oswald left as soon as the cameras departed.

That evening Bringuier sent an associate, Carlos Quiroga, "to infiltrate Oswald's organization if he could." Quiroga went to Oswald's house on Magazine Street and spent an hour talking to him. According to Quiroga, Oswald claimed he'd learned Russian at Tulane University, in New Orleans. He offered to let Quiroga join the FPCC for a dollar, and "stated that if the United States should invade Cuba, he, Oswald, would fight on the side of the Castro government." Quiroga contacted Lieutenant Martello of the New Orleans police—the officer who'd previously dealt with Oswald—and offered to join the FPCC if the police or FBI approved. Martello, according to a Secret Service report, "forgot about it."

At last, those "pamplets" appeared to be paying off. The next day Bill Stuckey, an advertising agent, visited Lee at home, and invited him to appear on his local radio show. Lee was interviewed that evening on WDSU's *Latin Listening Post*. Stuckey gave Oswald plenty of rope, and Lee hung himself with it, denying he was a communist, and claiming his New Orleans branch of the FPCC had more than one member. His most serious misstep came when Stuckey asked him about his personal background. Oswald replied,

"I entered the U.S. Marine Corps in 1956. I spent three years in the USMC, working my way up through the ranks to the position of buck sergeant and I served honorably, having been discharged. Then I went back to work in Texas, and have recently arrived in New Orleans with my family, with my wife and child."[41]

Why did Oswald ignore the most significant aspect of his life to date—his failed defection to Russia? This was a matter of the public record: it had been in the newspapers, and was well known by the FBI and by his associate Guy Banister. Did Lee hope to keep his Russian activities a secret from Stuckey and his radio listeners, or was he deliberately setting himself up for a fall? Four days later, his fall occurred.

On August 18, the Alliance for Progress marked its second anniversary with plans to "streamline its leadership"; Haiti's foreign minister reported another attempted invasion by exiles based in the Dominican Republic; 15,000 Buddhists in Saigon began a hunger strike in protest at the government of America's client, Ngo Dinh Diem; and James Meredith received a B.A. in political science from the University of Mississippi, becoming its first black graduate. On August 21, Ellen Rometsch was deported to West Germany, by order of the Attorney General. That evening, WDSU Radio broadcast *Conversation Carte Blanche*, featuring Oswald, Stuckey, Bringuier, and Edward Butler. Butler was a professional PR man, and director of the Information Council of the Americas (INCA), the anticommunist, CIA-connected outfit.[42]

Oswald did most of the talking and, as usual, he did nothing to help the FPCC or Castro's cause. Soon, Stuckey revealed Oswald's checkered past to his radio listeners:

> Stuckey: Mr. Oswald, if I may break in now a moment, I believe it was mentioned that you at one time asked to renounce your American citizenship and become a Soviet citizen, is that correct?
>
> Oswald: Well, I don't think that has particular import to this discussion. We are discussing Cuban-American relations.
>
> Stuckey: Well, I think it has a bearing to this extent. Mr. Oswald, you say apparently that Cuba is not dominated by

Russia, and yet you apparently, by your own past actions, have shown that you have an affinity for Russia, and perhaps communism... Are you a Marxist?

Oswald: Yes, I am a Marxist.

Brilliant! The "Cuban sympathizer" was exposed—by himself—as a Marxist! But worse. from the FPCC's point of view, was to come. After the commercials, Stuckey pursued Oswald's Russian connection.

Stuckey: Mr. Oswald... so you are the face of the Fair Play for Cuba Committee in New Orleans. Therefore anybody who might be interested in this organization ought to know more about you. For this reason I'm curious to know just how you supported yourself during the three years that you lived in the Soviet Union. Did you have a government subsidy?

Oswald: Er, well, as I, er, well—I will answer that question directly then since you will not rest until you get your answer. I worked in Russia. I was under the protection of the—that is to say, I was not under the protection of the American government, but I was at all times considered an American citizen. I did not lose my American citizenship.[43]

And so it went. Stuckey, Butler, and WDSU's Bill Slatter pursued Oswald on his Russian connections, indelibly tarring the FPCC with Marxism and anti-Americanism. Oswald seemed thrown off-base by Stuckey's initial questions—he started to tell them he was in Russia "under the protection" of the U.S. government—but, as the "debate" progressed, no one worked harder than Lee to smear the FPCC with guilt by association. Oswald claimed his fantasy league had several officers and a number of members. When he refused to reveal their names, Ed Butler accused the FPCC of being a "secret society." Then Oswald volunteered the news that "the Fair Play for Cuba Committee is now on the Attorney General's subversive list." At every turn, he said things which damaged the group. Instead of discussing Cuba and the successes of the Castro government, he repeatedly denied any linkage between the FPCC and Russia. The way Oswald phrased it made the FPCC seem subversive and communist-run, even as he tediously stressed it wasn't:

Oswald: We are not at all communist-controlled regardless of the fact that I have experienced living in Russia, regardless of the fact that we have been investigated, regardless of any of those facts, the Fair Play for Cuba Committee is an independent organization not affiliated with any organization.

A tape of the "debate" was soon in the hands of the FBI. It also became one of the *Truth Tapes* which INCA sent to over 100 radio stations in Latin America. Thus the FPCC was discredited, and Lee Harvey Oswald was newsworthy again.

(Ed Butler had some highly placed political associates. He boasted in writing about INCA's "contacts with CIA through General C.P. Cabell, Deputy Director." Cabell, Allen Dulles' deputy, had lost his job after the Bay of Pigs; his brother, Earle, was mayor of Dallas. Immediately after the assassination, Butler flew to Washington and played his tape for Senator Thomas Dodd and Representative Hale Boggs, the future Warren Commissioner.)[44]

Oswald seemed unmoved by the fiasco. Next day he visited the library to return another science fiction book—*The Worlds of Clifford D. Simak*—and checked out two more s-f collections and a James Bond book, *From Russia With Love*.

In Washington, the Kennedys were preoccupied by the March on Washington, a civil rights demonstration scheduled for August 28. The brothers had characterized it in the most violent terms, calling it "a gun to the head" of Congress. They'd urged the cancellation of the March; when this proved impossible, they diverted it to a "containable" area, in case a riot broke out. The sound system was rigged so that all audio could be cut off if one of the speakers got "out of hand." To the embattled brothers, Martin Luther King and other black activists were adversaries, not allies. Civil rights *had* to compete with the Test Ban Treaty and the tax cut and how to deal with Vietnam. It was all politics, cautiously negotiated, secured by deals, not fine words. This was something King and his colleagues didn't seem to understand.

On August 24, the Defense Department stated that the White House had ordered a "sharp expansion" of underground nuclear testing.

On August 28, the March on Washington took place. A quarter of a million Americans, black, white, and otherwise, showed up in support of labor unions and civil rights. There was no violence, despite a massive police and military presence. An FBI phone blitz—threatening participants with violence and the blacklist—did not deter a handful of Hollywood celebrities, including Marlon Brando, Harry Belafonte, Steve McQueen, and Charlton Heston, from attending. President Kennedy, relieved that there had been no riot, met the principal speakers in private afterwards. He seemed unimpressed by the turnout, and condescending toward the last speaker, Martin. Dr. King had just delivered, mostly impromptu, his "I Have A Dream" speech—perhaps the greatest and most important series of words ever uttered in the United States.

For a self-proclaimed radical, whose life's story was driven by his sympathy for the oppressed, Lee Harvey Oswald seems to have been ignorant of these events. An authentic, leftist, existentialist drifter would have been aware of the March, would have had something to say about it. Ruth Paine took her children to Washington to participate in it. Lee, rather than join the March or watch it on TV, wrote a letter to the American Communist Party, about himself:

> August 28, 1963
>
> Comrades:
> Please advise me upon a problem of personal tactics.
>
> I have lived in the Soviet Union from Oct. 1958 [sic] to July 1962.
>
> I had, in 1959, tried to legally dissolve my United States citizenship in favor of Soviet citizenship, however, I did not complete the legal formalities for this.
>
> Having come back to the US in 1962 and thrown myself into the struggle for progress and freedom in the United States, I would like to know weather [sic], in your opion [sic], I can continue to fight, handicapped as it were, by my past record, can I still, under these circumstances, compete with anti-progressive forces, above ground or weather [sic], in your opion [sic] I should always remain in the background, i.e., underground.
>
> Our opponents could use my background of residence in the USSR against any cause which I join, by association, they could say the organization of which I am a member, is Russian controled [sic] ect [sic]. But what do you think I should do? which is the best tactic in general?

Should I disassociate myself from all progressive activities?

Here in New Orleans, I am secretary of the local brach [sic] of the 'Fair Play for Cuba Committee', a position which, frankly, I have used to foster communist ideals. On a local radio show, I was attacked by Cuban exile organization representatives for my residence ect [sic] in the Soviet Union.

I feel I may have compromised the FPCC, so you see that I need the advice of trusted, long time fighters for progress. Please advise.

With Freternal [sic] Greeting,
Sincerely
/s/ Lee H. Oswald

As Philip Melanson observed, this is "an incredible letter." It was certain to be intercepted by the FBI and shared with other intelligence agencies. It contained a self-professed defector's report that his branch of the FPCC was a front for "communist ideals" and his proposal that he go "underground." Like Oswald's radio "debate" the letter would confirm any reasonable person's worst suspicions of the FPCC. And the postal employees and FBI agents who read his mail were not necessarily reasonable persons. In the process of smearing the FPCC, Lee also incriminated himself, suggesting that he was considering illegal actions.[45]

On September 1, Lee Oswald wrote again to the Communist Party. This was a one-sentence letter: "Please advise me as to how I can contact the Party in the Baltimore-Washington area, to which I shall relocate in October." The Warren Commission made no comment on this remarkable note. Did Oswald really plan to relocate to the DC area? Was he fishing for communists there, in the aftermath of the March? In both letters to the Communist Party he gave his post office box in New Orleans as his return address. But was he even there? Oswald's "official history" goes blank after his radio "debate": surprisingly, given how intense and picayune some of the FBI's investigations were, the Bureau could offer no information whatsoever as to Oswald's whereabouts between August 21 and September 17.

At the beginning of September, state troopers and sheriff's deputies fired tear gas into a crowd of black civil rights demonstrators in Plaquemine, Louisiana. On the Senate floor, Russell Long of

Louisiana demanded a reservation to the Test Ban Treaty—a specific statement that the U.S. would use nuclear weapons "if it felt its vital interests were in danger." The White House opposed the revision of the Treaty, saying it wasn't needed. Having "officially" supported the Treaty, Generals Curtis LeMay and Maxwell Taylor both briefed against it: Taylor said he expected the Russians would "cheat." White violence flared up again in Birmingham, when two black children tried to register at a previously all-white school. And Admiral George Whelan Anderson, Chief of Naval Operations during the blockade of Cuba, complained to reporters that "a lack of confidence and trust" was developing between the civilian and military wings of the Defense Department.

At some point in late August or early September, an anti-Castro Cuban activist flew to Dallas, Texas, to meet with his CIA handler. The activist was Antonio Veciana, who had received several years' CIA funding for his outfit, Alpha-66: a terrorist group which had made sea raids against Cuba, and Russian ships. Veciana's case officer went by the name of "Maurice Bishop," though that was not his real name: "Bishop" was Texan CIA man David Atlee Phillips, who had run the illegal domestic operation against the FPCC, and recently been promoted—to CIA grade 15—with new duties as Chief of Cuban Operations, in Mexico City.[46]

Veciana and his case officer met in the public area of one of the city's new skyscrapers, the Southland Center. Veciana told Anthony Summers:

> "Maurice was accompanied by a young man who gave me the impression of being very quiet, rather strange, and preoccupied. The three of us walked to a cafeteria. The young man was with us ten or 15 minutes, until Maurice told him something like, 'All right, see you later,' and dismissed him."

Veciana told Summers and the HSCA that the man he met that day was Lee Harvey Oswald, or, if not Oswald, then his "exact double." Lee certainly could have gone to Dallas: other than a visit to his uncle Dutz on Labor Day, September 2, his activities around this time are unknown. All that exist are employment office documents, cashed unemployment checks, and library book records. Regarding Lee's search for work, Summers wrote, "the FBI was able to authenticate

Oswald's signature on hardly any of the unemployment documents. Of the 17 firms where Oswald said he applied for work, 13 denied it, and four did not even exist."[47]

On September 5, according to a Hertz agent, Martha J. Doyle, Lee and Marina Oswald attempted to rent a car at San Antonio Airport. Oswald didn't identify himself but Doyle recognized him after the assassination and volunteered her story to the FBI. She said that the man who tried to rent a car claimed to have no credit card, charge account, or passport. He said he had come to the airport in a friend's car. Doyle asked him what business he was in, and the man replied, "I am in the publishing business."

Doyle: "Do you mean magazines?"

Oswald: "No, schoolbooks."

If this story is true then Oswald was once again prescient, since he was allegedly still living in New Orleans, and knew nothing about a job at the Texas School Book Depository. It's possible that the man, woman and baby who Doyle met weren't the Oswalds, of course, but an impersonation, like the bizarre "family portrait." But who would impersonate them, at an auto rental shop?[48]

On September 9, someone visited the Napoleon branch library and, using Lee's card, borrowed a copy of *Ben Hur*: a Christian epic written by an army general, Lew Wallace. This was unusual reading for the Marxist espionage enthusiast. Was Lee still in New Orleans? Or was someone else filing his unemployment slips and using his library card?

In Saigon, rumors of an impending *coup* abounded. At a press conference, the president spoke of "victory" in Vietnam. The *Dallas Times Herald* of September 13 announced an upcoming Kennedy trip to Dallas; no date was given. On September 14, two nuclear bombs— one as large as a million tons of TNT—were exploded beneath the Nevada desert. On September 15, a black church in Birmingham was bombed, and four girls were killed. Rioting followed, in which two black boys were shot to death. Governor Wallace called out the federalized Guard and State Police. King, Abernathy, and other black leaders urged the president to send in troops. But he demurred.

Suddenly, Lee Harvey Oswald involved himself in the civil rights movement. In the company of friends, he visited the small rural towns of Jackson and Clinton, Louisiana, about 130 miles from New Orleans. Over a three-day period he had a haircut, inquired about a job, and stood in line to register to vote. His first appearance was in Jackson, where he asked the local barber, Edwin McGehee, about finding work at the nearby East Louisiana State Hospital. McGehee advised Oswald to register to vote in the Parish, to improve his chances of getting a job. He also recommended Oswald visit the local State Representative, Reeves Morgan, and gave him directions to Morgan's home. Oswald visited Morgan that evening, and spent half an hour with him.

Next day, Oswald showed up in Clinton in a black Cadillac. With him in the car were David Ferrie, his old Civil Air Patrol captain, and Clay Shaw, a New Orleans businessman. Both would later become notorious as a result of Jim Garrison's investigation into the Kennedy assassination. Ferrie was a pilot who had worked for Carlos Marcello and Guy Banister; like Lee, he was a denizen of the Newman Building. Shaw was one of the founders of the International Trade Mart in New Orleans; he was also connected to the CIA. Ferrie's politics were extremely right-wing; Shaw's were liberal. Both Shaw and Ferrie were gay. What were they doing in Oswald's company that day? Several witnesses reported that they waited in the parked Cadillac while Oswald stood in line to register to vote.[49]

Oswald had picked no ordinary registration line to stand in. This was a drive organized by The Congress on Racial Equality (CORE) and, apart from Oswald, everyone in it was black. CORE had focused its attention on Clinton, in part, because of the behavior of the county's voter registrar, Henry Earl Palmer. Palmer had hung a black doll by a noose from his office door, disqualified black voters on technical grounds, and wore a handgun while registering voters. Robert Kennedy's Justice Department was simultaneously investigating East Feliciana Parish, Palmer's bailiwick. The CORE organizers had anticipated a visit from the FBI, and initially they thought Shaw's Cadillac was it. Ferrie and Shaw, despite their political differences, had driven Oswald into the thick of the civil rights struggle. The town of Clinton was also a focus of mobile reactionaries on the speaking circuit. Kent Courtney had recently spoken at the Clinton Courthouse on the topic of "The Right to Work."

The line moved very slowly. Everyone noticed Oswald. The town marshal, John Manchester, checked Shaw's driver's license and ran a trace on the Cadillac: it belonged to the International Trade Mart, in New Orleans. After waiting for hours, Oswald presented himself to the voter registrar, Henry Earl Palmer. Palmer sent Oswald on his way. Later he recalled seeing Oswald's U.S. Navy ID card, and telling him that he couldn't register to vote as he was not a resident of the parish. Palmer told Garrison's investigators that he'd heard— from Marshal Manchester—that "right around the time the black Cadillac was in Clinton, he remembers seeing a boy who fit Oswald's description coming out of a CORE meeting."

This was potential dynamite. The right wing viewed CORE and the civil rights movement as "communist-inspired" and/or "communist-infiltrated." Here was Oswald, helping to prove them right. Once again, he'd made contact with a corps of influential right-wingers (Palmer and Reeves Morgan were business associates; when Palmer retired, McGehee, the Jackson barber, succeeded him as voter registrar), then engaged in leftist street theater. The self-professed Marxist and underground agitator was standing in CORE voter registration lines, and, allegedly, attending CORE meetings. As with his FPCC activities, Oswald was laying a highly visible trail which might discredit the group with which he sought to be associated. This time, his accomplices were identified: Ferrie and Shaw.[50]

On the third day, Oswald showed up at East Louisiana State Hospital and filed an employment application. The application, which presumably bore a date, is lost. Where he went after this, and whether he traveled with Ferrie and Shaw or others, is unknown. The exact dates of his adventure in Jackson and Clinton remain unclear: the HSCA reports it as taking place in "August–September 1963."

During this period, another Oswald sighting occurred. Robert Ray McKeown, a club owner and former arms dealer based in Houston, Texas, told the Warren Commission that Jack Ruby had visited him in 1959. Ruby, he said, was trying to sell Jeeps and slot machines to the Castro regime. McKeown had supplied arms to Castro, and been busted for it: now he was on probation. He said he met Ruby several times, but nothing came of Jack's various proposals. In 1975, McKeown added to his story the detail that a man calling himself "Lee Oswald" had visited him—one Saturday in September or October, 1963. From his description, the man doesn't sound like Oswald: blond, 5'6", in his late 30s. But he certainly promoted the *concept* of Lee Oswald, international assassin and revolutionary. According to McKeown,

Oswald showed up in Bay Cliff, Texas, with a silent Latino partner, and announced, "We're thinking about having a revolution in El Salvador." He wanted McKeown to supply them with bazookas and machine guns. McKeown, still on probation, refused to assist.

According to McKeown, the men left, and then "Lee Oswald" returned. This time he offered to pay $10,000 for four .300 Savage automatic rifles. McKeown observed that "Oswald" could buy the rifles himself at Sears for a few hundred bucks, and sent him on his way. McKeown told this story to the HSCA, where Representatives Fithian and Christopher Dodd (son of Thomas J.) pursued him relentlessly over inconsistencies in his testimony, and his failure to tell the entire story to the Warren Commission. McKeown's situation was not helped by the absence of his attorney, Mark Lane, on other business. But he insisted that the visit from "Oswald" had occurred.[51]

On September 16, the president found himself again dealing with his least favorite material: nuclear war-fighting, and the Net Evaluation Sub-Committee Report. But this time he did not walk out of the briefing, despairing of the human race. The composition of the Joint Chiefs had changed: they were still pushing him to approve a new first-strike system, but not in the injured, blustering manner of General LeMay. The atmosphere was calmer, and McNamara had Kennedy's back. Air Force General Leon Johnson said all their estimates showed Russian fatalities, in the event of nuclear war, as at least 140 million. McNamara responded that U.S. deaths would be in the region of 30 million, plus. Therefore, he observed, "there was no way of launching a no-alert attack against the USSR which would be acceptable. No such attack, according to the calculations, could be carried out without 30 million U.S. fatalities—an obviously unacceptable number." The calculations had spoken. The president agreed. McNamara pressed on: "The president deserves an answer to his question as to why we have so large a force."

The Joint Chiefs could not answer. They wanted an expanded nuclear force so as to retain a first-strike capacity between 1964 and 1968—the period under discussion. Losing the ability to destroy all Russia's nukes in one surprise attack was deeply troubling to the Pentagon, but these Chiefs were politicians too, and for now they let the matter rest. Left undiscussed was the premise of the first Net Report: "a surprise attack in late 1963, preceded by a period of heightened tensions."

Oswald surfaced on September 17 at the Mexican Consulate in New Orleans, where he obtained a 15-day tourist card, No. 824085. When the FBI released a copy of the Mexican tourist documentation, there was a blank adjacent to No. 824084. The FBI annotated the blank as "no record located" but this was untrue. The person who got the tourist card ahead of Oswald was a CIA agent, William Gaudet, as researchers learned when his redacted name was accidentally revealed in 1975. Gaudet ran a CIA-funded publication, *Latin American Newsletter*. HSCA investigators saw Gaudet's CIA file, and a memorandum which stated that he "provided foreign intelligence information on Latin American political and economic conditions" and that he had been a "casual contact" of the New Orleans office from 1955 to 1961. Gaudet himself claimed CIA contacts until 1969. He admitted knowing Oswald, having seen him handing out his circulars at the International Trade Mart, but denied traveling to Mexico with him. Gaudet was on first-name terms with Guy Banister. He told Summers:

> "I saw him [Oswald] one time with a former FBI agent by the name of Guy Banister. Guy of course is now dead. What Guy's role was in all of this was [sic] I... I really don't know."[52]

Later, Gaudet told a different story. Interviewed by Michael Kurtz, Gaudet claimed that "he and Oswald were sent to Mexico City to survey the scenes at the Cuban and Russian embassies and to report their findings to the CIA." Since both embassies were already subject to intense CIA bugging and photographic surveillance, one wonders what insights Gaudet and Oswald might provide. Gaudet also claimed that he and Oswald were sent by U.S. intelligence to Mexico City "to look for pro-Castro spies among the large community of Cuban exiles living there." This is ludicrous. Oswald, who spoke no Spanish, was going on a five-day trip to ferret out spies in Mexico City? But one thing is clear: Gaudet was actively involved in creating the "legend" of Lee Oswald's Mexican travels.[53]

The same day as Oswald and Gaudet picked up their tourist cards, Senator Richard Russell took the floor to oppose the Test Ban Treaty: he called it "a step towards unilateral disarmament." And the State Department presented Kennedy with plans for two policy tracks for Vietnam, called "Reconciliation" and "Pressures and

Persuasion." The first involved continuing to fund the Diem regime in South Vietnam; the second entailed a partial cut in U.S. aid, and backing a *coup* attempt. Ironically, both policy tracks seemed to require the services of Ed Lansdale. Diem always asked to deal with him, in preference to other Americans, while Ambassador Lodge thought Lansdale might be able to split Diem from his corrupt associates, or secure their removal.

In New Orleans, Lee Oswald, or someone using his card, visited the Napoleon branch library and borrowed two more James Bond books, *Goldfinger* and *Moonraker*, plus two novels by Aldous Huxley: *Ape and Essence* and *Brave New World*. Where was he getting his reading list? From someone he was meeting, at the library?

Civil rights were on the back burner once again. On September 19, the writer James Baldwin warned Clarence Jones that many blacks now viewed King as too conservative and too close to an inactive president. The same day Premier Khrushchev called on Kennedy and 16 other heads of government to join him for a summit conference in Moscow, to negotiate a treaty for "general and complete disarmament."

On September 20, President Kennedy addressed the United Nations General Assembly in New York. He told the delegates that he saw "a pause in the cold war" and proposed further disarmament, the reunification of Germany, and a joint American-Russian expedition to the Moon. While the president was making these historic proposals, a former Army Intelligence officer, Richard Case Nagell, fired several shots into the wall of a bank in downtown El Paso, Texas. He was arrested driving his car past the bank a few minutes later. In Nagell's possession were a California driver's license, a Colt .45 pistol, a notebook containing the names of six CIA employees, and an FPCC newsletter. On his way to the Federal Building for questioning, Nagell told the FBI "I would rather be arrested than commit murder and treason." (About a month after the murders of Kennedy and Oswald, Nagell—still in jail—advised the FBI that he had known Oswald socially, in Texas and Mexico. He also claimed to have sent a registered letter to J. Edgar Hoover, warning the FBI chief of the assassination plot. Over the years his story grew, till he was describing himself as an ex-CIA spy *and* Russian double-agent, tasked by his case officer to kill Oswald and save the president... Nagell was treated as a serious source by Garrison, and by researchers

Dick Russell and William Turner. CIA denied any relationship with him. Nagell claimed to possess tape recordings of the assassination plotters, a Polaroid picture of himself with Oswald, and the receipt for his registered letter to Hoover—which the FBI said it had not received—but he produced none of these things, and died in 1995.)[54]

Ruth Paine arrived in New Orleans in her station wagon on September 23, supposedly on a whim after visiting relatives. She invited Marina to return to Irving, Texas, and Marina agreed. Ruth told the Warren Commission that the decision was spontaneous, but her friends and relatives told the FBI she had been planning to collect Marina. Lee had also told his relatives in New Orleans that Marina was going back to Texas to have their second child. So it seems the only person who didn't know about the plan was Marina. Ruth, Marina and June reached Irving the next day.

With Marina and June out of the way, and no job, Lee Harvey Oswald was ready for the next stage of his Big Adventure: return a copy of *Bridge On The River Kwai* to the library, and take his alleged trip to Mexico. I write "alleged" because, of all the allegations leveled against Oswald, including accusations of murder and attempted murder, his bus trip to Mexico City seems the least believable. Not that the Warren Report wasn't exact as to Lee's movements during this supposed journey. First, he made his way from Irving to Houston, by unknown means; on the evening of September 25, he telephoned a Socialist Labor Party official and spoke to his wife about the FPCC; he took another bus to Laredo, crossed the border, and took a third bus to Mexico City, arriving at 10 a.m. on September 27; the same day he visited the Cuban Consulate, then the Russian Embassy, then the Cuban Consulate again; on September 28 he visited the Russian Embassy again; on October 1 someone speaking poor Russian called the Embassy twice; on October 2 he left Mexico City for Laredo, with a bus ticket purchased in the name of "O.H. Lee"; from Laredo, still traveling as "O.H. Lee," Oswald proceeded to Dallas.

That is the official story of what Lee Oswald did. *Somebody* certainly visited the Cuban Consulate in Mexico City, claimed to be Oswald, showed his FPCC card, demanded an immediate transit visa to Russia, via Cuba, and started shouting when told he would have to wait. And somebody, also claiming to be Oswald, called and visited the Russian Embassy (the Russians reported him as packing a pistol, and weeping hysterically). And somebody rode back and forth on buses, claiming in one direction to be Oswald, and in the other, "O.H. Lee," bragging about his time in Russia and his plans to visit Cuba.

But it may not have been Oswald. The evidence collected by the Warren Commission suggests that it was not. Arrested in Dallas, Oswald told the police that he had never been to Mexico. Marina told Mark Lane the same thing, adding that the FBI had threatened her with deportation unless she changed her story.[55]

Oswald's name appears in the register of the Hotel Comercio in a different handwriting from that which transcribed all the other guests'. The passenger who sat next to "O.H. Lee" on the Mexico-Laredo bus said the young man wasn't Oswald: he described "Lee" as "29 years of age, 5'8", 150 lbs., thin blond hair, dark complexion, probably Mexican or Puerto Rican descent." The Mexican border guard who relieved the mysterious traveler of his tourist card listed him as "Harvey, Oswald Lee," recorded his departure vehicle as a car, not a bus, and his destination as New Orleans, not Dallas. And the FBI, when supplied with CIA tape recordings of the American caller to the Embassy, could not identify the voice as Oswald's.[56]

But the most concrete evidence that Oswald was impersonated in Mexico City comes from CIA itself. The Agency had an intelligence-gathering post across the street from the Russian Embassy and photographed all visitors to the building. For some reason the Warren Commissioners weren't aware of this until Marguerite Oswald, who had been shown a picture by the FBI, brought it to their attention. They requested a copy of the photograph, and CIA provided it. It is Fig. 5.

Who was this individual? As far as I know, he has never been credibly identified. The photo was allegedly taken on October 1, when someone identified as Oswald phoned, but did not visit, the Embassy. So why did CIA permit it to be misidentified as Oswald? And why could the Agency not produce a surveillance photograph of the real Oswald, if surveillance was continuous, and Oswald was really there?

Comm. Exh. 237

Fig. 5: CIA surveillance photo of "Oswald" at the Russian Embassy in Mexico City.

David Atlee Phillips was based in Mexico City when Oswald supposedly visited. In 1975, he had just organized the Association of Former Intelligence Officers—a group 5,000 strong—and was keen to publicize it. So he agreed to debate Mark Lane, author of *Rush to Judgment*, at the University of Southern California. Per Lane, during the debate Phillips stated:

> "When the record comes out, we will find that there never was a photograph taken of Lee Harvey Oswald in Mexico City. We will find out that Lee Harvey Oswald never visited, let me put it, that is a categorical statement, there, there, we will find out there is no evidence, first of all there was no proof of that. Second, there is no evidence to show that Lee Harvey Oswald visited the Soviet Embassy."[57]

Yet someone went to a bit of trouble—perhaps not quite enough trouble—to fabricate Lee Harvey Oswald's trip to Mexico City's diplomatic quarter. Why? Possibly to establish a connection between Oswald, notorious Marxist, and the KGB. Valery Vladimirovich Kostikov, the Russian consul who met someone claiming to be Oswald twice during this period, was more than a mere diplomat. CIA told the Warren Commission that Kostikov (no relation to the KGB Kostikov from Minsk, apparently) was the local leader of the KGB's "Thirteenth Division"—a specialist in sabotage and assassinations.

Much happened during Oswald's alleged trip abroad. Taylor, now chairman of the Joint Chiefs, and McNamara flew to Saigon "to review the military effort against the communists." The Senate ratified the Test Ban Treaty by 80 votes to 19. On September 25 a CIA *coup* overthrew Juan Bosch, democratically elected president of the Dominican Republic. The same day, an individual calling himself Harvey Oswald showed up at the Selective Service Office in Austin, Texas. "Harvey" asked the assistant director of the Office's administrative section for help in fixing his discharge from the Marine Corps. He told the assistant director, Mrs. Lee Dannelly, that he had been discharged under "other than honorable conditions" and that the Governor's office had told him the Selective Service Office might be able to deal with it. "Harvey" complained to Dannelly that "he was having difficulty in obtaining a job, and holding a job, with that type discharge." Dannelly could find no record of his case under the name he gave, and advised him to contact the Veterans Administration. After the assassination, Dannelly identified "Harvey" as Lee Harvey Oswald, and remarked that he had been "courteous" throughout the interview. (The Warren Commission declared Dannelly mistaken, since its own Oswald was supposed to be on a bus to Mexico.)[58]

On September 26 the White House announced the president's visit to Dallas and Fort Worth, now scheduled for November 21 and 22. Kennedy simultaneously embarked on an 11-state cross-country barnstormer with the uncontroversial theme of "conservation." He was thus out of the office—pulling switches at dams, and such—while the Dominican *coup* occurred and a minor scandal erupted at State. This involved Otto Otepka, former head of the State Department's Office of Security, who was said by the *New York Times* to have "violated regulations" in connection with Senator Dodd's Subcommittee on Internal Security. Otepka was the official who had initiated State's enquiry into Oswald and other alleged defectors, back in 1960. Now, the FBI told him, he was being charged with espionage: for leaking government documents to the Subcommittee.

While still "in Mexico," Oswald showed up in Dallas, Texas, at the home of Silvia Odio. Odio was a Cuban refugee whose parents had been imprisoned by the Castro regime. She and her sisters were active in anti-Castro politics, and one evening in late September—either 26th or 27th—she was visited by three men who wanted her to translate into English a letter soliciting funds for their CIA-created outfit, JURE: the Cuban Revolutionary Junta. Two of the men seemed to be Cubans, or Mexicans, she said. One of them used a "war name" of Leopoldo. The third was an American, whom they called "Leon Oswald." Next day, according to Odio, Leopoldo called and told her Leon had been in the Marines and was an excellent shot. Leopoldo claimed that Oswald said "President Kennedy should have been assassinated after the Bay of Pigs, and some Cubans should have done that." After the assassination, both Silvia and her sister Annie were convinced that "Leon" was Lee Harvey Oswald.[59]

Odio's story of the three men's visit, substantiated by her sister, created two major problems for the Warren Commission. The first was that, on the dates in question, the "historic" Oswald had to be en route to Mexico City, or already there. The second was that Odio's tale embroiled Oswald in a political conspiracy where his shooting skills and the murder of the president were being discussed. In a real criminal investigation, Odio's report would have been treated as a breakthrough: at last, two other conspirators had been identified! For the Warren Commissioners, it was a problem to be sidestepped, like Mrs. Dannelly's story. The FBI provided a half-hearted solution: an individual named Loran Eugene Hall, interviewed in California, claimed he had been fundraising for JURE in Dallas, Texas, accompanied by two men, one of whom looked like Oswald. Hall named as his companions Lawrence Howard and William Seymour (Seymour being the alleged lookalike). The Warren Commission accepted this story, even though Howard and Seymour both denied it, and, at his second FBI interview, Hall retracted it.[60]

Who was Loran Hall? He claimed to have been a mercenary and anti-Castro fundraiser; certainly he showed self-promotional skills. He told a newspaper reporter that while fundraising and speaking in Los Angeles, "On almost every occasion after I finished talking at one of those meetings, I'd overhear some people there discussing the possibility of assassinating Kennedy—and how it might be done."[61]

Hall told the tabloid *National Enquirer* that he had attended a meeting of paramilitary fanatics in Dallas prior to October 17, and that "one of the men, a fascist... said, 'You kill Kennedy and the $50,000 is yours.'"[62]

Hall claimed to have rejected the offer and departed. Lawrence Howard was a Mexican-American with a fine, waxed moustache. He denied being at Odio's house, but conceded he had "helped train guerrilla forces for a proposed invasion of Cuba." He stated that he had no knowledge of any conspiracy to kill the president.

William Seymour, the alleged Oswald lookalike, came from Arizona, and said he was in Miami on the days in question. Was he, like Hall, a "soldier of fortune"? In 1982, the mercenary magazine *Gung Ho!* published an article written by one William Seymour: a biography of Helmut Streicher, a top Nazi intelligence officer who was PAPERCLIPPED and worked at a high level of CIA till his retirement in 1980. In Seymour's adulatory story, Streicher described how the Agency "handled" a double agent named Geyer:

"Two of our people went into East Berlin... and staked him out at his building. When Geyer came out at noon, one agent created a noisy car wreck down the street by driving through a shop window. While pedestrians were looking at this, our man leaned a silencer-equipped rifle out of a rented room across the way and put Geyer out of business permanently."[63]

Was Seymour trying to send a message via this story of a political assassination, by rifle from an upper window, by the CIA? Garrison thought all three men worthy of investigation, and tried to extradite two of them from California. After interviewing Hall and Howard, he decided they were not connected to the assassination, implying that their introduction into the record by the FBI was a deliberate distraction...

On October 2, the president received the report of McNamara and Taylor's mission to Saigon. Their main recommendations were that a phased withdrawal from Vietnam be completed by the end of 1965, and that the "Defense Department should announce in the very near future presently prepared plans" to withdraw 1,000 troops by the end of the year. Press Secretary Pierre Salinger made a public announcement that evening of McNamara and Taylor's recommended timetable for withdrawal. On October 3, a holiday called the "Day of the Soldier," a *coup* led by a Honduran colonel, Osvaldo López Arellano, overthrew the government of President Ramon Villeda Morales. Villeda was sent into exile in Costa Rica. The *Times* observed that this was the fourth military *coup* in Latin America this year, and speculated that Kennedy might refuse to recognize the new Honduran government, or break diplomatic relations. But he didn't, and it is hard to imagine that any of these events were a surprise to the president. Jack Kennedy's response to a military *coup* in Honduras was the same as Barack Obama's: no response at all. As Kirk Bowman wrote,

"When López went ahead with the coup, his conservative allies scoffed at the threatened suspension of U.S. aid and a break in diplomatic relations: The U.S. 'would be back in six months.' The U.S. threat was hollow. Numerous democratic presidents were ousted in 1962 and 1963 and all of them were friends of Villeda."

"Coups in El Salvador, Guatemala, Peru, Argentina, the Dominican Republic, and Ecuador were followed closely in the press and the conservative opposition in Honduras could track the pattern: The U.S. in every case suspended relations, publicly exclaimed support of democracy, and then quickly renewed relations with the generals. The pattern would be no different in Honduras."[64]

On the day of the Honduran *coup*, William Fulbright met Jack Kennedy and urged him not to go to Dallas. "Dallas is a very dangerous spot. I wouldn't want to go there myself," the Arkansas senator told him. "Don't you go there either." The president was en route to a meeting with John Connally to discuss his Texas trip.

Lee Oswald resurfaced on October 3, checking into the Dallas YMCA. He registered as a serviceman and gave El Toro, California, as his address. Later, he went to the unemployment office and filed a claim. The same day, four books he'd borrowed in New Orleans— the Huxleys and the Bonds—were returned to the Napoleon branch library. The Warren Commission did not speculate as to who returned Lee's books for him. On October 4, he applied for a job with a printing company, and made a favorable impression. But the printer called Jaggers-Chiles-Stovall and they did not give him a good reference. Lee called Marina and asked her to get Ruth Paine to come and pick him up. Marina refused. Lee hitchhiked out to Irving.

On October 4, Kennedy recalled the CIA's Saigon station chief, John Richardson, who had fallen foul of Ambassador Lodge. Madame Nhu, the sister-in-law of South Vietnamese President Diem, flew to New York to begin a speaking tour which would include stops in Dallas and Los Angeles. Two days later, Edwin McChesney Martin, Assistant Secretary of State for InterAmerican Affairs, issued a policy statement: when military *coups* occurred in Latin America, he said, "we must use our leverage to keep those new regimes as liberal and considerate of the welfare of their people as possible... and press for new elections as soon as possible." In other words, there would be no meaningful action against right-wing *golpistas*. On October 7, the president signed the Nuclear Test Ban Treaty, and Robert Kennedy gave the FBI written permission to wiretap the telephones in Martin Luther King's home in Atlanta. The same day, the House Appropriations Committee eliminated from the civil defense budget the $200 million fallout shelter program authorized the previous month. The Committee allocated over five billion dollars to NASA—a sum space agency officials complained was insufficient to put Americans on the Moon.

Ruth Paine drove Lee Oswald to the bus station in Irving on the morning of October 7. Marina had declined to accompany him; he was going back to Dallas to look for work. In Dallas, Lee moved into a rooming house at 621 Marsalis Street. He paid the weekly rent of seven dollars. Supposedly, he continued to look for a job.

On October 9, the president announced his approval of a huge wheat sale to the Russians: 250 million dollars' worth of wheat would be sold commercially, at world prices, for use only by Russia and her satellite states. Kennedy assured the public that there would be no sales to Cuba or to Communist China.

The same day, an FBI official named Marvin Gheesling "disconnected" Lee Harvey Oswald from the system designed to identify potential national security threats. In 1959, after Oswald's Moscow Embassy performance, the FBI had placed a FLASH notice on his file, instructing all agents who received information on him to notify the Soviet Espionage Section, Division 5. For unknown reasons, Gheesling, a supervisor in the Espionage Section, removed the FLASH notice on October 9. A few hours later, the first CIA report on "Oswald's" alleged activities in Mexico City reached the Bureau, but triggered no alarms. As James W. Douglass wrote, "Had the FBI alarm sounded, Oswald would have been placed on the Security Index, drawing critical law enforcement attention to him prior to Kennedy's visit to Dallas."[65]

The House of Representatives rejected Kennedy's proposed joint Russian-American Lunar mission, by 125 to 110 votes, on October 10. Governor Nelson Rockefeller declared the Alliance for Progress a failure; he produced a six-point Latin American assistance program of his own. On October 11, the White House issued NSAM 263, which confirmed the Vietnam withdrawal plan but directed that no formal announcement be made. John Newman, in his book *JFK and Vietnam*, argues that secrecy was important because Kennedy's decision to withdraw troops from Vietnam was not contingent on a U.S. "victory" there. (On the multiple bases of Newman's book, Robert McNamara's memoir *In Retrospect*, the White House tapes, and contemporary newspaper accounts, there can be very little doubt that Kennedy planned to withdraw American troops from Vietnam.)[66]

It was a bad week for Lee Oswald, also. There were no job offers. He phoned Marina twice a day. When he told his landlady, Mrs. Bledsoe, that he would return on Monday, she refused to rent him the room again; she didn't like him. Lee spent the weekend of October 12–13 with Marina, Ruth, and June. On October 13, Ruth gave him a driving lesson. The same day, Sunday, General Walker attended a fundraiser for Cuban exiles in Dallas. Silvia Odio, also in attendance, thought she saw Lee Oswald in the audience. Next day, Ruth drove Lee back to Dallas, where he picked up his bag and rented a new room, at 1026 North Beckley Avenue, under the name of "O.H. Lee."

That evening, when Lee called to speak to Marina, Ruth told him of a possible job at the Texas School Book Depository, in downtown Dallas. A friend had mentioned it to her, she said, and she'd already called the superintendent of the Book Depository, Roy Truly, who'd told her Oswald should stop by. Truly, however, had not told her of an available job: he said he *didn't* know whether he had an opening. Who was the friend who thought a job might be available? Ruth claimed it was Mrs. Bill Randle, whose younger brother, Buell Wesley Frazier, worked there. But Mrs. Randle denied this: she told the Warren Commission, "I didn't know there was a job opening over there." Still, Oswald went to see Truly the next day, and was offered a temporary job, filling book orders, for $1.25 an hour. That evening, Robert Adams of the Texas Employment Commission called the Paines to speak to Lee about a job referral. Trans Texas Airways was looking for ramp agents; the salary was $310 a month. This was almost two dollars an hour, and the position was permanent.

Adams called again, the next morning, looking for Lee. He was told Oswald had already found work. It was Lee's first morning at the Book Depository: October 16.

And what of the Book Depository? Thirty years after the assassination, one writer, William Weston, focused his research on the notorious building at 411 Elm Street, its ownership, and purpose. What he unearthed and reported in the *Third* and *Fourth Decade*[67] is as follows: the seven-story building where Lee Oswald went to work was owned by a very wealthy Texas oil man, Colonel D. Harold Byrd. Byrd had the ultraconservative views of his class; he was a frequent guest of the Murchisons and Hunts at Del Mar; he was also the founder of the Civil Air Patrol, which he had organized to assist the Coast Guard during World War II. (Lee Oswald and David Ferrie were alumni of the Patrol.) Byrd had bought the Elm Street building in 1936, supposedly to use it as a manufacturing site. In 1940 he rented it to the John Sexton Company, a grocery warehouse firm. Sexton occupied the building till the fall of 1962, when they received notice to vacate. A new tenant, the Texas School Book Depository, rented the building.

Texas law mandated that schoolbooks be kept in depositories so as to hold the publishers accountable, and secure a ready supply of books. There were two such companies, the other being the Lone Star Book Depository. Until the summer of 1963, the TSBD had been based in the first floor of the Dal-Tex Building, also on Dealey Plaza. This was a big move, into much larger premises. So in addition to relocating its stock of boxed schoolbooks to the new building, the TSBD would be acquiring more stock, and taking on more staff.

This is the "innocent" explanation for the TSBD and how Oswald got his job there. Weston offers a "guilty" explanation for these matters, too. If there were a conspiracy to murder the president in Dealey Plaza, possession and control of the Book Depository building would be crucial to its success. Crucial because one or more rifle teams could be based there, and because Oswald must also be present, as the designated patsy. The passenger elevator in the TSBD only went up to the fourth floor; this, and the recent closure of a northwest stairway, made the fifth and sixth floors effectively "off limits" to those who didn't work there. Who worked on the building's upper floors? Only the warehousemen. There were 15 warehousemen, including Oswald. Unlike the TSBD office staff, they were all paid in cash. Oswald's supervisor, William Shelley, told a reporter he had worked as an intelligence officer during World War II and then joined the CIA. According to the Warren Commission, Shelley was born in 1925, which made him 19 or 20 when the War ended—pretty young to be a military intelligence officer. As Weston observes, if Shelley really was a CIA agent, then his job at the Book Depository was concurrent with his intelligence career, in which case Weston speculates that the Depository itself may have been a front for CIA activities.

> "Since Dallas was a source of munitions going to New Orleans in the drive to overthrow leftist governments in Central and South America, then a way had to be found to move them secretly. Big, heavy boxes marked 'Schoolbooks' would have been a handy way of delivering the goods safely and securely."[68]

Weston posits a "secret history" in which the Book Depository served as a conduit for illicit CIA arms shipments. M-16 rifles and other military equipment were indeed being stolen from storage at Fort Hood, Texas, and finding their way south. But the TSBD link is speculative. And it's possible Shelley was being untruthful when he claimed to be a CIA agent. Having worked for the TSBD for 18 years, Shelley was described as its assistant manager, yet he was still being paid in cash.

On October 17, President Kennedy welcomed President Tito of Yugoslavia to the White House. While anticommunist pickets protested, Tito received lunch, a champagne toast, and a 21-gun salute. The same day, the U.N. General Assembly voted unanimously to outlaw the placing of nuclear weapons in orbit around the Earth.

Buell Wesley Frazier, Lee's colleague from the warehouse, gave him a ride back to the Paines'. Buell was from Huntsville, Alabama. New in town, he too had just begun working at the TSBD. In Irving, Ruth and Marina threw a party for Lee. It was his 24th birthday: Friday, October 18. The next evening, according to Marina, she and Lee watched movies on TV: *We Were Strangers* and *Suddenly*. Both are films about political assassinations. In *We Were Strangers* (1946), the hero, played by John Garfield, assassinates a Cuban dictator. In *Suddenly* (1954) a malcontent ex-serviceman, played by Frank Sinatra, plans to assassinate the president with a high-powered German rifle. This was a sensational double bill, from the point of view of the "historic" Oswald, since it depicts both a heroic assassin (Garfield) and a sniper shooting at the presidential limo from an upper window (Sinatra). Case closed in the court of pop culture! If Oswald saw those movies.

Most likely, he didn't, though. Marina gave her story a date—the day after Lee's birthday—in a book written by Priscilla Johnson McMillan, *Marina and Lee*.[69]

Texas-based researcher Gary Mack trailed through antique Dallas TV guides for the weeks of October 13–19 and October 20–26. *Suddenly* appears nowhere in those lists. *We Were Strangers* was broadcast on Sunday, October 13, at 1 p.m., so it's possible the Oswalds saw it that afternoon. But the *Suddenly* portion of the double bill appears to be an invention.[70]

Next day, October 20, Lee stayed with June and Ruth's children while Ruth drove Marina to Parkland Hospital. There Marina gave birth to her second daughter, Audrey Marina Rachel. Lee worked the next day, but visited Marina in the evening, and spent the night in Irving, at the Paines'.

On October 21, as the president relaxed at Cape Cod, the press reported that he now thought Barry Goldwater was the "man to beat" in the 1964 election. This was shrewd media politics on Kennedy's part: the voluble Goldwater was the most right-wing of all the likely Republican candidates. Jack naturally preferred a fight with Goldwater versus one with Rockefeller, or a rematch with Nixon. The same day, Robert Kennedy signed an order authorizing wiretaps on the four phone lines into Martin Luther King's offices in Atlanta.

On October 23, Oswald attended an "ultra-right" rally headed by General Walker. The Warren Report suggests this was the same event as a John Birch Society meeting secretly taped "on the outskirts of Dallas" in October, but it was not. That meeting featured three "rabidly anti-Castro" Cuban exiles, one of whom made a speech against Kennedy:

> "Get him out! Get him out! The quicker, the sooner the better... He stinks... We are waiting for Kennedy the 22nd, buddy. We are going to see him one way or the other. We are going to give him the works when he gets in Dallas."[71]

The HSCA obtained a copy of the tape from Dallas researcher Mary Farrell; it seems they were unable to identify the Cubans. If they were based in Dallas, they may have been involved with the Alpha 66 terrorist group, which was being monitored by the sheriff's office, and had been meeting in a house at 3126 Harlendale Avenue. The principal Alpha 66 organizer in Dallas was Manuel Rodriguez.[72]

Walker's rally took place at the Dallas Auditorium, and was followed by a near-riot at the same venue the next night. It was United Nations Day—October 24—and Adlai Stevenson, President Kennedy's Ambassador to the U.N., was heckled, pushed, struck, and spat on by flag-waving demonstrators. One of the rioters, Robert Hatfield, was arrested. Though the melee was less violent by far than Walker's Ole Miss insurrection, the out-of-town press still disapproved of it. For a brief moment it seemed that President Kennedy might not visit Dallas. But this would have been a political setback for Connally and, to a lesser extent, Johnson; and, after "one hundred Dallas civic leaders" sent a telegram of apology to Stevenson and the president, plans for the Texas trip advanced.

On October 25, Khrushchev told a Moscow press conference that Russia was "not at present planning flights by cosmonauts to the Moon." His statement that the Russians "do not want to compete with the sending of people to the Moon without careful preparation" seemed to close the door to any joint mission with the Americans.

That evening, Oswald and Michael Paine went to a meeting of the American Civil Liberties Union (ACLU) at Southern Methodist University. According to the Warren Report, someone made a statement to the effect that members of the John Birch Society should not be considered anti-Semitic. Oswald then spoke, stating he'd heard anti-Semitic and anti-Catholic remarks "at the meeting he'd attended two days earlier."[73]

On October 26 the Rometsch story broke, in the pages of a provincial newspaper, the *Des Moines Register*. It moved on to a couple of other papers, as part of the newly emerging Bobby Baker scandal. None of the call girls' clients were named, though they were said to be highly placed, and it was immediately rumored that John Kennedy was one of them. Kennedy tried to defuse the story in a conversation with Ben Bradlee. "I thought of him [Baker] primarily as a rogue, not a crook," the president told the MONGOOSE asset and *Newsweek* bureau chief. "He was always telling me he knew where he could get me the cutest little girls, but he never did." Kennedy reassured Bradlee he had no plan to dump Lyndon Johnson, who was thick with Baker: "That's preposterous on the face of it. We've got to carry Texas in '64, and maybe Georgia." In Vietnam a *coup* was imminent: CIA advised Lodge, who advised the State Department, that Diem would be overthrown by November 2. Following the discovery of a Russian spy ring, three members of the Soviet mission to the U.N. were ordered to leave the country within 48 hours. A fourth Russian and a New Jersey engineer, accused of passing Strategic Air Command secrets to the diplomats, were held without bail.

On October 29, FBI agent Hosty, apparently unable to locate Lee Oswald, interviewed Ruth Paine's neighbor, Mrs. Roberts.

On October 30, President Kennedy made a political trip to Philadelphia. His motorcade, following a route 13 miles in length, encountered almost-deserted streets. Tom Wicker, a journalist covering the trip, called it "one of the poorest receptions Mr. Kennedy has had in a major city since he became president."

The same day, police in Denton, Texas, advised the Secret Service of a potential threat: a John Bircher and "former member" of the KKK and NSRP had stated, "We have something planned to embarrass President Kennedy during his visit to Dallas, Texas." The same day another report reached the Secret Service via the Denton police, this one from a student informant at North Texas State University: several students had visited General Walker and then participated in the demonstration against Adlai Stevenson; one of these students "told the informant that something was being planned for President Kennedy when he visited Dallas on November 22." Both reports were investigated. The Bircher was not considered dangerous, and his case was closed on November 6. The student was deemed not to have made any threats; the report states, "Pictures were obtained of the subject and others of the group, and were provided all security personnel (Trade Mart, behind the head table, etc.)."

The reader may recall Abraham Bolden, the first black agent on the president's security detail. Bolden had returned to the Secret Service office in Chicago. The same day as the Denton reports came in, SAIC Maurice Martineau advised agents in the Chicago office that the FBI had learned of a plot to murder the president *there*. Kennedy was due to visit Chicago in three days' time. The FBI's informant—code-named 'Lee' (!)—stated that four snipers planned to shoot Kennedy with high-powered rifles during his motorcade. The next day brought another referral from the FBI: a North Side landlady had reported that two tenants were stashing rifles with telescopic sights in their room. Martineau sent agents to investigate, and two men were apparently picked up and questioned, though no record of this—or of their names—exists.[74]

Also on October 31, Fidel Castro protested that an American ship, *The Rex*, was being used for CIA-backed missions against Cuba. He told reporters that a team of CIA assassins, armed with high-powered rifles, had been arrested on a Cuban beach. Next day, the *New York Times* confirmed that *The Rex*, a decommissioned U.S. Navy sub-chaser, was docked at Palm Beach, Florida, and was missing a couple of its launches. *The Rex* was also known as "the flagship of the JM/WAVE fleet," JM/WAVE being the name of the CIA's massive operations and intelligence-gathering station at the University of Miami.[75]

On November 1, Oswald wrote to the ACLU, applying for membership. He also wrote to the Communist Party, asking them their "general view" of the ACLU, and whether he should "attempt to heighten its progressive tendencies." And he opened a P.O. Box—Number 6225—at the Terminal Annex a block from Dealey Plaza. He gave his correct name but a false address—3610 North Beckley—and listed as corporations entitled to use the box the FPCC and the ACLU, both of which he described as "non-profit." While Lee was out doing this, Agent Hosty interviewed Marina and Ruth Paine; and a young man who claimed to be an ex-Marine acted "rude and impertinent" in a Fort Worth gun shop. After the assassination, several witnesses said this individual resembled Oswald. Who was he?

The same day, President Diem met with Ambassador Lodge in Saigon. Diem said he knew there was to be a *coup*; Lodge told him not to worry. Diem, clearly afraid, offered to capitulate. The Ambassador sent this breakthrough news ("In effect he said: Tell us what you want and we'll do it") to Washington via the slowest means possible. Instead of urgently phoning his boss, Lodge waited until 3 p.m. to cable his report—an hour and a half after the *coup* had started. And he chose not to send it via "Critical Flash"—which would have got it immediate attention—but via a slower route used for less urgent messages.

Had Kennedy known of Diem's offer, he might have pulled the plug—or tried to. Lodge, clearly, did not want that. No provision was made by the Embassy or CIA to evacuate their former client. On the morning of November 2, Diem and his brother Nhu visited a Catholic church. Mass was over, but the brothers were able to receive communion from a priest. An army convoy pulled up and arrested them on the church steps. They were quickly killed.

When Jack heard the news he was distressed. He had authorized the *coup*, but had apparently believed that Diem could be exiled, and bloodshed avoided in the regime change. It's hard to see why he imagined this. Madame Nhu, in Los Angeles, publicly blamed the Americans for her husband's death.

And duty called: that same day, November 2, the president was scheduled to fly to Chicago for the Army/Air Force football game at Soldier Field. It was a politically important visit, as Kennedy had "stood up" Mayor Daley on a similar scheduled visit the previous year. He needed to bond with allies like Daley in good time for the

'64 election. But the 11-mile route from O'Hare Airport to Soldier Field was a concern for the Secret Service: the president's limousine would pass through a warehouse district, which the advance men considered "ten times more deadly than any building corridor," involving a "slow, difficult left-hand turn" and "a difficult 90-degree turn that would slow [the vehicles] to practically a standstill." Two suspected snipers were in custody, but two others were still on the loose. And, following another tip-off, Chicago cops were shadowing Thomas Arthur Vallee, an armed ex-Marine who had threatened to kill the president. This was the disturbing assessment which the Secret Service passed on to the White House.

The cops arrested Vallee at 9:10 a.m. Five minutes later, in Washington, press secretary Pierre Salinger announced that the president would not be going to Chicago. The news was entirely unexpected; the press corps was already in the air. Salinger said the Vietnam crisis obliged Kennedy to remain at his desk. It's more likely the White House felt the trip too risky, given the Secret Service's concerns.

Vallee turned out to be a schizophrenic Korean War veteran, 30 years of age. He had an M-1 rifle, a carbine, 2,500 rounds of ammo in his apartment and 750 rounds in his trunk. Vallee was said to be "a disaffiliated member of the John Birch Society." He claimed to have worked at a U-2 base in Japan—Camp Otsu—and to have trained Cuban exiles for the CIA. Having left New York for Chicago in August 1963, he told the police he had found work as a printer in a building at 625 West Jackson. Author James W. Douglass visited the building in 2005 and wrote,

> "From its roof I could look down and over to where JFK's presidential limousine had been scheduled to make a slow turn up from the Northwest Expressway... onto West Jackson on November 2, 1963."[76]

Was Vallee a potential killer—or a potential patsy who could be offered up by the Chicago conspirators as the lone assassin? He was released without charge after the president's visit was canceled, along with the two alleged snipers, whose names remain unknown. The principal source for most of this information is Abraham Bolden, but Bolden's accounts are inconsistent. Bolden told the HSCA and Douglass that two suspects were arrested and detained on the evening of November 1 in the Chicago Secret Service office; he told the HSCA that he saw one of the suspects in custody. In his own book, published the same year as Douglass', Bolden wrote that "the suspects bolted, and our guys lost them in traffic." Which is true?[77]

An obscure Warren Commission document supports the Chicago story. In his FBI interview, *Chicago Daily News* reporter Morton Newman stated, "William Mooney, Assistant City Editor of that newspaper, mentioned that four men were arrested in Chicago, IL, on November 2, 1963, for carrying a concealed weapon and that he (Mooney) believed one was named Oswald."[78]

For Jack Kennedy, this was a dark moment. He had approved a policy in Vietnam which led two fellow Catholics, one of them that country's president, to be killed. The same day a group of armed men, possibly Cubans, possibly Birchers, had assembled in Chicago, to murder him. There was a disturbing synchronicity to the two sets of events. And Vallee's claims to have worked for CIA must have made interesting reading, if any report of them reached the White House.

On November 4, an individual named Oswald left a rifle to be sighted by the Irving Sports Shop. The Warren Commission decided this individual was not Lee Harvey Oswald. The work involved drilling three holes in the rifle's stock; the Italian rifle ordered in Hidell's name had only two such holes. On November 5, FBI agent Hosty visited the Paine home once again, only to find Lee absent.

In response to this, perhaps, Lee Harvey Oswald visited the FBI office in Dallas looking for Hosty. Hosty wasn't in, so Lee left him a note. The contents of the note are unknown, since Hosty destroyed it, on the orders of SAC Gordon Shanklin, a few hours after Oswald's death. The FBI didn't tell the Warren Commission about the note, and it remained a secret until 1975. What did the note say? According to the FBI receptionist, Nancy Fenner, it read as follows:

> "Let this be a warning. I will blow up the FBI and the Dallas Police Department if you don't stop bothering my wife. Lee Harvey Oswald."

Agent Hosty remembered it differently:

> "If you have anything you want to learn about me, come talk to me directly. If you don't cease bothering my wife, I will take appropriate action and report this to the proper authorities."

Shanklin claimed no knowledge of the note, a lie which got him censured by Congress' Judiciary Committee. The HCSA "regarded the incident of the note as a serious impeachment of Shanklin's and Hosty's credibility." Yet Hosty continued to be cited by Warren supporters as an unimpeachable source, and to appear as an authority in BBC and PBS documentaries! Here is a documented instance of two of J. Edgar Hoover's agents destroying evidence pertaining to the president's alleged assassin, and then participating in a conspiracy to conceal the crime. Hosty and Shanklin should have seen the inside of a jail for doing this.[79]

Anthony Summers points to another FBI cover-up involving Hosty. When the Bureau provided a list of the contents of Oswald's address book to the Warren Commission, one contact was omitted: James Hosty, whose address, telephone number and car license plate had all been scrupulously recorded by Oswald, only to be concealed by the FBI. The HSCA explained this omission as the work of other FBI agents seeking "to protect Hosty from personal embarrassment."[80]

But there is an alternative explanation for the destruction or withholding of evidence in both cases: that Oswald was working undercover for the FBI, and reporting to Hosty, and that his note confirmed this.

This could mean that Oswald was "Confidential Informant NO/Dallas T-1," reporting on himself; or that he was informant 172, as Deputy Sheriff Sweatt claimed; that "Lee" in Chicago wasn't the code name of an informant, but the informant's actual name; and that Lee's visit to Hosty and subsequent note were either part of his normal process of communication, or an exceptional contact in exceptional circumstances, which a panicked Shanklin ordered his subordinate, Hosty, to conceal.

In the John le Carré version of this story, did Oswald—working undercover in New Orleans to destabilize the FPCC and track down right-wing gun-runners—stumble upon a plot to kill the president, and follow it to Dallas? Did Oswald visit the FBI in Dallas to make a bomb threat, or to tell the G-men what he had learned?

On November 4, Gerald Behn, Special Agent In Charge of the White House Secret Service detail, phoned Forrest Sorrels, SAIC of the Dallas field office, and advised him that the president would probably be visiting "about November 21." He said two locations had been suggested for a lunch site: the Trade Mart and the Women's

Building. Sorrels surveyed both places and called Behn back. He advised him that the Women's Building was preferable from a security standpoint. The same day, Byron Skelton, the Texan delegate to the National Committee of the Democratic Party, wrote to Robert Kennedy: "To tell the truth, I would be greatly relieved if the president would omit Dallas from his itinerary." Skelton, like many others, feared a right-wing provocation was in the works.

The next day Behn met Jerry Bruno, the advance man for the trip, and presidential aide Kenneth O'Donnell. Bruno was concerned that the catwalks of the Trade Mart could be occupied by protestors. Behn, who was supposed to be the ultimate authority, also preferred the Women's Building. O'Donnell insisted on the selection of the Trade Mart.

On November 6, Byron Skelton wrote to Lyndon Johnson's adviser, Walter Jenkins, expressing his "concern and distrust of Dallas." Premier Khrushchev, meanwhile, seemed to have changed course regarding a Moon mission. He told a group of visiting American businessmen that Russians would make the trip to the Moon, but at a more leisurely pace than the Americans.

On November 7, Nelson Rockefeller declared his candidacy for the Republican presidential nomination. But his star had faded as the Republican base grew smaller and more right-wing. In particular, Rockefeller's divorce and remarriage had lost him support. The same day, the press linked Bobby Baker with the mafia, and the United States extended diplomatic recognition to the new military regime in South Vietnam.

Byron Skelton's letter to Bobby Kennedy was passed to Kenny O'Donnell on November 8. Skelton had traveled to Washington to advise Jerry Bruno against a Dallas visit, but to no avail. O'Donnell considered Skelton's fears "an unfounded intuition."

The same day, Lee Oswald wrote a brief note, maybe:

November 8, 1963

Dear Mr. Hunt,
I would like information concerding [sic] my position. I am asking only for information. I am suggesting that we discuss the matter fully before any steps are taken by me or anyone else

Thank you
Lee Harvey Oswald

Who was Mr. Hunt? Some researchers believe it was the Dallas oil man, H.L. Hunt, the hardcore right-winger who funded the Life Line Foundation. The FBI believed the note was intended for one of Hunt's sons, Nelson Bunker Hunt. But Hunt had another son, Lamar, whose office Jack Ruby would visit the day before the assassination. And there was another infamous Hunt—E. Howard, the CIA agent whose path had crossed Oswald's in New Orleans. And there was also Hal Hunt, the right-wing publisher of the *Shasta County Chronicles* in California. Was Oswald involved with any of these? And if so, what did he think his position was? The note holds a threat, the possibility of further action. But its author sounds subordinate to Mr. Hunt, and worried.

Is the note genuine? It exists only as a copy, sent anonymously from Mexico City to the Texas newspaperman, Penn Jones. The Mexican connection points to E. Howard Hunt, who did CIA work there. The misspelling of "concerning" feels like an Oswald-ism, but Oswald had spelled the word correctly in the past. Is the handwriting really Oswald's? Three HSCA handwriting experts had different opinions. Two thought the note was *not* in Oswald's handwriting; a third concluded, "it is impossible to determine; if not genuine, [it is] a clever imitation."[81]

A former KGB man, Vasili Mitrokhin, would later claim that the Dear Mr. Hunt letter was a fake, made by the Russians in 1975 (Penn Jones received his copy two years later). Mitrokhin said that the purpose of the fake was to incriminate CIA, and the disinformation plot backfired when people assumed the recipient was H.L. Hunt, or one of his sons.[82]

Joseph Milteer, the leader of the Dixie Clan of Georgia, remained under police surveillance. On November 9, he was secretly tape-recorded, in Miami, by a police informant. Milteer told the informant, William Somersett, of a plot to assassinate the president with a high-powered rifle. It took the Miami Police intelligence officers three days to transcribe the conversation and provide a copy to the Secret Service. This read in part:

> Somersett: I think Kennedy is coming here on the 18th, to make some kind of speech. I don't know what it is, but I imagine it will be on TV...
>
> Milteer: You can bet your bottom dollar he is going to have a lot to say about the Cubans; there are so many of them here.

Somersett: Well, he will have a thousand bodyguards, don't worry about that.

Milteer: The more bodyguards he has, the easier it is to get him.

Somersett: What?

Milteer: The more bodyguards he has, the easier it is to get him.

Somersett: Well, how in the hell do you figure would be the best way to get him?

Milteer: From an office building with a high-powered rifle...

Somersett: They are really going to try to kill him?

Milteer: Oh, yeah; it is in the working. Brown himself, Brown is just as likely to get him as anybody in the world. He hasn't said so, but he tried to get Martin Luther King.

Who was Brown? Harry Jack Brown had represented the Dixie Clan at the Congress of Freedom meeting, where political assassinations were discussed. He held the title of the Clan's Imperial Wizard. At a meeting in Vero Beach, in early October, Milteer had told Somersett that Jack Brown was the author of the Birmingham church bombing, which left four children dead (the case remains unsolved today). At a convention of the Constitution Party, in Indianapolis a week later, Somersett and another informant stated that Brown was "virtually bragging" about his role in the bombing. Now, according to Milteer, Brown was planning to kill the President and Dr. King.

Somersett: ...Hitting this Kennedy is going to be a hard proposition... I believe you may have figured out a way to get him, the office building and all that. I don't know how them Secret Service agents cover all them office buildings or anywhere he is going. Do you know whether they do that or not?

Milteer: Well, if they have any suspicion, they do that, of course. But without suspicion, chances are that they wouldn't.

Somersett worried about a clampdown on the right-wing movement after the assassination. Milteer assured him it wouldn't happen: "No way. They will pick up somebody within hours afterwards, if anything like that would happen, just to throw the public off." Not only did the Dixie Clansman predict the means of the president's assassination, he also predicted the arrest, within hours, of an innocent patsy. He was wrong only about the location.

Harry Jack Brown certainly sounded like an individual worthy of FBI investigation. But he wasn't investigated, and neither Brown nor Milteer were under surveillance when Kennedy visited Miami. Why not? Milteer was a wealthy individual who traveled constantly, promoting the far-right cause. On July 31, he had opened a savings account under a false name—Samuel Steven Story—with an initial deposit of $5,000. There were two more deposits: $5,000 on August 20 and $2,000 on September 24. On January 31, 1964, all $12,000 was withdrawn and the account closed. Where was that money coming from? What was it for?[83]

The same day as Milteer was tape-recorded, Oswald borrowed Ruth Paine's typewriter. According to the Warren Report, he used it to write to the Russian Embassy in Washington. He surely knew that this, like his other letters, would be read by the FBI, CIA, and other agencies. That was perhaps the point. It is the only one of his letters written on a typewriter:

> From: Lee H. Oswald, PO Box 6225, Dallas, Texas
> Marina Nichilayeva Oswald, Soviet Citizen
>
> To: Consular Division
> Embassy U.S.S.R.
> Washington D.C.
>
> Nov. 9, 1963
>
> Dear Sirs;
>
> This is to inform you of recent events sincem my meetings with comrade Kostin in the Embassy Of The Soviet Union, Mexico City, Mexico.
>
> I was unable to remain in Mexico indefinily because of my mexican visa restrictions which was for 15 days only. I could not take a chance on reqesting a new visa unless I used my real name, so I retured to the United States.
>
> I had not planned to contact the Soviet embassy in Mexico so they were unprepared, had I been able to reach the Soviet

Embassy in Havana as planned, the embassy there would have had time to complete our business.

Of corse the Soviet embassy was not at fault, they were, as I say un-prepared, the Cuban consulate was guilty of a gross breach of regulations, I am glad he has since been replced.

The Federal Bureu of Investigation is not now interested in my activities in the progressive organization 'Fair Play For Cuba Committee', of which I was secretary in New Orleans (state Louisiana) since I no longer reside in that state. However, the F.B.I. has visited us here in Dallas, Texas, on November 1st. Agent James P. Hasty warned me that if I engaged in F.P.C.C. activities in Texas the F.B.I. will again take an "interrest" in me.

This agent also "suggested" to Maria Nichilayeva that she could remain in the united States under F.B.I. "protection", that is, she could defect from the Soviet Uion, of course I and my wife strongly protested these tactics by the notorious F.B.I.

Please inform us of the arrival of our Soviet entrance visa's as soon as they come.

Also, this is so inform you of the birth, on October 20, 1963 of a daughter, Audrey Marina Oswald in Dallas, Texas, to my wife.

Respectfully
Lee H. Oswald

On the surface, this may seem like vintage Oswald. The pomposity, the self-involvement, and the spelling mistakes all seem familiar. But this one has *an unusual number of mistakes* (so many that I omitted the customary [sic] after each one), and they seem evenly distributed. Several words spelled correctly in his handwritten draft are spelled wrong in the typewritten version. If Oswald had been coached in his near-perfect letter to John Connally, something else was going on here. The typed version is longer and more incriminating than Lee's handwritten draft. And why is the letter in English? Oswald could write Russian; it was Marina's native language; and Ruth Paine had a Russian typewriter, recently repaired. Why contact the Embassy in English, if the recipients, whom one was trying to impress, were Russian speakers?

Given the lack of language skills within the FBI and CIA, it would be more logical to write the letter in English, especially if they were its creators, as well as its recipients. William Weston writes, "These verbal expressions give the impression that the writer who penned this letter must have been one of Moscow's most valuable agents," and speculates that Oswald was trying to get one of the Russian spymasters to initiate contact with him.[84]

It's certainly full of red flags: references to "our business" and the use of false names. But the brightest red light is in the opening mention of meetings with "comrade Kostin." Western intelligence would inevitably speculate that this was Valeriy Kostikov, the alleged KGB assassinations boss in Mexico City.

In 1999, Russian president Boris Yeltsin apparently gave U.S. president Bill Clinton a file of 80 documents from the KGB concerning the Kennedy assassination.[85]

One of them was a report expressing suspicion over the November 9 letter; noting that it was typewritten, unlike Oswald's other letters, and different in "tone," the KGB speculated that it was a "fake."

A fake Oswald document? Gambling, in this casino? The very idea! There were three versions of this suspicious letter; only two survive. The first is Oswald's undated handwritten rough draft (reproduced as Commission Exhibit 103); the second is Ruth Paine's handwritten copy of the above, which she made surreptitiously and gave to the FBI (this was not published by the Commission, and is apparently lost!); the third is the letter itself, presumably supplied by the Russian Embassy and the FBI (it is reproduced twice, as Commission Exhibits 15 and 986).

This is an incriminating document, whose author claims he went to Mexico City and met with KGB agents. Was it really written by Oswald? The reader may compare the handwritten draft—Commission Exhibit 103—with one of Oswald's other letters: for example, his letter to the FPCC requesting more "pamplets"—the Lee (Vincent T.) Exhibit No. 2—in Figs. 6 and 7.

Does this look like the same handwriting to you? It does not to me. In general, the lower-case characters are larger relative to the capitals, and more rounded in the FPCC letter than in the "comrade Kostin" draft. Consider just one character, the lower-case "t." In the FPCC letter the "t"s are often looped, i.e. open, with a cross-bar heading downward, from left to right. In the "Kostin" draft, almost all the "t"s are narrow, i.e. closed, with a cross-bar heading upward, or horizontally, from left to right.

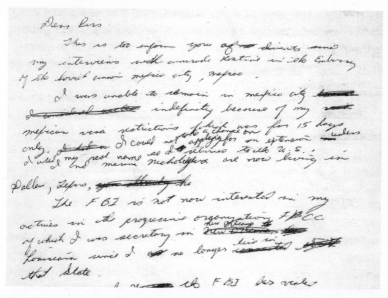

Fig. 6: Fragment of draft of a letter to the Russian Embassy, Commission Document 103.

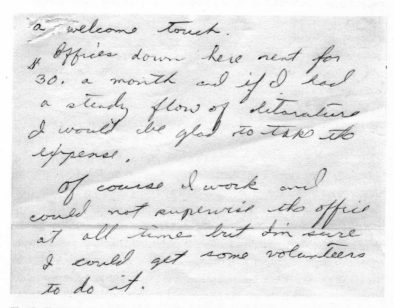

Fig. 7: Fragment of a letter to the FPCC, Commission V.T. Lee Exhibit No. 2.

If we assume that Oswald's letter to V.T. Lee was genuine, i.e. written by Oswald, then the case of the "comrade Kostin" letter is not closed. This and his tourist card are the only signed documents connecting him to Mexico. Since there is no photographic or audio evidence linking Oswald to Mexico City, and the embassy staff did not identify him, the case for his being there rests on the contradictory recollections of some bus passengers, his name in the hotel register, and this incriminating letter.

Ruth Paine claimed she read the draft and, concerned by its contents, copied it secretly while Oswald was in the shower, and took it to the FBI. What a pal! It's very strange that the Warren Commission didn't include a copy of her transcript among its exhibits, and disturbing (to say the least) that the original has apparently vanished from the National Archives. Author Carol Hewett has determined that the KGB *did* have an agent named Kostin: Valery Dimitrevich Kostin, who worked for Russian intelligence in the Netherlands from 1966 to 1969, and in Finland, in 1971. His whereabouts in the early sixties are unknown.[86]

That same day, November 9, a man calling himself Lee Oswald visited the Downtown Lincoln-Mercury showroom near the Book Depository, and took a car for a test drive. He alarmed the salesman, Albert Bogard, by driving dangerously fast. Back at the showroom, in front of two additional witnesses, the man objected to the high prices of the cars, and said he might "go back to Russia, where they treat workers like men."[87]

Since Lee Oswald couldn't drive, who was this person, and why was he drawing attention to himself, or, rather, to Lee Oswald? Around this time someone calling himself Lee Harvey Oswald applied for a job with Allright Parking Systems at the Southland Hotel. The manager, Hubert Morrow, recalled this Oswald asking him how high the Southland building was, and whether it had a good view of Dallas.

The weekend in question was a holiday weekend, which the "historic" Oswald spent in Irving, shopping with Ruth and playing with his children. He already had a job, and wasn't likely to be applying to be a parking lot attendant. So who was using Oswald's name, and why was he asking these questions? And who was the man at the Sports Drome Rifle Range, who drew attention to himself by being loud and obnoxious, and shooting at his neighbor's target?

Once again, witnesses after the assassination said the individual with the gun resembled Oswald.[88]

On November 12, at an Alliance for Progress meeting in São Paulo, Brazilian president João Goulart criticized Alliance policies, and said Latin American countries should unite in their trade and aid policies. Goulart would be gone within five months, the victim of yet another military *coup*. President Kennedy had less than ten days to live, and many reasons to be disappointed. His tax cuts were still stalled. Civil rights progress was glacial, and Kennedy was surprised by the anger his mixture of fine words and small, symbolic efforts had generated, on both sides of the racial divide. At home and abroad, his tendency to reach out to opposing sides had led to contradictory policies, inaction and worse. Kennedy wanted to win the trust of foreign leaders—Castro, Diem, Goulart—while simultaneously plotting to have them removed or killed. In Latin America he undermined his own Alliance for Progress by sending counterinsurgency troops, and permitting CIA to foment military takeovers.

The official history of Kennedy's presidency focuses on Cuba, where his attempt at regime change failed, and ignores *nine successful military coups* in Latin America alone on Kennedy's watch. The countries were El Salvador, the Dominican Republic (twice), Ecuador (twice), Argentina, Peru, Honduras, and Guatemala; coups took place in Brazil and Bolivia the following year. The denial of the franchise to so many Latin Americans in such a short time is quite remarkable, something of which Nixon or Reagan would have been proud. Elsewhere the policy was the same: in South Vietnam and Iraq, the installation and funding of increasingly repressive military regimes. The only break in the clouds was the Nuclear Test Ban Treaty—plus, if one includes negatives, that Jack Kennedy had not provoked atomic war in Cuba, nor approved the Pentagon's proposal for a "preemptive" nuclear strike on Russia.

On November 12, Special Agent Winston G. Lawson, of the White House Secret Service detail, flew to Dallas to view potential sites for the president's speaking engagement, and to inspect possible motorcade routes. In Washington, the NSC met, and CIA's Desmond Fitzgerald described an ongoing plan to identify Cuban leaders who might prove plausible rivals to Fidel Castro. NSC memorandum number 271 was issued, addressed to the NASA Administrator. It instructed him to personally develop "a program of substantive cooperation with the Soviet Union in the field of outer space... including cooperation in Lunar landing programs..."

Next day, the president convened the first planning meeting for his reelection campaign. Among those present were Robert, Ted Sorensen, Lawrence O'Brien, and Richard Scammon, the director of the Bureau of the Census. Jack pointed out that his approval rating had dropped from 76 percent at the start of 1963 to 59 percent today; Scammon said his statistical fall in popularity was due to civil rights. But the polls also showed that Kennedy would beat Barry Goldwater by 55 percent to 39 percent. "Give me Barry," the president exclaimed. "I won't even have to leave the Oval Office!"

Kennedy told his staff he wanted "Peace and Prosperity" to be the theme in '64. That very morning he had announced a crash program to bring food and public works to eastern Kentucky, which he called "the most severely distressed area in the country." But Scammon counseled against emphasizing the anti-poverty program or photo opportunities with the poor. "You can't get a single vote more by doing anything for poor people," Scammon warned the president. "Those who vote are already for you. I was thinking of photographs with policemen..." For two hours they discussed the numbers: which states Kennedy could lose, which ones he had to hold, or win. Kennedy felt the key to winning easily was to carry both Texas and Florida, which would more than compensate for other Southern losses. The trips he was about to take, to Florida and Texas, were crucial to this plan.

In Dallas, the same day, Secret Service agent Lawson visited the Trade Mart with Dallas SAIC Sorrels. After viewing the site he reported favorably on it: it had good internal security, and a kitchen, something the Women's Building lacked. According to the HSCA, "Lawson agreed with Sorrels that the interior decor at the Women's Building was unseemly for a president."

The Dallas public library didn't keep a list of members, only one of delinquent books. So the only book we know Oswald borrowed in Dallas was one he didn't return: *The Shark and the Sardines*, a political story by a former president of Guatemala, Juan Jose Arevalo. Lee checked the book out on November 6; due back on November 13, it was not returned, nor was it found among Oswald's possessions.[89]

On November 14, the FBI in San Antonio interviewed an unnamed informant who "stated that he is a member of the Ku Klux Klan; that during his travels throughout the country, his sources have told him that a militant group of the National States Rights Party plans to assassinate the president and other high-level officials. He stated that he does not believe this is planned for the near future, but he does believe the attempt will be made."

The informant had been arrested in Piedras Negras, Mexico, for car theft. The FBI reported that he remained in jail at the time of the assassination, and the Warren Commission—though it included the Secret Service's report as part of Commission Document 762[90]— did not consider it worthy of comment. Twice in one week, police informants had implicated the NSRP in a militant right-wing plot to kill the president. The Miami informant thought the assassination would take place on or around November 18, and named one of the plotters: Harry Jack Brown. Yet there was no alarm.

At a press conference the same day, President Kennedy was upbeat: optimistic about the new government in South Vietnam, he planned to bring "several hundred" U.S. troops home before the new year. On November 15, the head of the U.S. Military Assistance Group in South Vietnam confirmed that 1,000 U.S. troops would be withdrawn in December. Their departure would reduce the American military presence in that country to 15,500 men. Meanwhile, the president condemned the arrest of an American political scientist, Frederick C. Barghoorn, in Moscow. Kennedy told reporters Barghoorn was not a spy, as the Russians claimed, and ruled out any prisoner exchange. On Capitol Hill, he continued to suffer setbacks, as the Senate cut almost $800 million from his $3.7 billion foreign aid bill, and his tax-cut bill crept along.

The president spent the weekend in Florida, where he visited Cape Canaveral and witnessed the firing of a nuclear-capable Polaris missile from a submarine. He also toured the Space Center, and saw the *Saturn 1* launching vehicle. Professor Barghoorn, looking haggard and nervous, showed up in London after being held by the Russians for 16 days. They did not withdraw their charge that the Yale academic was a spy, but said he was being released and expelled because of the "personal concern" of President Kennedy.

Lee Oswald's activities during this weekend are obscure. He did not visit the Paines. On Saturday, November 16, someone calling himself "Oswald" was back at the Sports Drome Gun Range, showing off his Italian carbine. According to the *Dallas Morning*

News[91], Lee was interviewed by the FBI in Dallas that same day; for some reason, this meeting is not part of the FBI's official list of its Oswald interviews. On Sunday, at Marina's request, Ruth called Lee's rooming house and was told that no one by the name of "Lee Harvey Oswald" was staying there.

According to William S. Walter, a security patrol clerk with the New Orleans FBI, early the same Sunday morning a PBX message arrived from the Washington FBI office. It warned of an attempt to be made on Jack Kennedy's life during his upcoming visit to Dallas. Walter, testifying to the HSCA, said he immediately called the Special Agent responsible for threats against the president, read him the teletype, and followed his orders as to which agents to call. No copy of the PBX message has ever surfaced: if it really existed, it was "disappeared"—like Oswald's note to Agent Hosty—within the FBI. Walter said he made a copy of it, from memory, but he did not tell his story until 1967. The G-man recalled the urgent teletype as follows:

URGENT: 1:45 AM EST 11-17-63 HLF 1 PAGE

TO: ALL SACS
FROM: DIRECTOR

THREAT TO ASSASSINATE PRESIDENT KENNEDY IN DALLAS TEXAS NOVEMBER TWENTY TWO DASH TWENTY THREE NINETEEN SIXTY THREE. MISC INFORMATION CONCERNING. INFO HAS BEEN RECEIVED BY THE BUREAU. BUREAU HAS DETERMINED THAT A MILITANT REVOLUTIONARY GROUP MAY ATTEMPT TO ASSASSINATE PRESIDENT KENNEDY ON HIS PROPOSED TRIP TO DALLAS TEXAS NOVEMBER TWENTY TWO DASH TWENTY THREE NINETEEN SIXTY THREE. ALL RECEIVING OFFICES SHOULD IMMEDIATELY CONTACT ALL CI'S; PCIS LOGICAL RACE AND HATE GROUP INFORMANTS AND DETERMINE IF ANY BASIS FOR THREAT. BUREAU SHOULD BE KEPT ADVISED OF ALL DEVELOPMENTS BY TELETYPE. OTHER OFFICES HAVE BEEN ADVISED. END AND ACK PLS.

The HSCA pointed to various errors of terminology and procedure in the reconstruction. Walter replied he had not intended to fake a document, but to reconstruct it from memory. If it's genuine, it shows that J. Edgar Hoover had just been advised of an assassination conspiracy—hence the odd hour of the message—and was acting appropriately. It also suggests a disciplined capacity for *omerta* on the part of every FBI office in the country, where, presumably, a clerk such as Walter would have received the PBX, and alerted the appropriate special agent.

Was Walter faking, or was he the only agent telling the truth? In his long interview with the HSCA, Walter said that his colleague Agent Quigley, having interviewed Oswald in jail, asked him to pull the ex-Marine's files. Walter followed Lee Harvey Oswald's trail among the index cards, only to find his files missing. "When I searched for these files in the normal filing area of the Bureau, which was in an open bay filing, the files were not there. From looking at the numbers... they fell in the category of security-type, informant-type files, 105 classification, 134 classifications," Walter told the HSCA investigators.[92]

On Monday, November 18, the president met with Florida senator George Smathers, then addressed the Tampa Chamber of Commerce. There followed a lengthy motorcade through the city: according to Tampa police chief J.P. Mullins, the Secret Service told him the only longer presidential motorcade had been through the streets of Berlin. The Secret Service were aware of Milteer's threat (though they may have assumed Milteer was talking about Miami, not Tampa), and told Mullins there had been three other threats, as well. A Secret Service memo dated November 8 said a "white male, 20, slender build" had threatened to shoot the president. Mullins and Sarasota County sheriff Ross E. Boyer both told the *Tampa Tribune* that they had been warned in advance of an assassination attempt.[93]

In such circumstances, it is strange that they held a motorcade, especially one with two stops: first at MacDill Air Force Base, then at the downtown Armory. Obviously the air base was accessible by air, so why didn't the Secret Service insist the president cancel the Armory gig, and fly securely into and out of MacDill? Mullins said the Tampa police hadn't been advised of the Chicago assassination plot, but the White House Secret Service detail certainly knew about it. Yet they seem to have learned nothing from it, and to have ignored Milteer's threat and the three Tampa-specific warnings (though the Miami office did ascertain that Milteer was in Georgia, and not in Florida). Once again, the planned route was a dangerous one: it breached the Secret Service's own safety rules with a 90-degree turn directly in front of a tall, unsecured building, the Floridian Hotel. The "bubble top" which fitted over the presidential limo was not used (it was not bulletproof in any case), and President Kennedy stood up several times during the long ride, perhaps to relieve the pressure on his back.[94]

Still, the Tampa police and the federal authorities put on an impressive show of force. Six hundred officers lined the route. Overpasses were supposed to be guarded by police or military units, while the sheriff's office secured the roofs of major buildings. After the Armory, President Kennedy was flown by helicopter to Miami, where he addressed the InterAmerican Press Association in very intemperate terms—calling yet again for a *coup* in Cuba and promising U.S. backing to any Latin American nation to prevent "a communist takeover."[95]

The same day, Abraham Bolden flew to Washington, DC. There, the IRS offered him an undercover job, investigating corrupt practices on Capitol Hill. He was told the job was so secret that he would be given a new identity: "David Baker." Bolden felt uncomfortable about the proposal, and turned the offer down.[96]

Also in Washington, John Robert Glenn testified before the House Committee on UnAmerican Activities: Glenn (no relation to the astronaut) was a former Air Force Intelligence officer who had learned Russian in the military and become an outspoken left-wing activist. Glenn visited Russia and Eastern Europe, supposedly as a travel guide, and joined the FPCC in 1962. After they overstayed their Cuban tourist visas, Glenn and his wife were repatriated at State Department expense. Like Oswald's radio performance, Glenn's HUAC testimony branded the FPCC as a communist front.

According to the Warren Commission, on November 19, both Dallas daily newspapers reported on the president's forthcoming motorcade. The route they described, with its zig-zag turns, was uniquely dangerous. The whole diversion around Dealey Plaza— right on Houston Street, then left onto Elm—was unnecessary. Where the Chicago and Tampa motorcades had involved one risky sharp turn in an area surrounded by tall buildings, this Dallas route involved two.

Some of those involved denied that the route was finalized this early. Secret Service agent Lawson told the Warren Commission that the route was planned along main thoroughfares because "it afforded us a chance to have alternative routes if something happened along the motorcade route." But according to the *Times Herald* dated November 19, Chief Curry, Sheriff Decker, and Department of Public Safety Major Guy Smith had all "been in on the planning" of the parade route, and "a White House representative in Dallas released the motorcade route." Who was that? The HCSA revealed it was Bill Moyers, the director of the Peace Corps and a Texan friend of Lyndon Johnson. Moyers had been persuaded by O'Donnell and the president to go back to Texas and calm infighting among the Democrats. He told the HCSA that he'd insisted the route be published, so that large crowds would turn out. This was what the president wanted: it was the reason for the motorcade.

That day, President Kennedy met with Jean Daniel, a French journalist, and friend of Ben Bradlee's. Daniel passed along a message from Castro: that he would meet an American official if the U.S. was interested in "normalizing" relations. Kennedy declined to send an envoy, but expressed interest in hearing more. Meanwhile, CIA plans to kill the Cuban leader continued, as did the search for a "suitable" replacement.

November 20 was Bobby's birthday. The Attorney General was 38. The president attended his party on Hickory Hill, then returned to the White House to prepare for his Texas trip. In New Orleans, General Walker had a long meeting with Leander Perez, the political boss of Plaquemines Parish. He later met with a group of 35 "conservative political leaders," according to a police spy who was unable to gain entrance. At Red Bird Airport, outside Dallas, three young people enquired about renting a plane in two days' time, to fly to the Yucatán. Wayne January, the plane's owner, declined to do business with them, suspecting they were hijackers. After the assassination, January identified one of the three as Lee Harvey Oswald. The same day, most of the cabinet and senior military left Washington, DC, for Honolulu, where they were to confer on the situation in Vietnam.

That evening, police in Eunice, Louisiana, picked up a heroin addict, Rose Cheramie, who had been hit by a car. She told State Police lieutenant Francis Fruge that she had been traveling from Miami to Dallas with two men, who had stopped at a bar in Eunice, and threw her out. Cheramie said the purpose of their trip was "to pick up some money, pick up her baby, and to kill Kennedy." She told a complex tale in which the two men would kill the president in Dallas while she checked into a hotel in Houston and collected ten kilos of heroin from a sailor. Fruge, who checked Cheramie into East Louisiana State Hospital, did not believe her.[97]

At 2 a.m., the police spy, sitting in the lobby of the Hotel Jung in New Orleans, saw General Walker head upstairs.[98]

On November 21, Jack Ruby, proprietor of the Carousel Club in Dallas, visited the office of oil man Lamar Hunt. Around the same time, Hunt also received a visit from a Los Angeles gangster, Eugene Brading, a.k.a. Jim Braden. Recently out of prison, Braden had received permission from his parole officer to travel to Texas "on oil business." The nature of Braden's and Hunt's business is unknown. Agent Hosty advised the local Secret Service office of a handbill, circulating on the streets of Dallas, which featured Jack Kennedy's mugshot and the words WANTED FOR TREASON. Undeterred, the president departed for his Texas campaign trip. Jackie accompanied him: it was the first political journey she had taken since the election campaign of 1960. At 5 p.m., the Dallas Police Department and the Secret Service held a joint coordinating meeting: among those present were Chief Curry, assistant chief Charles Batchelor, and Secret Service agents Sorrels and Lawson. Lawson told Curry that he could not include a DPD car in the parade, and warned the Dallas officers that the president did not want any motorcycles alongside his limousine; the police bikes were to stay back behind the presidential car.

Curry gave a brief interview to NBC, where he was asked about the possibility of anti-Kennedy demonstrations in Dallas the next day.

> Q: Has any order gone out for special surveillance of any persons for tomorrow?
>
> A: We have one or two persons under surveillance and have interviewed one or two people previous to today and I would say we would probably be aware of the movements of a few people tomorrow.[99]

Was Curry referring to two potentially violent, Dallas-based suspects, or four, or more? Who were they?

1963 YEAR OF THE PATSY

Crowds cheered the president in San Antonio and Houston, where his limousine was flanked, as usual, by six police motorcycles. In San Antonio he dedicated the Aerospace Medical Center; in Houston he attended a testimonial dinner for the local congressman. In New Orleans, General Walker met with 90 adherents at the Jung Hotel.

Lee Harvey Oswald spent the evening in Irving, at Ruth's house, with Marina and the kids.

In the film *Nixon* there is a scene where, the night before Jack Kennedy's murder, Richard Nixon, Lyndon Johnson, and J. Edgar Hoover meet in the home of Clint Murchison, in Dallas, to plot the assassination, and the division of the spoils. This meeting is a conspiracy theorist's golden dream, since it places the next two presidents, Republican and Democrat, in the same room as the men who made their presidencies possible: the chief of the secret police and a homicidal Texas oil man... It's a formidable image, highly dramatic. Its print source was a short article by Penn Jones in the *Midlothian Mirror*. Jones was convinced the story was true, but would not reveal his source: according to Texan researcher Gary Mack, Jones heard the story from a chauffeur at the event. The Murchison in question was presumably Clint Jr., since his father, "Big" Clint, had suffered a stroke in 1958 and was extremely frail.[100]

The story of a conspirators' party at Murchison's resurfaced in 1992, when Madeleine Brown announced, on the TV show *A Current Affair*, that she had been Johnson's mistress and had attended the planning meeting with her lover. Brown confirmed Penn Jones' story, adding Clyde Tolson (Hoover's lover and FBI top brass), John J. McCloy, and H.L. Hunt to the guest list. Brown published a book in which she expanded the list further. According to Brown, Lyndon told her, "After tomorrow those goddamn Kennedys will never embarrass me again!"[101]

Was Brown telling the truth? Was she really Johnson's mistress? Johnson had mistresses, but there is no corroborating evidence that Brown was one. Brown also had a history of dishonesty, having been convicted of forging a relative's will.[102]

Her story—ghostwritten by an assassination researcher, Harrison Livingstone—appears to be an invention. Penn Jones definitely believed the meeting had occurred. As he wrote, it would make sense that the plotters and principal beneficiaries of a close-knit *coup* plot would get together for a last-minute "planning session." But did they? Richard Nixon was in Dallas that night, acting as a lawyer for the Pepsi-Cola company, attending a bottlers' convention. He had a partial alibi, as he was seen escorting Joan Crawford to a comedy show at the Statler Hilton. There is no firm evidence that J. Edgar Hoover was in Dallas. Lyndon Johnson was never far away, but his itinerary kept him beside the president for dinner and speeches at the Houston Coliseum, then in flight to Carswell Air Force Base, then in a convoy with the president to the Hotel Texas, arriving around 11:50 p.m.

Jack and Jackie slept that night in a Fort Worth hotel suite, decorated with Picassos, Monets, and Van Goghs borrowed from local art collectors.

notes

1 George de Mohrenschildt, *I Am A Patsy! I Am A Patsy!* (Appendix to HSCA Report on George de Mohrenschildt, 270 pp.).
2 Martha A. Moyer and R.F. Gallagher, "The Babysitters," *The Fourth Decade*, Vol. 3, No. 6, Sept. 1996, pp. 3–10; Carol Hewett, Esq., "The Paines Know: Lurking in the Shadows of the Walker Shooting," *Probe*, Vol. 5, No. 1, Nov.–Dec. 1997, pp. 11–18; Barbara LaMonica, "Michael Paine and his $300,000 Trust Fund," *Probe*, Vol. 5, No. 5, Jul.–Aug. 1998, pp. 6–7.
3 Carol Hewett, Barbara LaMonica and Steve Jones, "Ruth Paine: Social Activist or Contra Support Networker?", *Probe*, Vol. 3, No. 5, July–Aug. 1996, pp. 8–11.
4 Paul Lewis & Rob Evans, "Mark Kennedy: A Journey From Undercover Cop to 'Bona Fide' Activist," *The Guardian*, Jan. 10, 2011; "Mark Kennedy Case: Independent Inquiry Ordered Over CPS Claims," *The Guardian*, June 9, 2011.
5 Trevor Aaronson, "Terror Trials by the Numbers," *Mother Jones*, Sept.-Oct. 2011, pp. 36–37.
6 Ray and Mary La Fontaine, *Oswald Talked: The New Evidence in the JFK Assassination*, Pelican, LA, 1996, pp. 280–91, 316; Michael L. Kurtz, *The JFK Assassination Debates*, UP Kansas, 2006, p. 152.
7 Whether or not the FBI really opened and closed Oswald's file is unclear. According to John Newman and James W. Douglass, Oswald remained of interest to the FBI via a FLASH notice, designating him a possible enemy agent, throughout this period. Newman, "Oswald, the CIA and Mexico City", *Probe*, p. 4; Douglass, *JFK & The Unspeakable*, Orbis Books, NY, 2008, p. 178.
8 Timothy Cwiek, "Backyard Photos and the Paine Connection," *The Third Decade*, Vol. 1, No. 6, Sept. 1985, pp. 10–13.
9 HCSA, Vol. 4, Para 427.

10 John J. Johnson, "Bobby Brown and 'Oswald's Ghosts,'" *The Fourth Decade*, Vol. 5, No. 1, Nov. 1997, pp. 3–7; La Fontaines, *Oswald Talked*, pp. 385–7, 440).

11 Edgar F. Tatro, "The Congress of Freedom Papers," *The Third Decade*, Vol. 2, No. 2, pp. 6–10.

12 La Fontaines, Oswald Talked, p. 143; Jerry D. Rose, "Nut Country: The Friends of General Walker," *The Third Decade*, Vol. 5, No. 5, July 1989, pp. 12–17; Jerry D. Rose, "Oswald and the Nazis," *The Fourth Decade*, Vol. 3, No. 2, Jan. 1996, pp. 21–25.

13 Lisa Pease, "Thomas J. Dodd & Son: Corruption of Blood?", *Probe*, Vol. 3, No. 5, July–Aug. 1996, pp. 18–23; George Michael Evica, "And We Are Still Mortal: Thomas Dodd & Lee Harvey Oswald", *The Assassination Chronicles*, March 1996, p. 22.

14 Evelyn Lincoln, *Kennedy & Johnson*, Holt, Rinehart, NY, 1968, p. 182.

15 Jerry D. Rose, "A Fine Basic Pamplet: Oswald and Corliss Lamont," *The Fourth Decade*, Vol. 7, No. 5, July 2000, pp. 3–7.

16 James DiEugenio, *Destiny Betrayed: JFK, Cuba, and the Garrison Case*, Sheridan Press, NY, 1992, pp. 218–219.

17 Edisen's story was published for the first time in the Nov. 1991 issue of *The Third Decade*—Vol. 8, No. 1—as "From April to November and Back Again," under the pseudonym of "K.S. Turner".

18 Bill Kelly, "Follow Up: In Search of Jose Rivera," *The Third Decade*, Vol. 9, No. 1, Nov. 1992, pp. 43–44; Alan Houston, "An Update on Jose Rivera," *The Fourth Decade*, Vol. 4, No. 6, pp. 7–8.

19 WH 22, CE No. 1404, p. 786.

20 David Wise, *The Invisible Government*, Random House, 1964; Peter Whitmey, "The Man Who Heard Too Much," *The Third Decade*, Vol. 7, No. 1, Nov. 1990, pp. 23–24; Peter Whitmey, Letter to the Editor, *The Third Decade*, Vol. 9, No. 5, July 1993, pp. 13–14.

21 Clarence B. Jones, *Behind The Dream*, Palgrave 2012, pp 73-77.

22 CIA memo to file from M.D. Stevens, dated January 31, 1964, document # 1307-475.

23 Kurtz, *The JFK Assassination Debates*, pp 158, 189. Regarding Leake, Jim DiEugenio, in *The Obstruction of Garrison*, *The Assassinations*, p. 44, refers to him as "of the New Orleans [CIA] office"; a CIA document dated 1967 and released in 1993—Record Number 104-10133-10441—entitled *Memo re. Interview With Hunter C. Leake* is *not* an interview with Leake; it is an account of an interview, *by* Leake "of this office," of Carlos Bringuier.

24 According to the FBI report, Oswald received his library card five days later, on May 27. This and subsequent New Orleans library visits are listed in WH 25, CE No. 2650.

25 Jerry D. Rose, "You Don't Know Me But You Will," *The Third Decade*, Vol. 4 No. 1, Nov. 1987, pp. 17–19; WH 26 CE No. 2981: FBI Report on William McEwan Duff.

26 Frank de Benedictis, "Oswald, Banister and V.T. Lee," *The Fourth Decade*, Vol. 3, No. 4, May 1996, pp. 18–24.

27 Bryant, *The Bystander*, p. 406.

28 Jim Marrs, *Crossfire*, Carrol & Graf, 1989, pp. 275–276.

29 Rose, *You Don't Know Me But You Will*, pp. 17–19; WH 26 CE 2981, FBI Report on William McEwan Duff.

30 It's also been suggested that the misnaming of documents, including Oswald's, was part of a mole-hunt instigated within CIA by James Angleton. In spy

jargon this was apparently called a "barium meal." For a long discussion, see Peter Dale Scott, "Oswald and the Hunt for Popov's Mole," *The Fourth Decade*, Vol. 3 No. 3, Mar. 1996, pp. 3–38.

31 Turner, *Power on the Right*, pp. 106–8.

32 Kurtz, *The JFK Assassination Debates*, pp. 159–160. It is unclear whether "Connie" Martin was related to Jack Martin, one of Banister's investigators.

33 La Fontaines, *Oswald Talked*, pp. 181–182.

34 Summers, *Conspiracy*, pp. 312–313. Summers interviewed Alba.

35 William Weston, "Oswald: Peace Activist in Pennsylvania?", *Probe*, Vol. 4, No. 3, March-April 1997, pp. 4–8.

36 Michael L. Kurtz, "Lee Harvey Oswald in New Orleans: a Reappraisal", *Louisiana History*, Louisiana Historical Society, Winter 1980, Vol. XXI, No. 10, pp. 7–23.

37 Patsy Sims, *The Klan*, Stein & Day, NY, 1978, pp. 163, 291, per *The Fourth Decade*, Vol. 3, No. 1, p. 27.

38 Rose, *Nut Country*, pp. 13–15.

39 Sylvia Meagher, "Oswald's Arrest In New Orleans," *The Third Decade*, Vol. 1, No. 2, Jan. 1985, pp. 1–12.

40 Schlesinger, *A Thousand Days*, p. 833.

41 WH 21, Stuckey Exhibit No. 2, p. 631.

42 Jerry D. Rose, "INCA Dinka Do," *The Fourth Decade*, Vol. 4, No. 3, March 1997, pp. 28–31.

43 For some reason the Warren Commission's transcript of Oswald's words is incorrect. WH 21, p. 639, Stuckey Exhibit No. 3, quotes Oswald as saying "I was not under the protection of the—that is to say I was not under the protection of the American government." In fact, Oswald did not repeat himself: he corrected himself. Today, an Internet search for the audio file of the Oswald / Stuckey debate is easy; in 1964, most people were obliged to rely on Warren's entirely misleading transcription.

44 Lisa Pease, "Dodd Part II: New Orleans and the Cover-Up," *Probe*, Vol. 3, No. 6, Sept.–Oct. 1996, pp. 12–13.

45 Philip Melanson, "'Leftist' Lee At Work: The Great Debate & The Paper Chase," *The Third Decade*, Vol. 2, No. 5, July 1986, pp. 1–6; Melanson's *Spy Saga: Lee Harvey Oswald and U.S. Intelligence*, Praeger, NY, 1970, pp. 71–74, pursues the evidence that Oswald was deliberately trying to link U.S. leftist groups to the American Communist Party.

46 Thomas Donahue, "Gaeton Fonzi and Anthony Summers on 'Maurice Bishop': A Synthesis of the Key Evidence," *The Fourth Decade*, Vol. 1 No. 4, May 1994, pp. 14–19.

47 Summers, *Conspiracy*, pp. 356–7.

48 William Weston, "The Schoolbook Businessman," *The Fourth Decade*, Vol. 6, No. 5, July 1999, pp. 4–10.

49 HSCA, *Oswald in Clinton, LA, Final Assassinations Report*, pp. 170–171.

50 William Holden, "New Evidence Regarding Oswald's Activities in Clinton, Louisiana," *The Fourth Decade*, Vol. 4, No. 1, Nov. 1996, pp. 5–18.

51 HSCA Vol. 9, 5F viii. *Robert Ray McKeown*, pp. 587–801.

52 Summers, *Conspiracy*, pp. 363–365.

53 Kurtz, *The JFK Assassination Debates*, pp. 161–162, 167.

54 The tale of Nagell is scrupulously told by Dick Russell in *The Man Who Knew Too Much*, Carroll & Graf, NY, 1992 (824 pp.); his demise is recorded in "The Life & Death of Richard Case Nagell," *Probe*, Vol. 3, No. 1, Nov.–Dec. 1995, pp. 1–3. Two pages of *The Private Correspondence of Richard Case Nagell* in the same issue of *Probe* (pp. 5–6) suggest that he was insane.

55 Mark Lane, *Plausible Denial: Was the CIA Involved in the Assassination of JFK?*, Thunder's Mouth, NY, 1991, p. 66.

56 Jerry D. Rose, "The Trip That Never Was," *The Third Decade*, Vol. 1, No. 5, July 1985, pp. 9–16; John Newman, "Oswald, the CIA and Mexico City: Fingerprints of Conspiracy," *Probe*, Vol. 6, No. 6, Sept.–Oct. 1999, pp. 1–5, 29.

57 Lane, *Plausible Denial*, p. 82.

58 WH 14 CE No. 2137, pp. 732–734.

59 Jim DiEugenio, "Silvia Odio vs. Liebeler & the La Fontaines," *Probe*, Vol. 3, No. 6, Sept.-Oct. 1996, pp. 6–9.

60 Turner, *Power on the Right*, pp. 105–106.

61 *New Orleans States Item*, May 1, 1968; Paris Flammonde, *The Kennedy Conspiracy*, Meredith, NY, 1969, p. 204.

62 *National Enquirer*, Sept. 1, 1968; Flammonde, *The Kennedy Conspiracy*, pp. 205–206.

63 William Seymour, "The CIA's Man For All Nations," *Gung Ho!*, May 1982.

64 Kirk Bowman, *Militarization and Democracy in Honduras, 1954–1963*, The Sam Nunn School of International Affairs, Georgia Institute of Technology, Atlanta, GA.

65 Newman, "Oswald, the CIA and Mexico City," *Probe*, p. 4; Douglass, *JFK & The Unspeakable*, p. 178.

66 See also James K. Galbraith, "Exit Strategy," *Boston Review*, Oct.–Nov. 2003; Bryan Bender, "Papers Reveal JFK Efforts on Vietnam," *Boston Globe*, June 6, 2005.

67 William Weston, "The Fifth Floor Sniper," *The Third Decade*, Vol. 9, No. 4, July 1993, pp. 22–33; "The Transplantation of the Texas School Book Depository," *The Third Decade*, Vol. 9, No. 6, Sept. 1993, pp. 23–32; "411 Elm St.," *The Fourth Decade*, Vol. 1, No. 4, May 1994, pp. 24–29; "The Glaze Letters," *The Fourth Decade*, Vol. 6, No. 4, May 1999, pp. 6–13; "The Schoolbook Businessman," *The Fourth Decade*, Vol. 6, No. 5, July 1999, pp. 4–10.

68 William Weston, "The Glaze Letters," *The Fourth Decade*, Vol. 6, No. 4, May 1999, pp. 10–12.

69 Priscilla Johnson McMillan, *Marina and Lee*, Harper and Row, NY, 1977, pp. 379, 380.

70 Martin Shackelford, "Frank Sinatra's Assassination Role," *The Third Decade*, Vol. 1, No. 6, Sept. 1985, pp. 13–17.

71 Philip H. Melanson, "Dallas Mosaic: The Cops, the Cubans, and the Company," *The Third Decade*, Vol. 1, No. 3, March 1985, pp. 12–13.

72 Melanson, "Dallas Mosaic," *The Third Decade*, pp. 8–9.

73 According to WH 22 CE No. 1151, an ACLU member, Barry M. Cohen, "appeared voluntarily at the Dallas office of the FBI," to report that Oswald was present at the meeting as a guest of Ruth, not Michael, Paine. The Report ignored his testimony.

74 The Chicago assassination attempt—once a mere footnote in "conspiracy" books—has been more thoroughly documented in recent years. The story broke with Edwin Black's "The Plot to Kill JFK in Chicago", published in the *Chicago Independent* of November 1975. James W. Douglass interviewed Abraham Bolden several times and provides a detailed narrative of the Chicago events in *JFK and the Unspeakable* (pp. 200–214). Bolden's own book, *The Echo from Dealey Plaza*, deals with part of the Chicago story.

75 Bill Kelly, *Collins Radio, Back Channels*, Vol. 1, No. 4, Summer 1992, pp 1–2.

76 Douglass, *JFK and the Unspeakable*, p. 206; Black, "The Plot to Kill JFK in Chicago", pp. 5–6.

77 Bolden, *Echo From Dealey Plaza*, p. 56.

78 WH 26, 85, pp. 460-462.

79 William Weston, "Oswald and the FBI: Part One," *The Fourth Decade*, Vol. 2, No. 5, July 1995, pp. 45–49.

80 Summers, *Conspiracy*, p. 587.

81 John J. Johnson, "Oswald's Hunt Note," *The Fourth Decade*, Vol. 5, No. 3, March 1998, pp. 23–28.

82 Christopher Andrew and Vasili Mitrokhin, *The Sword and The Shield: The Mitrokhin Archive and the Secret History of the KGB*, Basic Books, NY, 1999, pp. 228–229.

83 Dan Christensen, "JFK, King: The Dade County Links", *Miami Magazine*, Vol. 27, No. 11, Sept 1976; HSCA file 000591, Record Number 180-10090-10220, *Intelligence received by electronic device on Nov. 9, 1963 by the Intelligence Unit of the Miami Police Dept., Miami, Fla.*

84 William Weston, "Oswald & The FBI, Part 2," *The Fourth Decade*, Vol. 2, No. 6, Sept. 1995, pp. 24–31.

85 Jerry D. Rose, "Gifts from Russia: Yeltsin & Mitrokhin," *The Fourth Decade*, Vol. 7, No. 1, Nov. 1999, pp. 3–8.

86 Carol Hewett, Esq., "Ruth Paine 'Finds' Evidence: Oswald's Letter To The Soviet Embassy," *Probe*, Vol. 3, No. 4, March-April 1997, pp. 16–17.

87 Summers, *Conspiracy*, p. 402.

88 Armstrong, "Harvey & Lee," *The Assassinations*, p. 123.

89 WH 25 CE Nos. 2642, 2650.

90 WH17 CE No. 762 is a 50-page Commission Exhibit entitled *United States Secret Service Protective Research Section; Protective Research Cases November 1961 through November 1963*. It lists dozens of threats against President Kennedy, known to the Dallas, Houston, San Antonio and El Paso Secret Service offices.

91 James Ewell, "Oswald Interviewed by FBI on Nov. 16," *Dallas Morning News*, Nov. 24, 1963, sec. 1, p. 11.

92 La Fontaines, *Oswald Talked*, pp. 300–306; HCSA, Walter Testimony, pp. 3–5, 10.

93 "Threats On Kennedy Made Here," *Tampa Tribune*, Nov 23, 1963.

94 Waldron and Hartmann, *Ultimate Sacrifice*, pp. 684–696.

95 WH 26 CE No. 2695, "Kennedy Virtually Invites Cuban Coup," *Dallas Times Herald*, Nov. 19, 1963.

96 Bolden, *Echo From Dealey Plaza*, pp. 47–49; Douglass, *JFK and the Unspeakable*, p. 214.

97 Jim DiEugenio, "Rose Cheramie: How She Predicted the JFK Assassination," *The Assassinations*, pp. 225–237.

98 Jerry D. Rose, "Nut Country II: Whatever Happened to Elsa Silbernagel?" *The Third Decade*, Vol. 6, No. 4, May 1990, pp. 1–5.

99 WH 25 CE No. 2395.

100 Penn Jones, Jr. "Forgive My Grief III Revised," *Midlothian Mirror*, Texas, 1976, pp. 84–86.

101 Madeleine Brown, *Texas In The Morning: The Love Story of Madeleine Brown and President Lyndon Baines Johnson*, Conservatory Press, Baltimore, MD, 1997; "Dallas Woman Claims She Was LBJ's Lover," *Dallas Morning News*, Nov. 6, 1992.

102 F9103481 M. Brown vs. State of Texas.

CHAPTER 8

NOVEMBER 22, 1963
St. Cecilia's Day

★ ★ ★

The President, always of a fatalistic turn of mind, was increasingly preoccupied with matters of mortality. He spoke often about the assassination of Lincoln, and taught his infant daughter, Caroline, a poem by Alan Seeger, an American killed in World War I. It began, "I have a rendezvous with death..."

> "...But I've a rendezvous with Death
> At midnight in some flaming town,
> When Spring trips north again this year,
> And I to my pledged word am true,
> I shall not fail that rendezvous."

So here Jack Kennedy was, dressing, on a cold, wet morning in Fort Worth, Texas, in a suite filled with borrowed works of art, remarking to Jackie and Ken O'Donnell how, "if anybody really wanted to shoot the President of the United States, it was not a very difficult job—all one had to do was get on a high building some day with a telescopic rifle..."

How tired they must all have felt. Tired, partially, because they had been treated so well. Applauded, over expensive plates of bland food, as the president spoke of substantial increases in military expenditure, of economic growth, of the mission to the Moon and its multiple benefits to the great, Democratic state of Texas. The president and the first lady had been made welcome. There were no hostile, demented crowds, no spitting, placard-waving Birchers. The Texas trip had gone swimmingly so far. But next up was Dallas, and that was something else.

The *Dallas Morning News* carried a full-page, black-bordered ad, welcoming the president and asking him 12 loaded questions. Why was Latin America turning "either anti-American or Communistic"? Why was he selling wheat to the Russians and drinking toasts with Tito? Why had he scrapped the Monroe Doctrine "in favor of the Spirit of Moscow?" It was a Bircher diatribe, paid for by Dallas oil men. The president glanced at the ad and put the paper down. "We're heading into nut country today," he said.

Lee Oswald caught a ride to work from Wesley Frazier. Before he left the Paines' house, he placed his wedding ring and (according to some reports) his wallet on the bedroom table. He reached the Book Depository at eight.[1]

Dallas was the heart of Texas oil country. It was a hard city in a harsh landscape: 20 percent black, entirely unintegrated. But Dallas was also the fastest-growing city in the United States, with the greatest boom in office building anywhere outside New York. H.E. Chiles, one of the petroleum millionaires of neighboring Midland, described their world thus:

"I love this place. There aren't more than thirty days in a year when we can't play golf here. Of course, that means we're sometimes playing in a twenty-mile-an-hour wind, but we're out there..."

"We're on the desert. We might as well face it, and we do. All our windows are weather-stripped. We build walls to keep the sand out. And when the sand is blowing, we stay indoors, just like the goddam Arabs."[2]

Such conditions did not breed political moderates. H.L. Hunt funded numerous extreme-right groups, and had stepped up the attack against the Kennedys when their tax-exempt status was challenged. Hunt's *Life Line* radio broadcasts excoriated the president, accusing him of being a communist and calling for acts of "extreme patriotism." Big Clint Murchison was said to have financed the American Nazi Party: his favorite watering hole was a millionaires' hunting lodge with five artificial lakes—the Koon Kreek Klub. Showing similar taste, Fort Worth oil men wined and dined in a private, whites-only restaurant called the Blackamoor Room. Alongside such brutishness, the Texas rich showed an unquenchable thirst for European culture in the form of Impressionist paintings and Surrealist works by Magritte and Dalí. The art which so beautifully adorned the Kennedys' walls that morning might be seen as a product of cultural anxiety on the part of the recently rich, but it was also an investment.

The Texas super-rich bought art the same way as they reinvested their millions in politics and politicians: they were ambitious, and keen to diversify. An oil magnate might buy a Manet or a Monet and he might take out an advertisement in the newspaper, to "welcome the president." The newspaper ad was not the only document attacking Kennedy that day. There was the handbill (or was it a circular? or a "pamplet"?) which Hosty had warned the Dallas Secret Service about, declaring Kennedy WANTED FOR TREASON. Like the "Welcome Mr. Kennedy" ad, it featured an itemized list of the president's crimes.

The newspaper ad was put together by a group calling itself Conservatism, USA. CUSA was a small group of young Army enlisted men, who had been based in Munich, Germany. Under the influence of their then commander, General Walker, these former "Screaming Eagles" had vowed to resist communism both in Europe and on their return to the United States. The head of CUSA, Laurie Schmidt, had based himself in Dallas, where his brother was, like Scotty Duff, a handyman and chauffeur for the general. After the riot against Stevenson, Schmidt had managed to convince reporters that CUSA was running the conservative resistance; on the basis of this he persuaded two former Munich buddies, Bernard Weissman and William Burley, to join him in Dallas, finding them work as carpet salesmen. Weissman sold no carpets, but he was given the cash for the ad—$1,462—by Joe Grinnon, a Bircher who collected it from Nelson Bunker Hunt and two other oil men, Edgar R. Crissey and H.R. "Bum" Bright. Weissman was persuaded to put his name on the ad, along with a fictitious group, the American Fact-Finding

Committee. (Weissman and Burley quit their jobs and left Dallas a few days after the assassination.)[3]

The WANTED FOR TREASON handbill was the work of Robert Surrey, General Walker's Nazi associate and Agent Hosty's bridge partner. (Surrey and Walker were partners in the American Eagle Publishing Co., which, in January 1964, produced a booklet of clippings from the two Dallas newspapers, entitled *The Assassination Story.*) Surrey, whom the Warren Report described as "a 38-year-old printing salesman" ordered 5,000 of the TREASON flyers from a printer named Robert Krause. He refused to answer any of the Commissioners' questions regarding his handbill, or say who paid for it or who distributed it, pleading the Fifth Amendment.[4]

Why Chief Justice Warren treated this Nazi provocateur with such kid gloves is hard to say. Perhaps because the element common to Surrey's handbill and CUSA's newspaper ad was General Walker, whose particular concerns are evident in both: the handbill complains about Kennedy's support for "communist-inspired racial riots" and claims he "illegally invaded a sovereign state [Mississippi?] with federal troops"; while the newspaper ad questions the president's suppression of right-wing propaganda at U.S. military bases.

Richard Nixon left Dallas at 9:05 a.m., aboard American Airlines Flight 82, bound for New York.

At 9:45, some 200 city and county police officers gathered at the Trade Mart for the day's detail. Sheriff Bill Decker instructed his deputies that they were to be spectators along the motorcade route, and to "take no part in security."

In Fort Worth, Jack Kennedy spoke to a group of businessmen over breakfast. Jackie was late, and the president joked about it, assuring his guests that she was worth the wait. At 10:30 his party left the Texas Hotel for Carswell AFB. Around that time the FBI informant, William Somersett, received a call from Joseph Milteer, who was now in Dallas. Milteer told him that Kennedy would soon be there, and would not be visiting Miami again, then hung up the phone.

FBI agent Hosty had a morning meeting with an IRS agent, Frank Ellsworth, and Edward Coyle, of the 112th Military Intelligence Group—part of the Fourth U.S. Army Division at Fort Sam Houston, which had defied the president with its anticommunist call-to-arms. The meeting took place in Ellsworth's office. On the agenda was the ongoing theft of weapons from Fort Hood. Ellsworth was also running an ATTD investigation into illegal arms traffic in Dallas. His undercover operation to entrap the Minuteman arms dealer, Thomas Masen, had collapsed three days before, when the DPD interrupted an illegal arms deal in which Masen was involved. His cover blown, Ellsworth arrested Masen on lesser charges. He told the Warren Commission,

> "An organization known as the Minutemen is the right-wing group most likely to have been associated with any effort to assassinate the president... The Minutemen are closely tied to General Walker and H.L. Hunt."[5]

There's an obvious parallel between Oswald's recent activities—associating with right-wing groups and illegally purchasing firearms—and those of IRS agent Ellsworth, and of the Minuteman Masen. Ellsworth later told author Dick Russell that Masen was an Oswald "lookalike," and that he believed Masen had impersonated Lee at the Sports Drome Rifle Range.[6]

At 11:03, six members of the cabinet departed Honolulu for further meetings in Japan. Minutes later, Air Force One left Carswell on the short flight to Dallas Love Field, landing at 11:35. As many as 4,000 people were waiting to greet the Kennedys. The first lady was presented with a bouquet of red roses—a strange gift in Texas, where the yellow rose is traditionally preferred. There was a brief reception, much handshaking, and then it was time for Jack and Jackie to join Governor and Mrs. Connally in the limousine. The motorcade departed at 11:50. It was meant to last 40 minutes, and to deposit the president and party at the Trade Mart, where lunch and another speech were planned.

The Kennedys were looking at another busy day of political glad-handing. At 12:30 Jack was scheduled to address the Dallas Citizens Council at the Trade Mart. At 2 p.m. he and Jackie were to leave the Trade Mart for Love Field. At 2:30 Air Force One would take them to Bergstrom Air Force Base. Arriving at 3:15, the president and first lady were to travel, in convoy, to the Commodore Perry Hotel in Austin. An hour later, at 4:15, they would attend a reception given by the Texas State Democratic Committee. At 6 p.m. the Kennedys would leave the hotel for the Governor's Mansion, and a reception with the Connallys. They were scheduled to return to the hotel at 6:45.

It was not over! Ninety minutes later, the Kennedys would depart the hotel again, and convoy to the Municipal Auditorium, where Jack would address $100-a-plate Democratic diners. At 9:30, they would leave for Bergstrom AFB, for a 9:45 p.m. helicopter flight to Lyndon Johnson's ranch, scheduled to touch down at 10:20 that evening. It's possible, I suppose, that Jack Kennedy had grown to love the politics! politics! handshakes! rubber chicken! of it all. But Jackie had not. She disliked the political road, and worried about her husband's health problems. And their Fort Worth/Dallas/Austin itinerary, published in the *Dallas Morning News* three days before, was beyond ambitious—it was a punishing schedule.

With so many things to be done, in such a tight time frame, why have a motorcade at all? Much of the blame for the parade, and its severe security failures, has been placed with Kennedy and his supporters. It seems most likely that the president's staffers *did* want the parade route publicized: as Bill Moyers observed, the parade would only be a success if people knew about it, and turned out for it. But other, more culpable, lapses were blamed on Kennedy. The HSCA reported that "the president said that if the weather was clear, he did not want the protective bubble used on the presidential limousine." Similarly, the Warren Report told us that the president didn't want motorcycle outriders near his car, and didn't want Secret Servicemen riding on his car. Lewis Merletti, the head of the Secret Service during the Clinton presidency, repeated the allegation that Kennedy had ordered the agents off his car, "thwarting" them in their protective duties... We shall see, shortly, whether these claims were true.

Kennedy's visit to Texas was purely political: to raise money, to improve his public profile, and to heal a rift between the liberal wing of the party, led by Ralph Yarborough, and the conservative wing, led by John Connally. It was Connally who had insisted on the Trade Mart as a venue. This was problematic from a security standpoint, but it offered a two-tiered seating arrangement, thus enabling Connally and his cronies to lunch with Kennedy and Johnson while consigning Yarborough's faction to the bleachers.

All of this—the money-raising, lunch and a speech, the ritual humiliation of one faction by another—could have been achieved without a motorcade through the streets of Dallas. On November 15, the *Dallas Morning News* had called a parade "unlikely," citing "a tight schedule and security restrictions." On November 19, according to the

Warren Report, both local papers had carried the description of the uniquely insecure route (Robert Surrey's *Assassination Story* clipping book contains the *Times Herald* version). But this day, November 22, the *Morning News* published a map of the presidential motorcade route which showed the parade proceeding *straight down Main Street* to the freeway, avoiding entirely those deadly right-left turns.

The first vehicle in the procession was Police Chief Curry's car, driven by the Chief himself. Next to Curry sat Winston Lawson, the Secret Service's SAIC. In the back seat rode Sheriff Decker and FBI SAC Forrest Sorrels.

Behind them came the presidential limo, driven by Secret Service agent William Greer, with agent Roy Kellerman riding shotgun. On jump seats immediately behind them rode the Connallys. Mrs. Kennedy and the President sat in the back. Somehow, the press photographers, who usually rode in front of the limousine on a flatbed truck, were relegated to cars near the back of the parade. Two members of the president's Secret Service detail were accidentally left behind at Love Field: one of them, Henry Rybka, was caught on video, waving his arms, trying in vain to flag his vehicle down.

> "The further we got toward town, the denser became the crowds, and when we got down on Main Street, the crowds were extremely thick. They were pushed off of curbs; they were out in the street, and they were backed all the way up against the walls of the buildings... there were at least a quarter of a million people on the parade route that day, and everywhere the reception was good."

Thus remembered John Connally, who felt he could finally relax after worrying about some protest or demonstration. Yet there were incidents along the way. The motorcycle cops who usually flanked the limousine were missing. Twice, children stopped the motorcade: once so that Kennedy could sign an autograph for a little girl, a second time when he caught sight of a Catholic nun and a party of schoolchildren, and climbed out to shake hands.

Bobby Hargis, one of the motorcycle outriders, recalled the president jumping out of the limo to shake hands. "The Secret Service liked to had a conniption fit when he did that," he said, 40 years later. At that moment, Hargis felt a sense of dread wash over him. "They was hoppin' around like cats on a hot roof. It freaked 'em out big time. You could tell how nervous they were."[7]

Ralph Yarborough looked up at the tall office buildings, above the cheering crowds. Like Officer Hargis, he began to feel afraid:

> "They stood there rather stonily. They just stood there looking at the president. And they weren't saying anything... I'd look up there on the second, third, floor, I'd see people through glass windows up there, standing back... They'd be looking down at the president, it looked to me like, with positive hate. I saw them, and I grew apprehensive."

A young man dressed in green Army fatigues collapsed at the corner of Elm and Houston, in Dealey Plaza. He was reported to have suffered an epileptic fit. An ambulance arrived and took the man, Jerry Belknap, to Parkland Hospital. Belknap, claiming he felt much better, declined to see a doctor and walked away. Meanwhile, Lee Bowers, a railroad supervisor whose post overlooked the Plaza, watched three cars cruise through the yards beneath his tower. First came a station wagon with a Goldwater sticker. Then a black '57 Ford. Then a four-door, white Chevy Impala. Separately, each car circled slowly around the parking area. The driver of the Ford seemed to be talking on a two-way radio.

At 12:15, Carolyn Arnold, a secretary at the Book Depository, went to the lunchroom on the second floor. She saw Lee Oswald sitting in one of the booths. "He was alone as usual and appeared to be having lunch. I did not speak to him but I recognized him clearly." Arnold complained in 1978 to the *Dallas Morning News* that the FBI had misquoted her regarding this. The Warren Report places Oswald on the sixth floor at this time, preparing his sniper's nest.

Senator Yarborough saw the sunlit area up ahead. He felt relieved. "I thought, 'I'm glad to see daylight. I'm glad we're through.' I felt safe the minute we got [there]." The sunlit space which reassured him was Dealey Plaza. At the intersection of Main and Houston, Chief Curry's car turned sharp right, skirting the edge of the Plaza. The presidential limo followed it. Behind the limo came the main Secret Service vehicle, with no less than nine agents aboard, protected by their phalanx of motorcycle cops. As they left the corridor of tall buildings, Hargis began to relax. "I thought, 'Well, we've got it made now,'" he recalled. Behind the Secret Service and the bikers came the vice president's car, with Johnson, Lady Bird, and Yarborough...

The crowds were thinning out at last. To their left, Elm Street ran under trees and a railroad bridge, a haven of potential shade. Mrs. Connally turned and said, "Mr. President, you can't say Dallas doesn't love you."

"That's obvious," Jack agreed.

The motorcade made its second prohibited turn in front of the Book Depository, heading down Elm Street. It was 12:30 p.m.

Before Dallas, all Jack Kennedy's motorcades had received full motorcycle "coverage." Each of his previous Texas stops had involved between three and six police Harleys securing both sides of his limousine. Vincent Palamara interviewed a number of those involved in Secret Service preparations for the Texas trip and learned that: 1) Jack Kennedy had never ordered Secret Service agents not to ride on his car; 2) Special Agent Samuel A. Kinney— not Kennedy or Bill Moyers or Ken O'Donnell—made the decision to remove the "bubble top"; 3) the Secret Service in Washington was aware of several threats to kill the president, but had not advised SAIC Sorrels or the other agents in Dallas; 4) the Secret Service, not Kennedy, had ordered the removal of his flanking motorcycle coverage. (Palamara's book, *Survivor's Guilt*, is an extremely thorough examination of the Secret Service's performance in Dallas. He interviewed many of the original participants, and his work is essential reading. It's available in hard copy, and as a free download from the Assassination Research website.)[8]

Whether one approves of Jack Kennedy or not, it's important not to blame the man for things he didn't do. Both the Warren and HSCA Reports imply that Kennedy contributed to his own demise by rejecting Secret Service and police protection. These claims are untrue. Nor was Kennedy responsible for the lack of professionalism which Abraham Bolden observed on the White House detail. Kennedy's bodyguards were, in large part, racist white Southerners. Several had gone out partying in Fort Worth the night before. Now, hungover and sun-blinded, they were clinging to their limo as it made its 120-degree turn.

Just past the Book Depository, on the right, was a grassy knoll, which rolled up to a concrete ramada, and then a low wall and a white stockade fence, shaded by trees. At the foot of the knoll was a sign, black with yellow-white letters, reading *Stemmons Freeway—Keep Right*. Immediately beneath the sign, the president may have noticed something strange. Two men—one in a light blue jacket, one in a dark suit coat—were staring intently at him. The suit-coat man opened an umbrella, and held it above his head. It wasn't raining. Jackie said later:

> "It was terribly hot. Just blinding all of us... Mrs. Connally said, 'We'll soon be there.' We could see a tunnel in front of us. Everything was really slow then. And I remember thinking it would be so cool, under that tunnel."

When the fusillade began, the bodyguards all froze.

Was the first shot even a shot? Or was it a firecracker, or an explosive, tossed into the road in front of the presidential limo? Several witnesses thought they saw or heard a firework. And that might explain why Greer, who was already driving very slowly, *stopped the car*.

The first time it happens, it won't be real...

According to the Warren Report, the presidential limo was picking up speed as it passed the Book Depository. Greer claimed to be driving at 12–15 miles per hour. But many witnesses saw the limo stop. Police officer Earle Brown, standing on the triple railroad overpass—the "tunnel" Mrs. Kennedy had seen—testified that Greer halted the limo. Police officer Marrion Baker testified "several officers said it stopped completely." (Why didn't they testify themselves?) Ralph Yarborough, Mrs. Earle Cabell (in the motorcade), and Roy Truly (standing on the steps of the Depository) all testified that the motorcade came to a complete halt. *Time* and *Newsweek* both reported the motorcade as halting. Hugh Betzner, a witness in Dealey Plaza, told the DPD the cars had stopped. Billy Lovelady, an employee of the Depository, told the FBI, "I recall that following the shooting, I ran toward the spot where *President Kennedy's car had stopped*."[9]

Perched on a nearby plinth, a garment manufacturer, Abraham Zapruder, was one of several people filming the event. His film shows the president clutching his throat as the limo emerges from behind the Stemmons Freeway sign. It depicts the car moving constantly,

NOVEMBER 22,1962 ST. CECILIA'S DAY

though slowing down. While it reveals extreme negligence on the part of Greer, it does not show him bring the limo to a halt.

Yet how many times did Greer need to look back? His training and instructions were to put his foot on the accelerator at the first hint of danger. Instead, Zapruder's film shows the Secret Service driver turning around to look, once, then a second time. What did he expect to see? The bullets were flying. The president, according to Agent Kellerman, had cried out, "My God! I am hit!" The governor was down, too, yelling, "My God, they are going to kill us all!" *They, not he.* Connally had seen action in World War II; perhaps he knew what it felt like to be caught in a crossfire.

Adjacent to the limo now, the man in the suit coat was pumping his umbrella up and down. The man in the blue jacket lifted his right arm, kept it raised.

Hearing the shots ring out, Ralph Yarborough stared, astonished, at the frozen tableau. "All of the Secret Service men seemed to me to respond very slowly, with no more than a puzzled look," he later said. "Knowing something of the training that combat infantrymen and Marines receive, I am amazed at the lack of instantaneous response by the Secret Service when the rifle fire began."

A motorcycle cop, James Chaney, gunned his motor and raced forward, past the stricken limousine. He testified, "I went ahead of the President to inform Chief Curry that the President had been hit." Curry, in the lead car, ahead of the limousine, confirmed this: "A motorcycle officer, I believe it was Officer Chaney, rode up beside us and I asked if something happened back there, and he said, 'Yes.'" *Back there...* So the president's limo was still *behind* Chief Curry's car: Officer Chaney had passed it on his motorcycle, and pulled up beside the chief. Chief Curry's passengers, Lawson and Sorrels, confirmed Curry's and Chaney's testimony. So did motorcycle patrolman Bobby Hargis. *But the Zapruder film does not show Chaney's motorcycle pass.*

After the assassination the Secret Service accompanied Abraham Zapruder to a Kodak lab in Dallas, where his double 8mm film was developed. Supposedly, Kodak had no print stock to make copies, so the developed material was taken to the Jamieson Film Company in Dallas. According to the Warren Commission, Jamieson made three reversal duplicates: they numbered the original #1083, and the copies #1085, #1086, and #1087. One doesn't need to be a mathematical genius to ask, what happened to #1084? According to H.L. Hunt's chief of security, Paul Rothermel, Hunt "purchased" his own copy of the Zapruder film that same evening.[10]

And Homer McMahon, head of the color laboratory at the National Photographic Interpretation Center (NPIC)—a CIA subsidiary—told the AARB that he viewed and analyzed a copy of the Zapruder film that night, or first thing the next day, tried to determine "where the three shots hit," and made enlargements of various frames.[11]

Which version of the film did NPIC get: #1084? Or was that Hunt's personal copy? Neither print is accounted for by the official version, which claims two of the copies were kept by the Secret Service, and the third sold, along with the original film, to *Time* magazine. In 1975 *Time* returned the original film to Zapruder's family, who deposited it with the National Archives.

Several versions of the film have been released over the years. All are different; all have missing frames or frames whose order was reversed. Today, the "official" version of the film in the National Archives contains two splices: places where the film was cut, and frames were lost. The film shows visual and spatial abnormalities: photographic experts have declared it a multi-layered matte, more convincing than the Oswald "backyard" photomontages, but far from perfect. John Costella draws attention to several visual fabrications in his article "A Scientist's Verdict".[12]

Costella singles out as fraudulent the Stemmons Freeway sign, which blocks our view of the assassination for many crucial frames. The rest of the Zapruder film shows pincushion distortion: a noticeable warping of the image at the edges of the frame. Such a photographic phenomenon is to be expected, given the consumer camera Zapruder used: a Bell and Howell 414PD Zoomatic. But the Stemmons Freeway sign, entering frame right and exiting frame left, exhibits no pincushion distortion. Its lines, and the bright stanchions which support it, are straight at all times. If the sign was shot with a different lens, and matted into the Zapruder footage, then the film is a fake, and one must ask: what other alterations have been made to this "official" visual record? And why was the record altered? Two possible motives might be 1) to conceal the fact that Greer halted the limo, and 2) to shorten the "official" duration of the fusillade. The removal of frames would explain why Zapruder's film contradicts the witness testimony, and why we don't see Chaney overtake the limousine. Such visual effects as the frame deletions and the insertion of fake elements would have demanded skill to pull off, quickly, and without detection. But they were certainly possible.

The bullets were still flying. John Ready, a Secret Service agent, jumped down and ran for the limo. SAIC Emory Roberts called Ready back. Clint Hill, the agent tasked with protecting Jackie, ran for the limo anyway.

How long did it all last? Several seconds. Then a shot, fired from the front and to the right, tore the back off the president's head and sent a fine spray of blood and water into the air.

Jackie was on the trunk of the limo, scrambling to rescue her husband's brains. Agent Hill pulled her back into the seat as the convoy began to gather speed. A dispatcher or motorcycle cop had left his mike open, paralyzing police communications. SAIC Roberts picked up his in-car phone: "Escort us to the nearest hospital—fast but at a safe speed."

Who was shooting? The Warren Report placed Lee Harvey Oswald behind his sniper scope, on the sixth floor of the Book Depository, alone. Several eyewitnesses reported seeing an armed man up there, but none of them described Oswald. The HSCA located Oswald there as well, but with an accomplice, a second assassin, shooting from the fence behind the knoll. Immediately after the fusillade, as the motorcade sped up, police and bystanders were described as rushing "towards the grassy knoll." In fact some 13 people converged not on the knoll itself but on the northwest corner of the Plaza, where the railroad bridge and the stockade fence meet. Chief Curry's first orders after the shooting stopped were to "Get a man on top of that triple underpass and see what happened up there." Sheriff Decker, riding in the car with Curry, ordered his dispatcher to "move all available men out of my department back into the railroad yards."

No gunman was found on the bridge or on the grassy knoll. Years later, researcher Jack Brazil sent a man into the drainage system beneath Dealey Plaza. He found a dual storm drain opening at the northwest corner, behind the stockade fence. One drain runs to the County Jail on the east side of the Plaza. The other leads to the Trinity River. Brazil's investigator made it, via the storm drain, from Dealey Plaza to the River in 54 minutes.[13]

Several people saw smoke rising from the trees behind the knoll. Sam Holland, a signal supervisor standing on the railroad bridge, saw "a puff of smoke still lingering underneath the trees in front of

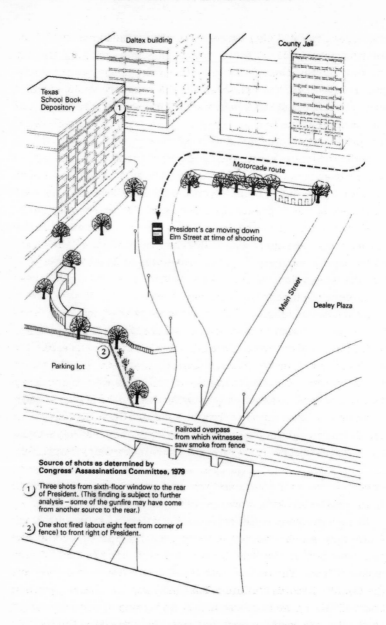

Dealey Plaza, November 22, 1963

Fig. 8: Elegant map of Dealey Plaza, from Anthony Summers' book *Conspiracy*.

the wooden fence." Other witnesses on the bridge agreed with him. Another witness, Ed Hoffman, saw a man in a dark suit, tie, and overcoat running through the railroad yards, carrying an automatic rifle. Per Hoffman, the man threw the rifle to an accomplice dressed as a railroad worker, and both walked in different directions. Lee Bowers, still at his post, reported two men behind the picket fence just prior to the fusillade.

Where had the other shots come from? Witnesses reported gunfire coming from above, and behind, the motorcade. The motorcycle cop, Marrion Baker, saw pigeons fly up from the Book Depository roof, and raced up the steps into the building. Roy Truly ID'd himself as the building manager, and tried to call an elevator, but both were locked in place on upper floors. So Baker and Truly took the stairs, and on the second floor ran into Lee Oswald. As Baker told the FBI, "On the second floor where the lunchroom is located, I saw a man standing in the lunchroom drinking a Coke."

At most, two minutes had passed since the last gunshot. When the Warren Commission reported Baker's testimony, his words "drinking a Coke" were omitted. Oswald, after murdering the president, had, per the Commissioners, run down four flights of stairs. He had not broken into a sweat. His hands were not shaking. The Report distorted Baker's testimony—as it did with many other witnesses—because the truth was problematic. Killing the president and then racing four floors down to the lunchroom... to buy a Coca-Cola? It was absurd. All within 120 seconds? Probably impossible. Back in the real world, Truly identified Oswald as an employee and Baker hurried on, up the stairs toward the roof, where the assassin might still be breaking down his gun...

But there were three other tall buildings behind the Book Depository which shared the same deadly trajectory. None had been searched by the Secret Service. And there were armed men in two of them. The first was the Dal-Tex Building. The second was the County Records Building. The third was the Dallas Criminal Courts Building, and County Jail. As one group of police cordoned off the Book Depository, another group began to search the Dal-Tex building, floor by floor. Almost immediately, a "young man" was arrested for being in the building "without a good excuse." Josiah Thompson interviewed two witnesses to the arrest and described their testimony thus:

"Dressed in a black leather jacket and black gloves, he was led out of the building by two uniformed police officers. To the catcalls of the assembled crowd he was ushered into a waiting police car, which quickly drove off."[14]

The Warren Report said that the young man was taken to the sheriff's office. But the sheriff's office had no record of his interrogation or arrest. Who was this man? A Cuban expatriate, Emilio Santana, allegedly testified to an Orleans Parish grand jury that he fired two shots at the motorcade. His sniper's nest, he said, was the Dal-Tex Building. He also claimed he'd been recruited by CIA in 1962. In return for his testimony, the story goes, Jim Garrison gave Santana immunity and let him leave the U.S. Numerous good-for-nothings have claimed to be Dealey Plaza assassins or facilitators, over the years, and this story may be just another fantasy. Santana's New Orleans testimony has not surfaced: he was one of two men Rose Cheramie named as being en route to kill the president, two days previously.[15]

Meanwhile, other men were being arrested in the Dal-Tex Building. One was Jim Braden, a.k.a. Eugene Brading, who had met Lamar Hunt (and possibly Jack Ruby) the previous afternoon. What was he doing there? Taking the freight elevator to the third floor, he explained, to use the pay phone. The sheriffs detained him for "acting suspiciously" and took him in for questioning. But he convinced them he was in Dealey Plaza by chance, and was released a few hours later. The other arrestee was Larry Florer, who, nabbed in the Dal-Tex Building at the same time, told the same story as Braden. Both men signed notarized statements that they had needed to use the phone, had been directed, by a lady who worked there, to the third floor of the Dal-Tex Building, only to discover no phones were available. Braden was arrested in the lobby; Florer on the street outside.[16]

Braden's and Florer's stories are so similar that they suggest coordination. It seems unlikely that an interviewing deputy got the two stories confused; each man signed his individual testimony, different notaries countersigned. Braden and Florer did not look similar: Braden was 49 years old, wearing a black hat with a wide band marked with Xs; Florer was 23, stout, and bare-headed. Interestingly, Florer's arrest was filmed by news cameras (a reporter said he had been arrested in the Book Depository), and footage was also shot of him being interviewed by a DPD detective. Was Florer's 15 minutes of fame coincidental, or was he being set up as an additional "patsy," if one were needed?

Like Braden and Santana, Florer was held and then released.

In a series of short articles, Penn Jones named one of Bill Decker's deputies as a possible sniper. Deputy Sheriff Harry Weatherford, Jones wrote, was "an expert rifleman, assigned to the top of the Dallas County jail with a rifle at the time the presidential parade passed." Jones had promoted the story of a conspirators' meeting at the Murchison mansion: was his information about Weatherford any more reliable? Other sources reported extreme right-wing tendencies among the peace officers of Dallas. This would not be surprising. If, as one informant claimed, many DPD officers were Klansmen, what about the sheriffs? Were there more violent, organized, racist right-wingers in their midst, or fewer? Jones wrote several articles about Weatherford, claiming the deputy sheriff had admitted extrajudicial killings. The deputy did not respond. The Warren Commission placed him "outside the Sheriff's Office watching the Presidential Motorcade."[17]

(Various witnesses saw one or more people in the windows of the Book Depository—on the fifth, sixth, and seventh floors. Some said they saw a man with a short, automatic rifle. Would professional assassins choose the Book Depository as a sniper's nest? It provided great views, but somewhat limited opportunities for escape. Two freight elevators would reach the ground floor slowly; two passenger elevators and one staircase led to the lobby, from which one could exit via the front, on Elm, or via the loading dock, on Houston. Strangers would have to leave fast, or risk getting arrested—as they were in the Dal-Tex Building. Only an employee, such as Lee Oswald, Buell Frazier, or the other warehouse men, could count on making an exit after the fusillade.)

Over the decades, numerous candidates have been proposed as the killer behind the fence, among them Dallas policemen in uniform (J.D. Tippit and Roscoe White), Watergate burglars (E. Howard Hunt and Frank Sturgis), a Corsican hit-man (Lucien Sarti), an American *mafioso* (Charles Nicoletti), a Native American gunman (Loy Factor), a Cuban terrorist (Luis Posada Carilles), a French terrorist (Jean-Rene Soutre a.k.a. Michael Mertz) and the father of the movie actor Woody Harrelson. A salesman at Downtown Lincoln-Mercury, Jack

Lawrence, was reported to have staggered into work, spattered in mud, and vomiting, a half-hour after the assassination. Lawrence—a colleague of Albert Bogard, who took "Lee Oswald" for that memorable test ride—had borrowed one of the dealership's cars, then abandoned it. Two salesmen later reported that Lawrence left the vehicle in the railroad yard behind the grassy knoll. Lawrence was never officially interviewed about these damning accusations, which he denied to researcher Sheldon Inkol. Another possible lurker behind that fence was Jack Ruby's handyman, Larry Crafard. Crafard (whose real name was Curtis Laverne Craford) fled Dallas the day after the president's murder, protesting his innocence. He later told author Peter Whitmey that, while living in San Francisco, he had been a hit man, i.e., a professional assassin, but maintained that he was innocent of any involvement in the Kennedy crime.[18]

And what of the umbrella man? As the convoy sped away, he and his dark-skinned companion sat calmly down at the foot of the Stemmons Freeway sign. They remained seated for a while, then got up, and walked in different directions. Years later a man named Louie Witt told the HSCA he was the umbrella man. He claimed his was a spontaneous political protest, and that he had not witnessed the killing as the umbrella blocked his view. This was not true: the umbrella was held high as the president passed. Both the umbrella man and his companion had a ringside view of the shooting gallery. R.B. Cutler, architect and author, told me that Gordon Novel, "the illegitimate son of the entertainer, Billy Rose," was the umbrella man. Novel was a CIA-connected electronics specialist, and Cutler believed that the umbrella was a CIA-developed weapon, capable of firing a poison dart, or *flechette*. Though this sounds entirely ridiculous, such weapons did exist, courtesy of the generous funding granted CIA by Presidents Eisenhower and Kennedy. A Department of Defense weapons engineer, Charles Senseney, testified to the Church Committee that he and colleagues had developed the M-1 dart launcher for the CIA: the device fired incapacitating darts out of a pen, an umbrella, or a cane.[19]

And what about the dark-skinned man? He has never been ID'd. While seated, he appeared to take something from his back pocket and hold it to his mouth. Was it a walkie-talkie? Why was this individual never identified, by the FBI or HSCA? He seems like a dead ringer for one of Oswald's New Orleans associates—the youth who helped him hand out flyers—late teens or early twenties, six feet tall, slender build, dark hair, olive complexion. Who was this man, signaling with an upraised fist as the crossfire occurred?

The convoy raced along Stemmons Freeway, toward Parkland Hospital. Why Parkland, when Methodist Hospital was nearer? Suddenly there was no plan at all... Communications within the motorcade were still paralyzed by the open microphone. The vice president's driver raced to keep up with the Secret Service and the president's limousine. SAIC Roberts waved him closer. "They got him! They got him," Roberts yelled, and pointed at Kennedy's car. Agent Rufus Youngblood, protecting the vice president with his body, shouted, "When we get where we're going, you and me are going to move off and not tie in with other people." For all Youngblood knew, there were more assassins waiting at the hospital. His job was to keep his man separate, and alive. "Okay. Okay, partner," Johnson replied.

At 12:37, Dallas police inspector Herbert Sawyer ordered two guards posted at the front door of the Book Depository. In theory, no one was to be allowed to enter or leave until the building was completely searched. Lee Oswald, along with numerous other employees, was already gone. According to James Bookhout, an FBI agent who was ubiquitous after the assassination, and present at Oswald's interrogation:

> "Oswald stated that he took this Coke down to the first floor and had lunch in the employees lunchroom. He thereafter went outside and stood around for five or ten minutes with foreman Bill Shelley, and thereafter went home. He stated that he left work because, in his opinion, based on remarks of Bill Shelley, he did not believe that there was going to be any more work that day due to the confusion in the building."

So Oswald left with the implicit okay of his boss, William Shelley (who like Lee was paid in cash, and claimed to work for CIA). Yet no sooner had Lee departed than Shelley apparently alerted Roy Truly that Oswald, unique among Book Depository employees, was missing.

Penn Jones, in the third of his *Forgive My Grief* books, reprinted a photograph first published in the *Saturday Evening Post*. It shows a motorcycle cop and the hood of the president's limo, racing for Parkland Hospital. In the background, on the roof of a structure

Fig. 9: Man with rifle on rooftop? The rush to Parkland Hospital, from *Forgive My Grief III* (WH 21 p. 782, Yarborough Exhibit A).

which Jones identified as the Green Stamp building, is a man holding some horizontal item. Is it a rifle? A policeman reported a rifleman on the roof of Cobb Stadium, on the far side of the freeway. Jones observed:

> "Military philosophy demands that some guns be held in reserve should the primary battle position fail, and in the military assassination of President Kennedy, we feel those reserve weapons were located along Stemmons Freeway, en route to the luncheon site."[20]

By this, I don't think Jones meant that the assassins were military personnel: he'd already identified a deputy sheriff as a potential rifleman. Rather, he was referring to an act of political violence—like CIA's assassination of Geyer or Trujillo—carried out with military precision. And, based on his own Army experiences, Jones posited a *fallback* position where a second crossfire would be possible, in case the first ambush failed. Imagine, for a moment, that someone in the Secret Service or the president's entourage had noticed the illegal turn onto Elm Street, and insisted that the motorcade proceed straight to the freeway via Main. Would the conspirators be content to risk total failure at this point? Murdering the president is a dangerous business. The plot had already failed in Chicago, and been abandoned in Florida. In Dallas, a second shooting gallery was crucial: this might be the last chance the conspirators would get.

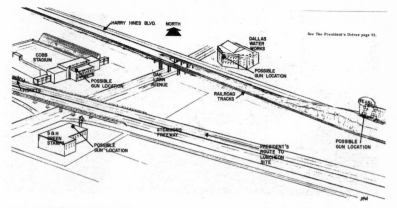

Fig. 10: Elegant map of the route to Parkland and the Trade Mart, annotated, from *Forgive My Grief III*.

Jones directed his readers, via a handy map, to the section of the Stemmons Freeway between the Dallas Water Department building, the Green Stamps building, and the Stadium.

According to Jones, another Cuban refugee, Luis Angel Castillo, was on the fourth floor of the Dallas Water Department building, with a rifle and orders to shoot at a man in an open car *carrying red roses*. The source of his information is unclear. The Rockefeller Commission would report that CIA maintained a 201 file on Castillo, who, arrested by the Philippine police, claimed to have been one of *14* Cuban assassins sent to Dallas by Fidel Castro. A different version of Castillo's story, featuring the red roses and CIA brainwashing, is told by Walter Bowart in his book *Operation Mind Control*.[21]

And there is a provocative footnote to this: in 1996, an accused Russian spy, Robert Stephen Lipka, claimed in court that, while at NSA, he had seen documents identifying the real assassin of President Kennedy. When a reporter asked who it was, Lipka answered, "Luis Angel Castillo."[22]

Penn Jones' map refers to "Pickets" adjacent to Cobb Stadium: "a group of young boys... who had tape across their mouths." Per Jones, these boys were accompanied by an adult, who told a reporter, "We are here as a silent protest. Kennedy has sealed our mouths." Who was the reporter? Is there confirmation for this? Jones speculated that the boys were meant to get into the road and slow the motorcade, for the benefit of the snipers. Surely this was crazy thinking, right? Yet we know that the motorcade had already stopped, twice, for groups of children. And we know that Greer was apt to jam on the brakes when danger threatened.

Before the first cars reached the hospital, ABC radio announced the shooting of the president, "perhaps fatally." Mrs. Connally recalled "a silent, terrible drive. We got to the hospital, I guess it was the hospital... people were swarming around the car." Another agent asked Clint Hill how badly the president was hit. "He's dead," Hill replied.

Dealey Plaza was quickly turning into a Strangelovian circus. Several witnesses claimed to have been stopped by men with Secret Service credentials, though officially there were no Secret Service people there. Unidentified men in suits gathered up evidence. A deputy constable, Seymour Weitzman, approaching the grassy knoll, was turned back by a man in a windbreaker with Secret Service ID.

Not long after the departure of the umbrella man and his friend, Sheriff's Deputy Roger Craig saw Lee Harvey Oswald, or someone closely resembling him, leave the Book Depository and get into a Rambler station wagon driven by a dark-skinned man. The Rambler headed under the triple overpass, in the direction of Oak Cliff. Simultaneously, according to the Warren Report, Lee Oswald walked in the opposite direction, looking for a bus. But the bus he caught took him back toward Dealey Plaza, where police vehicles were causing a traffic jam. Only one witness placed Oswald on that bus: his former landlady and nemesis, Mrs. Bledsoe. According to Mrs. Bledsoe and the Warren Commissioners, Oswald sat in traffic for four minutes, then got off the bus, and walked south toward the Greyhound station.[23]

At 12:40, aboard a Braniff Airlines jet en route from New Orleans, the pilot announced that shots had been fired at the motorcade. One of the passengers became agitated and began roaming the aisle, telling his fellow travelers to remember him, and asking the flight attendants to initial his ticket. It was General Walker.

At 12:45, 15 minutes after the shooting started, the Dallas Police dispatcher issued the description of a suspect: "an unknown white male, approximately thirty, slender build, height five feet ten inches, weight one hundred sixty-five pounds, armed with what is thought to be a 30-30 rifle." No information exists as to the source of this description. Three minutes later the dispatcher repeated the description, adding that the suspect was "believed to be in [the] School Book Depository."

At the bus station, we are told, Lee Oswald got into William Whaley's taxicab. He asked to be taken to 500 North Beckley—seven blocks past where he lived. Before they left, an old lady came up and Oswald, clearly in no hurry, offered her the cab. But she declined to take it. He was acting very relaxed and courteous for someone who had just murdered the president. He was also the first presidential assassin to attempt his escape by public transport... Whaley's testimony, like Mrs. Bledsoe's, is unpersuasive. Confused throughout, Whaley told the Warren Commission that he signed an affidavit identifying Oswald as his passenger before attending the police lineup. Mrs. Bledsoe admitted to the Commission that she had been coached and given written notes as to what to say.[24]

What is most puzzling is why the Commission chose to believe the chaotic and dubious claims of Bledsoe and Whaley over the testimony of a trained policeman, Deputy Roger Craig. It does not make sense. Wasn't Craig, who said he saw Oswald driven away by an accomplice, the more credible witness?

Meanwhile, Lee Bowers, the railroad dispatcher, observed several individuals board a passing freight train. He ordered the train stopped, and called the police, who arrested three men.

At a few minutes before 1 p.m., in the midst of the hurly-burly of incoming and outgoing messages at Dallas Police Headquarters, the dispatcher found time to order one officer, Jefferson Davis Tippit, to the Central Oak Cliff area—even though no crime had been reported there. Police dispatcher Murray Jackson gave Tippit perhaps the vaguest instruction a policeman ever received: "Be at large for any emergency that comes in."

At 12:57, a priest, Father Huber, gave the president the last rites. Jack Kennedy was pronounced dead, and the Secret Service ordered the room cleared.

Police Captain Will Fritz arrived at the Book Depository at 12:58 and ordered the building sealed (in theory, this had already been done). Almost immediately, a military intelligence officer from Fort Hood, Special Agent James Powell, was detained within the TSBD. He was carrying a 35mm Minolta camera and had been taking photographs.

Either by taxi or by chauffeur-driven Rambler, Lee Oswald returned to Oak Cliff. He got back to his digs shortly before 1 p.m., and went to his room. According to his landlady, a police car pulled up outside, honked, and drove away. Lee changed his shirt, collected his pistol and left the building. He either ran or caught a ride to downtown Oak Cliff, almost a mile away.

It's interesting how much of this story takes place in the couple of square miles that is Oak Cliff, Dallas. Oswald moved frequently, but when in Dallas he always rented in Oak Cliff, even though he never worked there. And all of his apartments were within walking distance of the Texas Theatre. Now Patrolman Tippit was cruising down Tenth Street in Oak Cliff, at large for any emergency. Jack Ruby's apartment at 223 S. Ewing was only five blocks away. It was just a three-minute drive from Jack's place to the Texas Theatre if he wanted to take in a movie. (In his Warren Commission testimony, Lee's brother Robert observed, "the route taken by my brother Lee from the place of his boarding house, or apartment, and prior to his capture, was in a direct or approximately a direct line to Mr. Ruby's apartment." His questioners changed the subject.)

According to Butch Burroughs, the ticket-taker of the Texas Theatre, Lee Oswald sneaked in, without paying, shortly after 1 p.m. He spent 15 minutes in the balcony, then came down and bought popcorn from Burroughs. After that he walked into the main theater and sat, in turn, next to three different people, the last being a pregnant woman. What was Oswald doing? Cinemas are, or were, good places for illicit meetings, especially in the afternoons when they aren't crowded. Who did he expect to meet there? What did he expect to receive—money? Further instructions? His ticket out?

Around 1:10 p.m., Patrolman Tippit stopped his car on Tenth Street, and beckoned to a pedestrian. The man walked over, and leaned down next to Tippit's passenger window. They talked for a few moments, then Tippit opened his door. As he got out, the man drew a gun and fired three shots. Tippit fell, and, according to one witness, his assailant fired a fourth shot into his head. First reports said the killer had an automatic pistol, which ejected its cartridges. Then the story changed. The suspect had a revolver, and so the killer coolly walked away, ejecting his empty cartridge cases and loading his handgun with fresh bullets.

At 1:16, a citizen, one T.F. Bowley, called the dispatcher on Tippit's car radio, and told him an officer had been shot. Naturally, the killing of a policeman will get the police's attention, but only

46 minutes had elapsed since the assassination of the president, and what took place next was bizarrely disproportionate. On hearing the news of the Tippit shooting, dozens of police officers raced to the scene. Assistant D.A. Bill Alexander caught a ride in Sgt. Gerald Hill's patrol car. First Lieutenant Elmo Cunningham and several other officers, directed by their captain to go to the School Book Depository, instead drove to Oak Cliff, where Cunningham felt they could "do more good." Captain Cecil Talbert, in charge of all police patrolmen in the city, raced to Oak Cliff, as did Captain W.R. Westbrook, a personnel manager whose duties, in theory, were entirely office-bound.[25]

According to the Warren Commission, Tippit's killer was Lee Oswald.[26]

But only one witness identified him, and her identification was tentative: Helen Markham told Mark Lane the killer was "a short man, somewhat on the heavy side, with slightly bushy hair."[27]

Others described the fleeing killer in similar terms. When Sergeant Hill arrived, a witness told him that the killer weighed 160–170 lbs. and had "brown, bushy hair". Officer J.M. Poe quoted Markham as saying the killer had "bushy hair" and a brown jacket. Ted Calloway, the manager of a nearby used car lot, described the fleeing suspect as "5'11", 165 lbs., black wavy hair" and carrying an automatic pistol.

The main feature at the Texas Theatre—*War Is Hell*—began around 1:20.

Already, *two* rifles had been found at the Book Depository. A news cameraman filmed Dallas Police officers displaying a rifle without a telescopic sight found on the roof of the building, while at 1:22, Deputy Sheriff E.L. Boone discovered a weapon on the sixth floor, in what would soon be termed the "sniper's nest": a 7.65mm German Mauser. Boone and deputy Weitzman both signed affidavits confirming they had found the Mauser. Sheriff's Deputy Roger Craig recalled seeing the word "Mauser" stamped on the weapon. Dallas D.A. Henry Wade would also describe the rifle as a Mauser.[28]

The problem with these discoveries was that the "historic" Oswald wasn't on the roof, and didn't own a Mauser. He, or Hidell, had allegedly ordered a cheap Italian rifle, a Mannlicher-Carcano. So, even though the Mauser was a better, more reliable weapon—more likely an assassin's choice—the Warren Commission ignored these early discoveries. ATTD agent Frank Ellsworth participated in a second search of the Book Depository and confirmed that the Mannlicher-Carcano was found around 1:30 p.m., on the fourth or fifth floor, by a DPD detective. If Ellsworth is correct, this was the third rifle found in the Book Depository within half an hour.[29]

Roy Truly approached Captain Fritz on the sixth floor, where he was studying one of these rifles. He said to Fritz, "I don't know if this means anything, but we have a man who is missing." He gave the captain Lee Oswald's name, address and physical description. Fast work, Truly! But why did he do it? To suggest that Oswald, alone among TSBD employees, had gone missing, was a lie. No fewer than 23 employees of the Book Depository or publishers based there had left the building or not come to work that day, including the company president, Jack Cason. For Truly and Shelley to single out Oswald is deeply suspicious.

Meanwhile, the DPD dispatcher advised car 87 to locate a white Pontiac station wagon, heading east on Davis Boulevard, with a rifle lying on the seat;[30] and, around 1:35, the manager of a nearby shoe store noticed a man slip into the Texas Theatre without paying. He advised the theatre cashier to call the police. Butch Burroughs, at the concession stand, thought Oswald was already in the building. Near the Tippit murder site, Captain Westbrook found evidence as to the identity of the killer: a gray jacket. And beside Tippit's car, a TV cameraman filmed DPD captain George Doughty and Sgt. Calvin "Bud" Owens, examining a wallet. According to FBI agents Hosty (who wasn't there) and Robert M. Barrett (who was), the wallet was Oswald's, and Captain Westbrook took charge of it.[31]

Police continued to pour into Oak Cliff; Dealey Plaza fell quiet as all radio traffic reported cars racing to the vicinity of the Tippit murder. A false alarm directed the cops to the public library, where Tippit's killer was believed to have fled. Then, at 1:46, in response to the cashier's call, a new wave of police vehicles raced for the Texas Theatre. The DPD dispatcher put out a call for the arrest of Charles Givens, another TSBD warehouse worker: "He has a police record and he left."

First at the theater, Lt. Cunningham led a phalanx of cops upstairs and began to question a young man in the balcony. Then a second wave of police arrived, the lights went up, and the cops started questioning the patrons on the lower level. There were 16 policemen in the body of the theater when officer Nick McDonald approached Oswald. They exchanged words, and there was a scuffle. Johnny Brewer, the shoe store manager, heard a cop cry out, "Kill the president, will you?" A cinema patron, George Applin, heard the click of a revolver—supposedly, Oswald drew his pistol but it misfired—and watched as Oswald was knocked down and subdued. As he was handcuffed, he shouted, "I am not resisting arrest!"

Lee offered no further resistance and the cops cleaned him up in the bathroom before leading him out. Captain Westbrook was the highest-ranking officer present; he told the Warren Commission that he ordered his men to take the names and addresses of all eyewitnesses, yet no such list was made. Of 15 cinema patrons, only two were ID'd by the police. Meanwhile press photographers, some of them brought to the scene in police cars, were gathering outside. Within, Applin saw someone he recognized, quietly watching the proceedings: Jack Ruby. Meanwhile, police continued to arrive—no less than two captains, one lieutenant, three sergeants, an FBI agent, an assistant D.A. and numerous patrolmen, detectives, and sheriff's deputies were now on the scene.

Butch Burroughs told James W. Douglass that he witnessed a second arrest in the Texas Theatre, only "three or four minutes later." Burroughs saw a man, who "looked almost like Oswald, like he was his brother or something," handcuffed by the police and taken out via the rear exit. Another local store owner, Bernard Haire, saw police lead a young white man out of the back door of the Texas Theatre, put him in a squad car and drive off. Haire believed for almost 25 years that he had seen Oswald under arrest. In 1987 he discovered that Oswald had been brought out through the front door.[32]

In the car on the way to the Police Station, Oswald said little. Indeed, the cops were impressed by how quiet he was. "He was real calm... extra calm," officer Charles T. Walker recalled. Sergeant Hill reported, "He gave the appearance of arrogance, but he did not talk boastfully. In fact, he talked very little." Oswald played the tough guy when they accused him of killing a policeman. When asked why he had done it, he did not reply. He even refused to reveal his name, according to the policemen. So Sergeant Hill suggested that detective Paul Bentley should search the suspect for ID. Bentley quickly discovered Oswald's wallet—this was his third wallet of the day!—containing ID in the names of Oswald and Hidell.[33]

Fig. 11: Defiant, revolutionary killer, Lee Harvey Oswald (version one—UPI).

Fig. 12: Defiant, revolutionary killer, Lee Harvey Oswald (version two—*Dallas Morning News*).

Fig. 13: Uncropped version of Fig. 12.

Shortly before 2 p.m., the police car drove into the basement of headquarters. A wedge of cops surrounded Oswald and he was taken to Captain Fritz's office, on the third floor. Reporters and photographers rode the elevator with them, shouting questions at Lee. Out of this impromptu photo session, two pictures showing the suspect making a famous revolutionary gesture emerged. They're reproduced as Figs. 11 and 12.

What does the picture above tell us? Well, that Lee Harvey Oswald was a smug, platitudinous, gesture-obsessed individual, right?

But what are we to make of the second picture, which is an entirely different angle on Oswald, with a different background—but *a near-identical image of his two manacled hands?* The position of Oswald's right fist—fingers, wrist and cuffs—is identical in both photographs. The position of his left fist is slightly different. As Timothy Cwiek wrote,[34] if Oswald's right hand is the same in both photos, then at least one of the photos must be a fake. The *Dallas Morning News* did not respond to Cwiek's enquiry as to who took the second photograph. But Bill Winfrey took credit for the picture at a conference in 1993, and was credited as the photographer in his obituary in 2009.

Is either genuine? Oswald's arms seem somewhat strangely positioned, and those Texas handcuffs certainly gave the wearer ample room to move his wrists around. According to two FBI agents, *Oswald had been handcuffed with his hands behind him*. All we can hazard is that if the Winfrey picture is genuine, then the UPI picture must be fake: created the same day, by someone with access to Winfrey's photograph, and widely distributed, presumably to emphasize that Oswald was a defiant revolutionary. But, as the arresting officers observed, Lee's behavior in custody was not at all defiant, and he denied killing anyone. When a reporter called out, "Did you kill the president?" the alleged killer-for-fame replied, "No, I have not been charged with that." When the reporters next saw him he cried out, repeatedly, "I am a patsy! I am a patsy!"

A few minutes later the DPD marched three suspects past the Depository and into the County Jail. Their passage was recorded by news photographers, and the men came to be known as "the three tramps." They were, supposedly, the men arrested aboard the railroad car.[35]

Their shoes look new, but their clothes have a certain jumble-sale quality. Who were these "tramps"? They went unidentified for many years. Even their pictures went unseen, until Jim Garrison produced them, with a theatrical flourish, on *The Tonight Show Starring Johnny Carson*, to his host's alarm. Penn Jones published some of them, as did the magazine *Computers and Animation*. Canfield and Weberman's book *Coup d'État in America*[36] reprinted the "tramp" photographs alongside pictures of E. Howard Hunt and Frank Sturgis.

The reader may consider the similarities between Sturgis and the "tall tramp" and ponder the photographs of E. Howard Hunt alongside the so-called "old tramp," seen over.

The resemblance between Hunt and the "old tramp" seems to me strong. Maybe it is coincidental. In 1992, Larry Howard located arrest records for three other men, naming them Harold Doyle, John Forrester Gedney, and Gus W. Abrams. Hunt, on the other hand, has been connected to the Kennedy assassination by

Fig. 14: The "Three Tramps" in custody.

various people—including his own children. Victor Marchetti, who told Anthony Summers about a false defector program run by the Navy, claimed in 1978 that CIA itself was about to finger Hunt as a Dealey Plaza assassin. Hunt sued Marchetti's publisher and, in a case defended by Mark Lane, lost. Hunt's "witnesses" at the Agency would not vouch for him; his own children, asked to provide alibis, refused to do so.[37]

Hunt died in Miami, Florida, in 2007, at the age of 88, leaving behind a memoir in which he claimed that a conspiracy, led by Lyndon Johnson, murdered the president. According to Hunt's memoir, the principal conspirators were David Atlee Phillips, Cord Meyer (the CIA disinformation specialist, and husband of Mary Pinchot), Bill Harvey (a senior CIA officer and assassinations specialist), Frank Sturgis, David Morales (Chief of Operations at CIA's JM/WAVE station), and *mafioso* Antonio Veciana. Hunt was a prolific writer of spy fiction; he ghost-wrote Allen Dulles' memoirs. Is his

Fig. 15: Watergate burglar and CIA agent Frank Sturgis; tramp; Sturgis.

Fig. 16: Watergate burglar and CIA agent E. Howard Hunt; tramp; Hunt.

"confession" credible? It certainly supports the visual evidence that Sturgis and Hunt were "tramps." Harvey and Morales were reported to be violently opposed to Kennedy. All but Meyer were involved in Cuban operations and the Bay of Pigs. Ironically, E. Howard Hunt's "confession"—if genuine—confirms Mark Lane's original conclusion that the Agency was behind the assassination.[38]

But why, if the assassination plotters were CIA, would they use Oswald, an obvious intelligence agent, as a patsy? Or did Oswald's "dual-use" aspect—as an FBI informant and *agent provocateur*— guarantee the Bureau's help in covering things up? Was David Atlee Phillips, under cover of a false name, so confident that he would risk being seen, in Dallas, in Oswald's company?

Phillips was, like Hunt, a fiction writer. He died in 1988, having, like George de Mohrenschildt, written the outline of a book about Oswald, this one featuring Lee as the patsy in an assassination conspiracy. Phillips' manuscript is titled *The AMLASH Legacy*, and its protagonist—"Harold Harrison"—confesses at the outset how he "created" Oswald:

"I was one of the two case officers who handled Lee Harvey Oswald. After working to establish his Marxist bona fides, we gave him the mission of killing Fidel Castro in Cuba. I helped him when he came to Mexico City to obtain a visa, and when he returned to Dallas to wait for it I saw him twice there. We rehearsed the plan many times: In Havana Oswald was to assassinate Castro with a sniper's rifle from the upper floor window of a building on the route where Castro often drove in an open jeep. Whether Oswald was a double-agent or a psycho I'm not sure, and I don't know why he killed Kennedy. But I do know he used precisely the plan we had devised against Castro. Thus the CIA did not anticipate the president's assassination but it was responsible for it. I share that guilt."[39]

Colonel Robert E. Jones was Chief of Operations for the 112th Military Intelligence group at Fort Sam Houston. In 1978, he testified before the HSCA that he had opened a file on Lee Harvey Oswald following his New Orleans arrest, and that he had provided a small force of military intelligence personnel—between eight and 12 men—to assist the Secret Service in Dallas. Colonel Jones said that several of his men were in Dealey Plaza, and that one M.I. agent—presumably James Powell—was trapped inside the Book Depository when the building was locked down. Colonel Jones said his men did not carry Secret Service ID, and told the HCSA that he had not known Oswald worked in the building.

Congressman Dodd (son and heir of Senator Dodd) had a question for Colonel Jones:

> Dodd: Did I understand you correctly to say that the agents who were assigned to Dallas on that day were in civilian clothes?
>
> Jones: Yes, sir.
>
> Dodd: Were they dressed in any specific way so as to hide their identity, or was it just coat and tie? Had they work clothes, or were they purposefully [sic] attired in such a way as to look as though they came from one stratum of society rather than another?
>
> Jones: They were dressed to blend in with the man on the street, the normal coat and tie. Some of them may have had on a sport coat without a tie with an open collar.

Was Congressman Dodd giving Colonel Jones an opportunity to say that his agents in Dealey Plaza *were not dressed like tramps*? It's hard to think of another explanation for the Congressman's fascination for the social strata of disguise. But he opened a can of worms, because what Colonel Jones described *was the wardrobe of the umbrella man and his friend.*[40]

Within the next few hours, the FBI received two tip-offs linking Jimmie George Robinson, a Dallas-area Klansman, to the assassination. The Houston FBI office reported that an official of the Anti-Defamation League had fingered Robinson as an NSRP associate who had purchased a sniper's rifle. A police official in Richardson, Texas, called the Dallas FBI office to advise them that Robinson and other NSRP members "should be considered possible suspects in the assassination of President Kennedy." There is no evidence that Robinson, who was in Alabama, was ever investigated. The FBI did investigate the whereabouts of Charles "Connie" Lynch, a Minuteman and head of the California NSRP: he was determined to be in Jacksonville, Florida, addressing a rally of the Ku Klux Klan.[41]

In California, two employees of Knott's Berry Farm advised the FBI that Joachim Rudolph Roehricht, a young German Nazi, had returned from a Texas vacation announcing that Kennedy would be killed there. Roehricht insisted that "many young men in Texas wore the swastika," and told his employer, Ken Knott, "that if Kennedy insists on continuing his trip to Texas he will not come out alive." After hearing of the assassination, Roehricht had laughed and stated that he knew all about it. The FBI interviewed the young Nazi the next day, and took his word that it was all a misunderstanding.[42]

Meanwhile, Colonel Jones was on the phone to the San Antonio FBI. He advised them that "A.J. Hidell" was an alias used by Lee Harvey Oswald. How he knew this is a mystery. Jones then called the Dallas FBI office, told them about the "Hidell" alias, and "mentioned of Oswald's defection, trip to Russia, his return, his marriage to a Russian national, his activity with Fair Play for Cuba." Of course, the FBI already knew this (perhaps from Oswald's own T-1 reports), but the colonel was certainly primed to release a lot of damaging information about the arrested man. Jones told the HSCA he had a source who was simultaneously a member of the Dallas Police Department *and* a military intelligence agent, but that without his records he could not identify the person. (When the HSCA asked to see Jones' records, they were told that all military files on Oswald were "destroyed routinely" in 1973.)

Soon after 2 p.m., Oswald's first interrogation began. Captain Fritz told the Warren Commissioners that he listened in on a call between FBI agent Bookhout and SAC Shanklin, in the Dallas office. According to Fritz, Shanklin told Bookhout he wanted—who else?— Agent Hosty present at the interrogation, because "he knew about these people, and had been investigating them." At 2:20, Hosty set off for the city jail. Who did Shanklin mean by "these people"? Hosty's work mainly entailed monitoring right-wing groups. Was Shanklin referring to the NSRP and the Klan, or to Lee and Marina? Oswald would be questioned several times during the next 48 hours—by the DPD, the sheriffs, the Secret Service, and the FBI. Astonishingly, no stenographer took any record of these interrogations, and they were not tape-recorded. Beyond his increasingly anxious exchanges with reporters, both the Warren Commission and the HSCA claimed that no record was made of anything Oswald said: what the cops asked him, or what his answers were.

This was not true. SAIC Sorrels kept written notes of Lee's interrogation (these were published as part of Sorrels Exhibit No. 3-A, his Jack Ruby notes); he noted that Oswald admitted to being a Marxist, and denied ordering guns by mail. In 1995, to promote a book he had written, *Assignment Oswald*, Agent Hosty produced a page of what he claimed were his original notes of Oswald's interrogation. And in 1997, an anonymous donor provided the ARRB with five pages of interrogation notes made by Captain Fritz. Why Fritz and Hosty concealed their notes for many years has not been satisfactorily explained. There is also the near-contemporaneous Warren Commission Exhibit 832: Hosty and Bookhout's own FBI report of Oswald's first interrogation, dictated the following day.[43]

At 2:45, the Dallas cops picked up another suspect, John Franklin Elrod, walking along the railroad tracks near Cobb Stadium, where a rifleman had been seen. Elrod was held, on suspicion of murder and vagrancy, for several days, and may have shared a cell with Oswald.

Fritz's scribbled notes of Lee's interrogation begin at 3:15, and note the presence of Agents Hosty and Bookhout. The agents' report states that they arrived at 3:15, and that "Captain Fritz had been previously interviewing Lee Harvey Oswald for an undetermined period of time." Captain Fritz and the G-men contradicted each other: Bookhout claiming he arrived at 3:15, Fritz saying Bookhout was in his office at two, on the phone to SAC Shanklin. (This pattern would persist—the DPD and FBI telling conflicting stories to make each other look bad—until the Texans turned up in Washington, DC, and accused the FBI, point-blank, of running Oswald as an agent. After that, as we shall see, the FBI bothered the DPD no more.) Fritz's notes tend to support his later written report to the Warren Commission. There, he wrote that he asked Lee why he was packing a pistol, and Oswald replied, "You know how boys do when they have a gun: they just carry it."

The FBI men's report is somewhat different, and contains more information. Oswald had been polite with Captain Fritz, but "adopted a violent attitude towards the FBI and both agents and made many uncomplimentary remarks about the FBI. Oswald requested that Captain Fritz remove the cuffs from him, it being noted that Oswald was handcuffed with his hands behind him. Captain Fritz had one of his detectives remove the handcuffs and handcuff Oswald with his hands in front of him. Captain Fritz asked Oswald if he ever owned a rifle and Oswald stated that he had observed a Mr. Truely (phonetic), a supervisor at the Texas Schoolbook Depository on November 20, 1963, display a rifle to some individuals in his office on the first floor of the Texas Schoolbook Depository, but denied ever owning a rifle himself."

So, during his first interrogation, Oswald denied owning a gun but told the DPD and the FBI that Roy Truly, the building manager, had brought a rifle into the Book Depository two days previously. Surely the finger of suspicion now pointed to Truly, who had hired Oswald and then reported him missing. Why wasn't he arrested?

Agent Hosty badgered Oswald about his time in Russia. For no apparent reason, he also asked Lee if he had been to Mexico City. According to Captain Fritz, "this irritated Oswald a great deal, and he beat on the desk and went into a kind of tantrum."[44]

Fritz's report suggests some private knowledge or agenda on Hosty's part. How did the FBI man know about Lee's alleged Mexican trip? Why did he think it was important? And why did Oswald get so upset about it? He admitted to having lived in Russia—something far more damning in the eyes of the Dallas cops—and to having been the secretary of the FPCC in New Orleans "a few months ago." But he was adamant that he had never been to Mexico, not even to Tijuana. While the questioning continued, the DPD dispatcher sent two cars to Love Field, to check out a report of several armed men in the Braniff Airlines Building. But the patrolmen found no one, and were back in service by 3:50.[45]

After it's over, the men will be out of the country...

Robert and Patricia Hester were two Dallas-based commercial photographers. They told Jim Marrs that they were called in by the police to help process photographs of Oswald, at around 4 p.m. According to the Hesters, the photos showed Oswald holding a rifle and a pistol, and the FBI had color transparencies of them, plus one color transparency with no one in the picture. If their story is true, it is noteworthy for several reasons: "officially" the backyard rifle-and-pistol photographs were not found until the following day; they were black and white negatives, not color transparencies; and the Hesters' reference to an FBI agent suggests that the FBI, as well as the DPD, were involved in the fabrication of these photo composites—perhaps at the same time as the "fist" photographs were faked.

At 4:05, Hosty and Bookhout recorded that the interview ended with Oswald being taken to a witness lineup. Fritz noted that Oswald left for the lineup at 4:15. Oswald participated under protest. After several false starts, Helen Markham tentatively identified him as the killer of Officer Tippit. He was returned to Captain Fritz's office for two more hours of questioning (there are no notes of this interview). Around this time, Captain Westbrook told Sergeant Hill that Oswald had admitted to being a communist, had a dishonorable discharge from the Marines, had been in Russia, and also in trouble with the police in New Orleans. Where Westbrook acquired this biography is unclear, since he was not present at either interview.[46]

Fritz let Oswald use the phone, and he tried twice to call Ruth Paine, who didn't answer. Unknown to him, she had already consented to a warrantless search of his property at her home. Meanwhile, his family—Marina, Marguerite and Robert—had gathered at police headquarters, trying to see him. Robert Oswald was introduced to the Paines and formed an instinctive dislike of them. He stayed in a hotel in Dallas that night and wrote in his diary, "I did not like the appearance of Mr. Paine, nothing really to put my finger on but I just had a feeling. I still do not know why or how, but Mr. and Mrs. Paine are somehow involved in this affair." (Marguerite also told the Warren Commissioners that she was "suspicious" of Mrs. Paine.)

Around 5:30, according to Sheriff's Deputy Roger Craig, Captain Fritz took him into an office where Oswald was being held. Craig positively identified Oswald as the man he saw leave Dealey Plaza in a Rambler station wagon. According to Craig, Oswald volunteered that the station wagon belonged to Ruth Paine, adding, "Don't try and tie her into this. She had nothing to do with it." But he did not deny departing the assassination scene in Ruth's car. What to make of this? Had Mrs. Paine really loaned her car to assist in the killers' escape? Or was Lee trying to implicate her, in a roundabout way? Then, per Craig, Oswald remarked (with a sigh? or a triumphant shout?), "Everybody will know who I am now." He was not asked to elaborate. But he clearly felt that Craig's report—and the link to the Rambler—had blown his cover.[47]

What was going on here? As we have seen, various people had been arrested, in and around Dealey Plaza, before and after Oswald's capture. A second man, who closely resembled Lee, had been spirited away in handcuffs from the Texas Theatre. Several suspects were in custody, yet the DPD suddenly gave up on all but one of them, and on the possibility of catching suspects still at large. Instead, the circus-like atmosphere which had greeted Oswald on his arrival intensified, as journalists, and others, piled into the corridors of the police station.

At 6:20, Oswald was taken downstairs for another lineup. Around 6:30, Captain Fritz, Forrest Sorrels of the Secret Service, and Assistant D.A.s Bill Alexander and Jim Allen all left the police station and went across the street to a café. While they were absent, Jack Ruby attempted to enter the Captain's office. He was prevented by two uniformed officers guarding the door. One of them told him, "You can't go in there, Jack." Was Ruby already gunning for Oswald? If so, Fritz and company had given themselves a handy alibi: only their timing was off. Ruby left, and, five minutes later, Oswald was returned to Fritz's office.

At 7 p.m., Captain Fritz signed a complaint against Oswald. Justice of the Peace David Johnston charged him with the Tippit murder: case number F-153. When Greg Olds, the president of the local ACLU, tried to see Lee, he was told by Captain Fritz that Oswald didn't want an attorney. Olds was not allowed to visit Oswald. A third lineup took place at 7:40, followed by a fourth interrogation session (also unnoted by Fritz), with several Secret Service and

FBI men present. Just before 9 p.m., Oswald was fingerprinted and paraffin casts were made of his hand and cheek. The paraffin test proved positive for his hand, negative for his face. If accurate, the test indicated that Oswald might have fired a pistol, but not a rifle. Fritz asked Lee what he thought of President Kennedy: according to Thomas Kelley, a Secret Service agent, Oswald replied,

> "My wife and I like the president's family. They are interesting people. I have my own views on the president's national policy. I have a right to express my views, but because of the charges I do not think I should comment further... I am not a malcontent. Nothing irritated me about the president."

Meanwhile, Oswald's old friends in the Newman Building were acting crazy. Guy Banister got drunk and pistol-whipped one of his investigators, Jack Martin. According to Martin, Banister accused him of going through his private files. David Ferrie, Oswald's old CAP leader and partner on the Clinton trip, left New Orleans in the middle of a rainstorm and drove 364 miles to Houston, Texas, allegedly to go ice-skating. But Ferrie did not put on skates. Instead he sat by the pay phone, waiting for a call. Next day Jack Martin dropped a dime on Ferrie to the New Orleans police, telling them he was connected to the assassination; and Dean Andrews, Oswald's New Orleans lawyer, received a call from a man named Clem Bertrand—most likely Clay Shaw, of the Clinton excursion—asking him to represent Lee.

At 10:45 in the evening, Oswald asked to make a collect, long-distance call—to Raleigh, North Carolina. Police and Secret Service listened in as Lee tried to telephone a man named John Hurt. He was unable to make contact. Of two John Hurts resident in Raleigh at that time, one had served in U.S. Army Counterintelligence. He denied calling Oswald or receiving a call from him (but as the call did not go through, this is not in dispute). Victor Marchetti suggested that Oswald's call to Raleigh was an attempt to contact an emergency "cutout": a middleman who could put him in touch with "his" agency. Per Marchetti, the ONI fake defector program was based in North Carolina.

Meanwhile, the Chief of Staff, Army Intelligence, at Fort Sam Houston, sent a secret cable to USSTRICOM, the U.S. Strike Command at MacDill Air Force Base in Florida, reporting:

> "Assistant Chief Don Stringfellow, Intelligence Section, Dallas Police Department, notified 112th Intelligence Group, this Headquarters, that information obtained from Oswald revealed that he had defected to Cuba in 1959 and is a card-carrying member of the Communist party."

Neither allegation was true, and it is unlikely Oswald lied about such matters. Stringfellow was a member of the Dallas Police Intelligence Unit, and USSTRICOM was a two-service (Army and Air Force) command, located within striking distance of Cuba. The HCSA asked Colonel Jones why such a cable—packed with disinformation—might have been sent. The Colonel replied,

> "I would assume that they would fear a national emergency and they would want to apprise this organization that was kind of the nerve center for activation and deployment of troops in case of emergency. This is the only reason that I can give as to why they would send such a cable."

Operation NORTHWOODS—proposed by the Pentagon, rejected by Kennedy and McNamara—had proposed violent acts on U.S. soil, so as to justify a retaliatory invasion of Cuba. Now, hours after the president's murder in Dallas, the alleged killer had been misidentified, in a secret military communication, as a Cuban communist.

notes

1 Timothy Cwiek, "The Wedding Ring Story: A Study in Manipulation," *The Third Decade*, Vol. 2, No. 4, May 1986, pp. 11–17.

2 John Bainbridge, *The Super-Americans*, Doubleday, NY, 1961, pp. 47–48.

3 Rose, *Nut Country*, pp. 15–16.

4 WH5, *Testimony of Robert Alan Surrey*, pp. 420–449.

5 Warren Commission Memorandum dated April 16, 1964.

6 Russell, *The Man Who Knew Too Much*, pp. 542–546.

7 Michael Granberry, "Those Who Rode With Kennedy Remember," *Dallas Morning News*, Nov. 22, 2003.

8   Vincent Palamara, *The Third Alternative—Survivor's Guilt: The Secret Service & the JFK Murder*, self-published, 1993, Trine Day, 2013.

9   Chuck Marler, "Questioning The Limousine's Speed on Elm Street," *The Fourth Decade*, Vol. 1, No. 4, May 1994, pp. 19–22; Betzner, WH 20, p. 467, Dekker Exhibit No. 5323. Lovelady, WH 22, CE No. 1281, p. 662. WH 21, p. 770—Willis Exhibit No. 1 (Slide No. 6)—shows a car in the motorcade stopped in the street, with its rear door open and a passenger stepping out.

10 Neil Twyman, *Chronology, The Great Zapruder Film Hoax*, ed. James H. Fetzer, Ph.D., Catfeet Press, Chicago, 2003, p. 461.

11 AARB reports dated 06/12/97 and 07/15/97 by Douglas Home; reproduced in *The Great Zapruder Film Hoax* pp. 456–460.

12 John P. Costella, Ph.D., "A Scientist's Verdict: The Film is a Fabrication", *The Great Zapruder Film Hoax*, pp. 163–221.

13 Grant Leitma, "Where Did the Front Shot Come From?", *The Fourth Decade*, Vol. 1, No. 1, Nov. 1993, pp. 31–32.

14 Josiah Thompson, *Six Seconds in Dallas*, Bernard Geis, Random House, 1967, p. 139.

15 Santana story told to me by R.B. Cutler; DiEugenio, "Rose Cheramie," *The Assassinations*, pp. 230, 235–236.

16 WH 19, p. 469 (Jim Braden's statement), p. 476 (Larry Florer's statement); Dekker Exhibit No. 5323.

17 Jones, *Forgive My Grief III*, pp. 35, 36, 100; WH20, pp. 502–4, Decker Exhibit No. 5323.

18 Peter R. Whitmey, "Creating A Patsy" (formerly *The Real Target*), *JFK/Deep Politics Quarterly*, April 1998, revised & expanded online.

19 *Testimony of Charles A. Senseney*, Church Committee, Volume V 1.6, pp. 167–169; J. David Truby, "The Poisoned President: JFK Hit by CIA Dart", *Special Weapons & Tactics*, Vol. 7, No. 5, Sept. 1988, pp. 34–39.

20 Jones, *Forgive My Grief III*, p. 94.

21 Walter Bowart, *Operation Mind Control*, Flatland Editions, CA, 1994, pp. 298–307.

22 *Philadelphia Enquirer*, March 22, 1996.

23 William Weston, "Marsalis Bus No. 1213," *The Fourth Decade*, Vol. 2, No. 3, Mar. 1995, pp. 3–10.

24 Weisberg, *Whitewash*, self-published, Hyattstown, MD, 1965, pp. 78–79, 108–109.

25 Ian Griggs, "Just Another Day At The Office...", *The Fourth Decade*, Vol. 3, No. 2, Jan. 1996, pp. 14–21.

26 Weisberg, *Whitewash*, p. 63, points out that, if Oswald was the killer, this was the moment for him to make his getaway. He had about $14 cash on him, and had left $170 in Irving. Instead of trying to escape, Lee went to the picture show.

27 Jerry D. Rose, "They Got Their Man On Both Accounts," *The Third Decade*, Vol. 3, No. 2, March 1988, pp. 1–15; William Weston, "The Arrogant Suspect," *The Fourth Decade*, Vol. 2, No. 2, Jan. 1995, pp. 3–10; Mark Lane, *Rush to Judgment*, Holt, Reinhard, NY, 1966, p. 180.

28 Robert Sibley, "The Mysterious, Vanishing Rifle of the JFK Assassination," *The Third Decade*, Vol. 1, No. 6, Sept. 1985, pp. 16–19; Sylvia Meagher, "Treasure-Hunting in the National Archives," *The Third Decade*, Vol. 2, No. 2, Jan. 1986, pp. 2–3.

29 Sheriff's Deputy Harry Weatherford was present on the roof and on the sixth floor of the Book Depository, according to his investigation report. He said he

was "about 10 feet from Deputy Boone when he found the rifle." Sheriff Decker then sent Weatherford to the Paine residence in Irving, where Ruth invited him in and agreed to a warrantless search of the Oswalds' possessions (WH 20, pp. 502–3, Decker Exhibit No. 5323).

30 WH17 CE No. 705, DPD Radio Transmissions, pp. 410–411, 413–414.

31 Dale K. Meyers, *With Malice*, Oak Cliff Press, TX, 1998, pp. 288–294.

32 Jim Marrs interviewed Burroughs and Haire and reported their remarkable stories in *Crossfire* (pp. 353–354). James Douglass also interviewed Burroughs, who told him he had seen the Oswald "double" under arrest—something he hadn't told Marrs (Douglass, *JFK and the Unspeakable*, pp. 291–293, footnotes pp. 460–461). The fact that Burroughs, like Ray McKeown, added things to his story in later interviews may suggest that they are unreliable witnesses. But there are other explanations for witness statements which expanded over the years: 1) that, in the immediate aftermath of the assassination, the witnesses were afraid of being killed; 2) that they only answered the questions they were asked (per Douglass, Burroughs was extremely taciturn); 3) that their original testimony was misreported. In the case of the Warren Commission, many witnesses complained they were misquoted, or ignored. Consider deputy Craig's testimony, and compare the Commission testimony of motorcycle officer Hargis—where he has the same "voice" as all the other witnesses—with his newspaper interview, where his colorful spoken style ("those boys liked to had a conniption fit") is highly distinctive. The Warren Report documents and exhibits are important evidence, but they can't be considered accurate, or complete.

33 Police Captain Fritz's inventory of Oswald's possessions—WH 22 CE No. 1148—lists $13 in currency; 87 cents in change; a bus transfer; a paycheck stub from a bakery dated August 22, 1960—on which date Lee was supposedly living in Russia; a black belt; a box top; a post office box key; his silver Marine Corps ring; and a chrome ID bracelet with the inscription "Lee." Fritz's list of the contents of one of the wallets is WH 24 CE No. 1986.

34 Timothy Cwiek, "Oswald's Revolutionary Salute: Did He Ever Make It?" *The Third Decade*, Vol. 5., No. 2, p. 11.

35 Alan Houston, "Tramp, Tramp, Tramp?" *The Fourth Decade*, Vol. 1, No. 5, July 1994, pp. 3–4.

36 Michael Canfield and Alan J. Weberman, *Coup d'État in America*, Quick American Archives (revised edition 1992). These pictures and others can be found in A.J. Weberman's extensive website about matters related to the assassination.

37 The story of the trial is told by Mark Lane in his book *Plausible Denial*, previously cited.

38 Carol J. Williams, "Watergate Plotter May Have a Last Tale: Two of E. Howard Hunt's Sons Say He Knew of Rogue CIA Agents' Plan to Kill President Kennedy in 1963," *Los Angeles Times*, March 20, 2007; Larry Hancock, "Evaluating the Howard Hunt "Confession," *Dealey Plaza Echo*, Vol. 13, No. 2, July 2009, pp. 13–18.

39 The direct quote is from the Internet. Phillips' use of the *nom de guerre* "Harold Harrison" anticipates Wikileaks' Julian Assange's calling himself "Harry Harrison" on an Internet dating site. Harry Harrison was in fact a noted science fiction writer. Among his books are *Bill, the Galactic Hero*, and *The Stainless Steel Rat*.

40 HSCA Executive Session, April 20, 1978, *Jones* 4-2-78, 78 pp.

41 D. Boylan, "A League of Their Own: A Look Inside the Christian Defense League," *The Fourth Decade*, Vol. 4, No. 5, July 1997, p. 11; WCDs 42, 1107.

42 WH 24 CE No. 2095 pp. 529–30.

43 WH17 CE No. 832, 2 pp.

44 WH 4, J.W. Fritz Testimony, p. 210.

45 WH 17 CE 705, DPD Radio Transmissions 432. Braniff flew from Dallas to several U.S. cities, including Houston, San Antonio, and Chicago. It seems unlikely that escaping snipers, carrying their guns, would travel by commercial airliner, even in Texas.

46 WH 7 Testimony of Gerald L. Hill, pp. 59–60.

47 Roger Craig said his testimony to the Warren Commission investigators (for example, WH 23 CE 1967) was substantially altered. He gave evidence at the Clay Shaw trial in New Orleans and self-published a book, *When They Kill A President*, in 1971. He died in 1974.

CHAPTER 9

November 23/24, 1963
THE PASSION OF
LEE HARVEY OSWALD

★   ★   ★

"This press conference was something akin, I guess, to something you might conjure up for the Middle Ages. Something like a press conference in Ancient Rome..."

Seth Kantor[1]

After midnight, the cops marched Oswald out to a "press conference." Jack Ruby was in attendance, handing out sandwiches. It was a brief appearance.

OSWALD: I positively know nothing about this situation here. I would like to have legal representation.

REPORTER: (unintelligible)

OSWALD: Well, I was questioned by a judge. However, I protested at that time that I was not allowed legal representation, during that very short and sweet hearing. I really don't know what this situation is about. Nobody has told me anything, except that I'm accused of murdering a policeman. I know nothing more than that and I do request someone to come forward to give me legal assistance.

Oswald didn't ask for any particular lawyer. He asked for help, and complained about being interrogated without an attorney present.

> OSWALD: These people have given me a hearing without legal representation or anything.
>
> REPORTER: Did you shoot the president?
>
> OSWALD: I didn't shoot anybody, no sir.

Asked, again, if he killed the president, he gave the same answer.

> OSWALD: No. I have not been charged with that. In fact, nobody has said that to me yet. The first thing I heard about it was when the newspaper reporters in the hall asked me that question.
>
> REPORTER: Mr. Oswald, how did you hurt your eye?
>
> OSWALD: A policeman hit me.

Lee was being treated terribly. A suspect, especially one in such a high-profile case, has rights. For the DPD to ignore those rights so excessively suggests that they had no expectation that Oswald would ever see the inside of a courtroom. Instead they marched him back and forth like some unfortunate scapegoat, insisting on his innocence, pleading for a lawyer.

As the suspect was led away, Jack Ruby introduced himself to the Justice of the Peace, David Johnston. He gave the judge his Carousel Club card, featuring a stripper and a martini glass.[2]

Next, D.A. Henry Wade held his own press conference. Asked what kind of rifle the assassin had used, Wade told reporters, "It's a Mauser, I believe." He said that Oswald had boarded a bus, announced that Kennedy had been shot, and laughed. Wade added that Oswald was a member of the "Free Cuba Committee"—the right-wing group founded by Edward Teller and Arleigh Burke. From the back of the room, Jack Ruby corrected him: "Henry, that's the Fair Play For Cuba Committee."

Oswald was put in a maximum-security cell on the fifth floor of the jail, on Dealey Plaza. He was taken out a few minutes later and fingerprinted again.

At 1:35 a.m. he was woken and formally arraigned with the murder of the president. In response he told Judge Johnston, "I don't know what you're talking about." Again he asked for legal representation, mentioning the Dallas ACLU.

At the *Dallas Morning News* the presses had begun to roll. The first edition of the day quoted D.A. Wade as saying that "more than one person was involved in the shooting."

Now in Shreveport, Louisiana, General Walker issued a five-sentence "statement of sympathy." "The death of Mr. Kennedy is not as surprising as it is tragic," the general wrote. "The sacrifice of our leading American family is the sacrifice of every American for peace." Simultaneously, at Walker's headquarters in Dallas, Robert Surrey read the general's statement over the phone to the *Dallas Times Herald*.

Allegedly, on this date, William Somersett and Joseph Milteer met at the Union Station in Jacksonville, Florida. Milteer, just in from Dallas, was jubilant. "Everything ran true to form," he told Somersett. "I guess you thought I was kidding when I said he would be killed from a window with a high-powered rifle." Is such a rail journey possible? Not anymore: since the Katrina disaster, there has been no service from New Orleans to Jacksonville. When there was, the train trip from Dallas to Jacksonville, via San Antonio, took around 40 hours. But in 1963, there was a faster connection from Dallas to Jacksonville—the train to Shreveport, connecting with the New Orleans-bound *Southern Belle*. Taking this route, Milteer could have met Somersett with time to spare. He could also have stopped off in Shreveport, *en route*, to share his sympathy with General Walker.

Several of the police officers who interrogated Oswald remarked how calm and in control he seemed, how he would converse with the cops freely, always deny killing anyone, then clam up when further questions came. His mother observed that, in spite of being the worse for a beating, Lee was "severely composed and assured." William Weston has a theory to explain Oswald's calm manner and his alleged refusal to talk: still working on his long-term project— the discrediting of communist groups—Oswald expected to be held in jail for a while, as he had been in New Orleans, and *then to walk away*. Weston writes:

"The assassination was too big an operation to allow an innocent patsy to say and do things unpredictably and thus expose the plot. It was essential to have a cooperating patsy who could be relied upon in a role that was to be extremely sensitive. Oswald's part in this highly complex operation was indispensible. Not only did he give time to the real assassins to make their getaways, but he was also laying down a trail of false clues indicating that the assassination was a Communist plot."[3]

If Weston is right, then Oswald was far from innocent. He was part of the plot, a witting accomplice, and his job was to stonewall the investigation for a couple of days, while the killers escaped. This, perhaps, is what he did. We don't know what Lee Oswald really said in his police interrogations because there is no genuine transcript. The cops claimed he was close-mouthed about serious matters. That may not be true. To reporters, Oswald denied killing anyone, and asked for legal assistance. Perhaps Lee acted confident, and surly, because he believed he was just a sideshow, a distraction, and that—like Braden, Santana, Florer, Doyle, Abrams, Gedney, and the other arrested suspects—he would be allowed to go free.

Waking on his second day in custody, it must have been harder to believe this.

At 10:25 in the morning he was taken from his cell to Captain Fritz's office. Chief Curry gave a press interview in which he complained that the FBI had failed to warn the DPD that Oswald was a potential threat. Curry remarked that the FBI had recently interviewed Oswald, and had him under surveillance. Director Hoover threw a fit, and told SAC Shanklin to get a retraction from Curry or lose his job. Curry obligingly withdrew his remarks. By now the third floor of his police station was overflowing with reporters, whose passes weren't being checked. One journalist, Ike Pappas, recalled, "It was chaos... I was stunned and amazed that we were permitted so close to the prisoner."

Fritz's notes about these interviews are remarkable for how little information the homicide detective wrote down. According to Fritz, Oswald denied bringing a package to work, or owning a rifle. He answered idle questions about sandwiches and asked to be represented by "Mr. Abt." Oswald again denied shooting the president, and would not admit to having signed a fake draft card with the name "Heidel."

At 11:40 a.m. Oswald was returned to his cell. He was back in Fritz's office at 12:35 p.m. for further questioning. In his report to the Warren Commissioners, Captain Fritz wrote,

> "I talked to Oswald about the different places he had lived in Dallas in an effort to find where he was living when the picture was made of him holding a rifle which looked to be the same rifle we had recovered. The picture showed to be taken near a stairway with many identifying things in the back yard."

Clearly Fritz is talking about one of the historic "backyard photos." There is a problem with this. Warren Commission Exhibits 133-A and B—the first two "backyard photos" showing Oswald with his guns— were officially discovered around 1 p.m. by DPD officers Stovall and Rose. The photos didn't reach police headquarters until three hours later, 4 p.m.

So how did Fritz know about the photographs?

From 1:10 to 1:30 p.m., Marguerite and Marina were able to see Lee. Separated by a glass partition, they spoke over the telephone. "Lee seemed very severely composed and assured. He was well beaten up. He had black eyes, and his face was all bruised, and everything... I said, 'Honey, you are so bruised up. Your face. What are they doing?' He said, 'Mother, don't worry. I got that in a scuffle.'" Marguerite asked if there was anything she could do to help. She told the Warren Commission that he replied:

> "No, mother, everything is fine. I know my rights, and I will have an attorney. I have already requested to get in touch with Attorney Abt, I think is the name. Don't worry about a thing."

At 1:40 p.m., according to the Commission, Lee "tried to call an attorney in New York."

Lyndon Johnson, meanwhile, had a disturbing visitor: CIA director John McCone. McCone briefed the new president twice that day: first advising him that an "international conspiracy" might be behind the murder, then claiming that Lee Harvey Oswald had, in Mexico City, met the Soviet assassinations specialist Valery Kostikov. It isn't known to what extent McCone asserted there had been direct Russian involvement. But he certainly planted the seeds. In the hands of a new president, inexperienced in foreign affairs, such information was potentially incendiary. What if Johnson believed the Russians were behind the killing, based on McCone's report, and asked the Joint Chiefs to prepare a military response?[4]

Sanity prevailed, from an odd source: Johnson's old crony, J. Edgar Hoover, whom the president telephoned as soon as McCone was gone.

> Johnson: Have you established any more about the visit to the Soviet Embassy in Mexico in September?
>
> Hoover: No, that's one angle that's very confusing, for this reason—we have up here the tape and the photograph of the man who was at the Soviet Embassy, using Oswald's name. That picture and the tape do not correspond to this man's voice, nor to his appearance. In other words, it appears that there is a second person who was at the Soviet Embassy down there.

The audio tape which Hoover mentioned, provided by CIA to the FBI, later disappeared. But the photos of a burly, middle-aged blond man, who CIA had falsely claimed was "Lee Harvey Oswald," remain. For a second time, the FBI chief was advising the highest authorities that Oswald was being impersonated. Was Hoover also implying that Lee was a patsy, set up by a conspiracy to which the FBI was not a party?

The same afternoon, according to Penn Jones, Captain Fritz received a person-to-person call from the new president. Johnson told the Dallas police chief to wrap up the murder investigation forthwith. "You have your man," the president counseled Fritz.[5]

Meanwhile, Elaine Mosby, who had interviewed Lee in his hotel room in Moscow just four years previously, filed a UPI report based on that interview. She repeated what Lee had told her: that he and his mother had moved to North Dakota when he was a teenager, and that he had studied Marxism there.

At 2:10 p.m., Oswald was taken to his fourth lineup, in the basement of the police station. Present were two taxi drivers, one of them William Whaley. Whaley later testified,

> "...directly they brought in six men, young teenagers, and they were all handcuffed together... you could have picked

> [Oswald] out without identifying him just by listening to
> him because he was bawling out the policemen, telling them
> it wasn't right to put him in line with these teenagers...
> they were trying to railroad him and he wanted his lawyer...
> Anybody who wasn't sure could have picked out the right one
> just for that..."[6]

At 2:30 p.m., Lee was returned to his cell. Fifteen minutes later
he was roused by detectives who took hair samples from his head,
chest, arms, armpits, legs, and pubic area. These samples were
forwarded to the FBI. At 3:30, he was returned to the fourth-floor
visiting area for a visit from his brother, Robert. On the far side of
the glass, Lee motioned to Robert to pick up the phone. The first
thing Robert heard Lee say was, "This is taped." (As far as we know,
nothing was taped or recorded during Lee Oswald's imprisonment
and interrogation. Or did Oswald know something we don't?) They
talked about family matters, then Robert demanded to know what
was going on. "I don't know," Lee replied.

"You don't know?" Robert catalogued the trouble Lee was in.
"They've got your pistol, they've got your gun, they've got you
charged with shooting the president and a police officer. And you tell
me you don't know what is going on?"

"I just don't know what they're talking about," Lee answered.
"Don't believe all this so-called evidence." Robert stared into his
brother's eyes, trying to figure him out. "You will not find anything
there," Lee told him.

After Robert left, Oswald made two more calls to the Paine house.

An hour later, Captain Fritz gave an impromptu press conference,
announcing, "I can tell you that this case is cinched. This man killed
the president. There's no question in my mind about it. I don't want
to get into the basis. I don't want to get into the evidence. I just want
to tell you that we are convinced beyond any doubt that he did the
killing."

By 5:30, Oswald was back in his cell. Here he received a visitor: H.
Louis Nichols, president of the Dallas Bar Association. They spoke
for three minutes. Twenty-seven minutes after that, Nichols told
the press that Oswald wanted John J. Abt, an attorney famous for
defending communists, to represent him. If Abt was not available,
Nichols said, then Oswald would accept an attorney from the ACLU.

Nichols went on to say he would not contact Abt, as Oswald's family were going to do it. This was untrue. One wonders what H. Louis Nichols, Esq.'s game was. Presumably he had gained access to the arrested man on the basis that he was going to assist him, and make sure he knew he had a right to legal counsel. Then, after the briefest of meetings, Nichols gave a press conference revealing everything Oswald had said. Later, Captain Fritz, the ubiquitous FBI agent, James Bookhout, two Secret Service agents, Forrest Sorrels and Thomas Kelley, a postal inspector, Harry Holmes, a young Texas reporter, Dan Rather, and Marguerite Oswald would all claim that Lee had asked for Abt.[7]

After it's over, he'll call Abt to defend him...

Some time after 5:30, John Currington, a member of H.L. Hunt's security staff, showed up at the County Jail. He would later testify that Hunt had tasked him to see what security the police had set up. Currington reported back to his boss that "there was no security whatsoever around the jailhouse." From 6 to 7:15 p.m., Oswald was returned to Fritz's office and interrogated. During this round of questioning, Chief Curry announced to the throng of journalists that Oswald would be transferred from the city jail to the county jail, probably next morning. Pressed for an exact time, Curry told the reporters they should show up around ten.

At that moment, Marguerite and Marina Oswald were being "detained" by the Secret Service in a Dallas hotel, the Executive Inn. Around 6:30, an FBI agent named Bardwell Odum knocked at the door, wanting to see Marina. Marguerite refused to let him in. According to Marguerite, Odum held a photograph in his hand—a picture of someone he wanted Marina to identify. Marguerite looked at Odum's photo; she didn't know the man. A few days later, she said, she realized that Odum had shown her *a picture of Jack Ruby*. The Warren Commissioners did not call Odum as a witness. In an affidavit, he stated that the photo he showed Marguerite was of "an unknown individual, furnished to the FBI by the CIA." Was it a photo of the Oswald impersonator at the Russian Embassy? Or was it Jack Ruby?

Back in his crowded office, Captain Fritz confronted Oswald with a "backyard" photograph of him holding a rifle. Lee remained composed. Fritz reported his response as follows:

> "He said the picture was not his, that the face was his face, but that this picture had been made by someone superimposing his face, the other part of the picture was not him at all and that he had never seen the picture before... He further stated that since he had been photographed here at the City Hall, and that people had been taking his picture while being transferred from my office to the jail door, that someone had been able to get a picture of his face, and that with that they had made this picture. He told me that he understood photography real well, and that in time, he would be able to show that it was not his picture, and that it had been made by someone else."

Such sangfroid! Oswald, who had worked for the photographic specialists Jaggers-Chiles-Stovall, saw the trick immediately. Still expecting to be exonerated and released, he offered to show the Chief how it had been done.

Fritz's notes for this interrogation session, starting at 6:35 p.m., are as follows:

> "Shows photo of gun. Would not discuss photo denies buying gun from Kleins Comp of wanting jacket for line up Says I made picture super imposed."

This is the one difference between Fritz's incomplete notes and his written report. Here we learn that Oswald accused Fritz of faking the picture himself! Given 1) Fritz's knowledge of the photographs before they were discovered, 2) detective Bobby Brown's admitted creation of composite materials, and 3) patrolman Roscoe White's possession of a third composite, I suspect Lee was right, and that the DPD fabricated the pictures, either before or immediately after his arrest.

At 8 p.m., Lee called the Paines' once again. He asked to speak to Marina. Ruth told him Marina was no longer staying there. He spent his second night in custody.

Of all the writers dealing with this material, Harold Weisberg shows the most empathy for Oswald in captivity. Weisberg, a journalist, Senate investigator, and waterfowl expert, saw Oswald's treatment as a violation of his civil rights.[8]

And indeed it was: from the moment the cops piled onto him in the Texas Theatre, Lee Harvey Oswald was denied any semblance of his rights as an adult, sentient American. First and second among these rights were the right to remain silent, and the right to an attorney. Neither was respected. Ironically, for a "leftist" who had shown no interest in the civil rights cause (beyond his CIA-chauffeured day trip to Clinton), Lee was now receiving the same treatment as the demonstrators in Birmingham and Albany. In some ways, his treatment was worse. Dr. King was allowed to contact his attorney, sometimes shared a cell with him, and had been released.

The Warren Report addresses the denial of Oswald's civil rights, very briefly:

> "Although he made remarks to newsmen about desiring a shower and demanding his 'civil rights' Oswald did not complain about his treatment to any of the numerous police officers..."[9]

That's all right then—the Chief Justice of the Supreme Court confuses a lawyer with a shower, and notes that Oswald didn't complain about his treatment to the cops who'd beaten him up! But at his one and only "press conference," Oswald begged for legal assistance. FBI agent Bookhout wrote that Oswald would not consent to a polygraph "without the advice of counsel." Secret Service inspector Kelley wrote that he "would not answer any questions until he had been given counsel." Perhaps this is the simple explanation for Lee Oswald's taciturn behavior in custody: he had requested a lawyer—not necessarily Abt, or the ACLU, but just "someone to come forward"—and was waiting for one to appear.

After it's over, someone will kill him...

During the small hours of November 24, the Dallas FBI office and the DPD switchboard received anonymous warnings that Oswald would be killed during the jail-to-jail transfer. At 8:15 a.m., SAC Shanklin phoned Chief Curry, and advised him of the warning the FBI had received.

In Columbia, South Carolina, Joseph Milteer had breakfast with Willie Somersett. The men had driven to Columbia as part of Milteer's ongoing reactionary outreach, this time to set up a new political unit, the Constitutional American Parties (CAP) with the assistance of the Ku Klux Klan. At 9 a.m., Milteer went out for coffee, and returned with a handful of change—leading Somersett to believe he had made a long-distance call, on a pay phone. "Oswald has not said anything and he will not say anything," Milteer told the police informant.

Oswald was signed out of jail at 9:30 a.m. They took him up to Captain Fritz's office for a final round of questioning. At 10:20, Chief Curry gave—what else?—another press conference. He announced that Oswald would be moved to the county jail by armored truck, as a security precaution. Afterwards, Captain Fritz objected, reasoning that a regular unmarked police car driven by an officer would be faster and more maneuverable. Curry agreed, but kept the armored truck on hand, as a decoy.

Captain Fritz returned to his office to question Oswald further. Not much interrogation went on. Instead, Secret Service agent Kelley asked Lee whether he thought religion was the opiate of the people, and Lee answered, "Very definitely." Then Fritz wanted to know if he believed in a deity, but Oswald refused to answer, "since this was an attempt to have me say something which could be construed as antireligious or anti-Catholic." Someone talked politics, and Lee replied, "Will Cuba be better off with the president dead? Someone will take his place, Lyndon Johnson, no doubt, and he will probably follow the same policy." After two days in chaotic custody, Oswald seemed remarkably rational, and calm. But H.D. Holmes, the postal inspector, observed that Fritz was getting his goat. When the Captain mentioned Oswald's dishonorable discharge, Lee "bristled noticeably" and insisted his discharge had been honorable. Having abandoned his wife, his family, his wedding ring and various wallets, Lee still wore his Marine Corps ring, just as he'd worn his dress gloves in Moscow on the day of his "defection." Was Oswald, through all these years of craziness, still following orders the Corps gave him, and never rescinded... *semper fi?*

Fritz asked Oswald again about Hidell. Oswald denied knowing Hidell, denied using his name to order guns, denied using his name as an alias, denied knowing who he was. Fritz asked about the fake Hidell ID. "I've told you all I'm going to about that card," Lee snapped back. "You took notes. [!] Just read them for yourself if you want to refresh your memory."

Just before they took Oswald down, a pathetic scene occurred. Thomas Kelley, the Secret Service agent, approached him out of the hearing of the others, and spoke to him quietly.

"I... said that, as a Secret Service agent, we are anxious to talk with him as soon as he had secured counsel; that we were responsible for the safety of the president; that the Dallas police had charged him with the assassination of the president but that he had denied it; we were therefore very anxious to talk with him to make certain that the correct story was developing as it related to the assassination."

By "the correct story" I hope that Agent Kelley meant the truth! Oswald responded favorably to Kelley's good-cop approach. According to Kelley, Lee's last words were as follows:

"He said that he would be glad to discuss this proposition with his attorney and that after he talked to one, we could either discuss it with him or discuss it with his attorney, if the attorney thought it was a wise thing to do but that at the present time he had nothing more to say to me."[10]

Is that all it would have taken—an attorney? And Oswald would have talked? Or would he still have stonewalled? We shall never know. Around 11 a.m., according to the cops, Lee received a clean shirt—his old one having been sent for analysis—and opted for a black sweater, which had arrived with "a bundle" of his clothes. One wonders why he wasn't dressed in jail clothes, like the other prisoners. Instead the police gave him a black top and a new pair of black pants. Now, clad all in black, Lee at last resembled the killer in those backyard photographs...[11]

In Washington, Lyndon Johnson signed NSAM Number 273, canceling President Kennedy's 1,000-troop withdrawal from Vietnam. The language of the document signaled a change in U.S. objectives: from "assisting" the South Vietnamese, to "assisting them to win" against the communists. In Mexico City, a young Nicaraguan, Gilberto Ugarte Alvarado, walked into the American Embassy and claimed to have seen Lee Harvey Oswald paid $6,000, in the Cuban Consulate, to murder the president. Ugarte's story, soon proven false, was part of an ongoing background of intelligence chatter linking responsibility for the assassination to the Castro regime.

At 11:19 a.m., running more than an hour behind schedule, Dallas detectives took Lee via the elevator from his fifth-floor cell to the basement of the city jail. At least 50 journalists had gathered in the basement, almost a third of them unidentified by the police. Jack Ruby joined the crowd just before Oswald and his guards emerged. Ruby sheltered behind a police friend, William "Blackie" Harrison, till Lee was level with him. Then, at 11:21, he stepped forward and shot Oswald at point-blank range. Oswald fell, and the cops grabbed Ruby, who offered no resistance. Lee was dragged back into the jail office and given artificial respiration by the police. This, for someone with ruptured organs and severe internal bleeding, was a death sentence.

Fig. 18: Dying Oswald gives his clenched fist salute, version 1.

Ruby was hustled upstairs and put in the cell Oswald had just vacated.

Then the ambulance came, and Lee was placed on a stretcher, where he was "photographed" for the last time, giving his trademark clenched-fist revolutionary salute.

Are these pictures real, or further photomontages? Video footage of the same event shows no clenched fist. And whose hand is Oswald "holding"? When Lee was shot, he was cuffed by the right wrist to the detective in the white suit, J.R. Leavelle. Now, with his left hand, he appears to be gripping the hand of a man in a black suit and hat. No cuffs

Fig. 19: Dying Oswald gives his clenched-fist salute, version 2.

are visible. Once aboard the ambulance, Lee was taken to Parkland Hospital, where President Kennedy had died. While a team of doctors struggled to keep him alive, one of them—Charles A. Crenshaw—was called to the phone. Lyndon Johnson was on the line. "I want a deathbed confession from the accused assassin," the president told the astonished surgeon. "There's a man in the operating room who will take the statement. I will expect full cooperation in this matter."

Lee Harvey Oswald died without talking, at 1:07 p.m.

notes

1   WH20 Kantor Exhibit No. 4, p. 413.

2   WH 20 Johnston Exhibit No. 1, p. 315.

3   William Weston, "The Arrogant Suspect," *The Fourth Decade*, Vol. 2, No. 2, Jan. 1995, p. 9.

4   Michael Bechschloss, *Taking Charge: The Johnson White House Tapes 1963–1964*, Simon & Shuster, NY, 1997, p. 22.

5   Jones, *Forgive My Grief III*, p. 101. Bechschloss (*Taking Charge*) makes no mention of any such call from Johnson to Fritz. But Johnson and his secretaries controlled the tape-recording of his calls; it's unlikely the president would have taped himself directing the DPD's investigation. Texas Attorney General Waggoner Carr testified to the Warren Commission that he received a call from the White House on the afternoon of November 22—"I can't for the life of me remember who it was"—regarding a rumor that Oswald would be connected to an international conspiracy in his indictment. Though he couldn't remember the White House caller's name, Carr had been able to report back to him after a conversation with D.A. Henry Wade (WH 5, p. 259). Wade told the Warren Commission that he received several calls from Lyndon Johnson's aide Cliff Carter, beginning the afternoon of November 22, "concerning the international conspiracy angle" even though, as Wade observed, "there is no such crime in Texas, being part of an international conspiracy" (WH 5, pp. 218–219).

6   WH 2, pp. 260–261.

7   Timothy Cwiek, "John J. Abt: Did Oswald Ask For Him?", *The Third Decade*, Vol. 3, No. 1, Nov. 1986, pp.1–6.

8   Weisberg, *Whitewash*, pp. 67–70.

9   Warren Commission Report, p. 188.

10 WH 20 Kelley Exhibit A, p. 444.

11 Timothy Cwiek, "The Final Framing of Lee Oswald," *The Third Decade*, Vol. 2, No. 3, Mar. 1986, pp. 9–13.

CHAPTER 10

AFTERMATH

★ ★ ★

Oswald was dead, but the NORTHWOODS-style chatter about Cuba continued. A long-distance telephone operator notified the FBI when she overheard a caller say, "The Castro plan is being carried out. Bobby is next." The call was traced to the phone of Emilio Nuñez Portuondo, Batista's former ambassador to the United Nations, and an agent of David Atlee Phillips.[1]

In Washington, leading figures from the Eastern establishment began to lean on Lyndon Johnson to establish a "blue ribbon" panel to investigate the crime. Among those pushing for such an entity were MOCKINGBIRD asset Joseph Alsop, Eugene Rostow, and Dean Acheson—establishment figures at the McCloy level. Johnson, in turn, leaned on Earl Warren, head of the Supreme Court, to chair the panel. The new president warned the Chief Justice that there was a real danger of nuclear war unless they both helped lay the ghost of any "international conspiracy." But, while Johnson agonized to Warren and others about the threat of imminent nuclear war, he made no effort to discuss these matters with the Joint Chiefs. Having aggressively reversed direction in Vietnam, Lyndon laid low where Russia and Cuba were concerned. This arm-twisting frenzy—a traditional Johnson tactic—seemed for domestic consumption only, to enshrine the notion that Oswald, an "authentic" communist and killer/nut, had acted alone.

President Kennedy was buried, with great honors, in Washington on November 25, 1963. A few hours later, Lee Oswald was interred in a Fort Worth cemetery, without honors, under a black slab bearing his surname. The gravediggers had been told they were burying a man named "William Bobo."

After it happens, the President's best friend will commit suicide.
He'll jump out of a window because of his grief...

Jack Kennedy was a charismatic man with many friends. The day after the funeral, one of them, Grant Stockdale, flew to Washington and talked with Bobby and Teddy Kennedy. Stockdale had served as Kennedy's first Ambassador to Ireland. After meeting the brothers, he returned to Miami. On December 1 he talked incoherently to his attorney about "those guys" trying to get him, and about the president's assassination. Stockdale died the next day, falling from his office window on the thirteenth floor of the duPont Building. He did not leave a suicide note.

On December 31, the Fair Play For Cuba Committee closed.

When a great tragedy such as the murder of a head of state occurs, one might expect misfortune to befall the city where it happened. There are historic precedents. Carthage was "to be destroyed" by the Romans, who sowed its streets with salt. The Athenians razed the city of the Melians. The "lone nut" theory allowed Dallas, in the aftermath of John F. Kennedy's assassination, to prosper, to expand. In due course, the city integrated its police force: the DPD is no longer a mob of white boys wearing cowboy hats. Clint Murchison Jr. purchased a football team, the Cowboys. American Airlines relocated its corporate offices from New York to Dallas. In honor of the fallen president, it was announced that Cape Canaveral would be renamed Cape Kennedy, but that pious promise was soon rescinded. Florida's political leaders christened it Canaveral again, and the federal government responded feebly, calling its NASA outpost the "John F. Kennedy Space Center at Cape Canaveral" instead.

Feeble too was the Report of the Warren Commission, a cartel of special interest representatives, none of whom served full-time or attended all the proceedings: Dulles, the former CIA boss, fired by

Kennedy; McCloy, Rockefeller's banker, the Pentagon's man; Russell, the senatorial voice of Southern racism and the Walker/NSRP faction; Ford, the simple-minded future president, snitching on the proceedings to the FBI... Denied information by the intelligence agencies it relied on, the Commission reached the same conclusion as Johnson had: that Oswald, a Marxist ex-Marine with no intelligence connections, on his own, killed Kennedy and Tippit, and wounded Connally. Thanks to its clever and persistent lawyers (all of them remunerated by the taxpayer) the Commission convinced itself that Oswald, a mediocre rifleman using a misaligned, bolt-action rifle, had shot Kennedy and Connally multiple times with only three bullets, one of which missed.

We should thank our lonely stars for Lyndon Johnson. Like Jack Kennedy, he resisted the NORTHWOODS-driven temptation to invade Cuba, or declare nuclear war. In the area of civil rights, he delivered what Kennedy had promised. In Vietnam, he encouraged a gigantic, criminal holocaust which killed millions, and greatly enriched his benefactors, the military contractors Brown and Root. No one is perfect. Some authors, especially Texans, believe Johnson was the instigator of the Kennedy assassination. One version of this theory places "Mac" Wallace, a killer alleged to be on Johnson's payroll, firing a rifle from behind the fence, across the Grassy Knoll. This theory relies on the Eastern establishment—people like Rostow, and Acheson, and McCloy—lining up to assist Lyndon, helping to orchestrate the best possible cover-up. Johnson was a powerful character with some influence in Texas and the South, but if he'd ordered the murder of Jack Kennedy, wouldn't the Eastern establishment have taken him down, on principle? This is not to say that Kennedy was popular with that establishment. He was not: as noted, he was a Roman Catholic, and they didn't like his dad; most of all, he had offended some very powerful interests, including banking, oil, and steel, during his brief presidency.

There is a tendency on the part of writers to exaggerate the significance of their subject. This book treats the parallel lives of Kennedy and Oswald as of equal interest and importance, when perhaps they are not. But, as Bertrand Russell wrote,

> "...there has never been a more subversive, conspiratorial, unpatriotic, or endangering course for the United States and

the world than the attempt by the United States government
to hide the murderer of its recent president."

If an assassination conspiracy took place, and the perpetrators got
away with it, then the rule of law and the will of the electorate were
truly scuppered in 1963. Its instigators may well have killed other
political and social leaders, and pulled off even greater political
scams and frauds, in the ensuing decades. Was there an assassination
conspiracy, as Bertrand Russell and his Committee feared? Over the
years, pretty much everyone Jack Kennedy offended, and everyone
Lee Harvey Oswald met, has been accused of some involvement: the
FBI; CIA; ONI; the KGB; Cuban intelligence; anti-Castro Cubans;
the mafia; White Russians; the KKK and NSRP. Of these, Oswald's
weakest links are to the mafia (solely via his uncle, the bookie) and
to the Cubans: despite his FPCC posturing, Lee showed little interest
in Cuba, spoke no Spanish, and was impersonated at the Cuban
Consulate. His Russian language skills were strong and his links to
the FBI, CIA, and KGB were serious, suggesting that he may indeed
have been a double agent. His strongest links of all were to George de
Mohrenschildt, who was CIA-connected and most likely his handler
in Dallas, and to Guy Banister, ex-FBI, Nazi, and Minuteman, who
gave Oswald office space and secretarial services in New Orleans.

For any assassination conspiracy to succeed, in an advanced
and partially transparent democracy such as the United States, it
requires three tiers: 1) the assassins themselves, who will presumably
be dispatched after the assassination; 2) those with advance knowledge
who "tidy up" the crime scene, help the killers disappear, and promote
the "patsy" story; 3) those in high authority, some with advance
knowledge, some without, who participate in the dissemination of an
official "lone nut" theory, and suppress alternate versions.

It is too late to hunt these scoundrels down. And in November,
1963, only the FBI had the power to pull it off. Given 30-odd arrests
within a week of the assassination, the crime could have been solved.
J. Edgar Hoover played his cards close to his chest, and his G-men
lived by his motto, *Don't Embarrass the Bureau*. But Hoover was an
old crony of Johnson, and, unlike CIA's McCone, he didn't lie to him
on Day One. While McCone was spinning tales of KGB assassins and
international conspiracies, Hoover was telling the new president
the truth: that Oswald had been impersonated, and that CIA were

feeding him false information. Imagine, for a fantastic moment, an alternate universe in which Johnson had empowered Hoover—whose nominal boss was still Robert Kennedy—to investigate the crime and arrest and interrogate the most likely suspects. Lee Harvey Oswald, instead of being damned as the lone assassin, might have been re-branded as the hero FBI informant, penetrator of the plot. Stranger things have happened. In such an alternate reality, who would the G-men have dragged in?

In terms of 1) the assassins themselves, the FBI should have re-arrested and interrogated those detained on the scene, including Jim Braden, Emilio Santana, James Powell, Larry Florer, and the so-called "tramps." As potential employers of the assassins, the FBI should have arrested and interrogated General Walker, his Nazi associate Robert Surrey, and the Dixie Clansmen Harry Jack Brown and Joseph Milteer. Surrey would almost certainly have spilled the beans: he seemed in a panic at his Warren Commission testimony, continually pleading the Fifth. Walker, at his testimony, named three individuals for the Commission to investigate, including George de Mohrenschildt. Given the third degree, the general might have revealed several more names.

In terms of 2) those who assisted the killers and framed the patsy, the FBI should have arrested and interrogated Sheriff Bill Decker, who told his men not to provide security; District Attorney Bill Alexander, and Captain W.R. Westbrook, uniquely prescient in their pursuit of Oswald; Captain Fritz, who stage-managed Oswald's last two days alive; and Roy Truly, who allegedly brought a rifle into the TSBD. On the assumption that Lee Oswald was one of the killers, the FBI should have arrested and interrogated George de Mohrenschildt, David Atlee Phillips, and the Paines, as his accessories. Similarly, his New Orleans associates—Guy Banister, Delphine Roberts, Clay Shaw, and William Gaudet—should have been picked up and grilled, as David Ferrie was, but more robustly. Naturally Jack Ruby's request to be allowed to testify in Washington, DC, rather than in Dallas where he was afraid, should have been granted.

Regarding 3), just as no effort was made to arrest members of the duPont family over the plot against FDR, and there was no prosecution of Standard Oil for its support of the Nazis during World War II, it would have been a tall order to locate, much less punish, the intellectual author/s of the Kennedy assassination. The rich can get away with almost anything, anywhere in the world. Still, if the investigators wanted to pinpoint the intellectual authors of the crime, they could have arrested and grilled: Secret Service head James Rowley, White House detail chief Roy Kellerman, the dysfunctional Emory Roberts, and another agent, Floyd Boring, all of whom could have explained the intentional security-stripping; the military men present at the dead president's autopsies, including Captain John H. Stover, Admiral George Burkley, and General Godfrey McHugh; military supporters of armed, racist groups such as the NSRP, including Admiral Crommelin; plus Dean Acheson, Allen Dulles, Joseph Alsop and other early promoters of a Warren-style Commission.

In January 1964, D.A. Alexander and Texas Attorney General Waggoner Carr flew to Washington to advise the Warren Commissioners of the Hosty/Oswald relationship, which the FBI had tried to keep secret, and to bring to their attention a rumor that Oswald was a paid FBI informant with a number—"Agent 179."[2]

This was the same story as Deputy Sheriff Sweatt had told journalist Alonzo Hudkins, though Sweatt reported Oswald's FBI informant number as 172, not 179. Whatever the number, the FBI seems to have been rendered powerless and inactive by this broadside from the Dallas cops. And these persons of interest are almost all dead now. Some of the most notable ones died early on: Guy Banister, of a heart attack, in 1964; David Ferrie of "natural causes" at the age of 49; George de Mohrenschildt of "suicide" just before he was to be questioned by HCSA investigators. Fifty years later, perhaps only Marina and the Paines survive.

But we can say, on the basis of the evidence we have, that the case is very much unclosed. Closure—a satisfactory explanation for the crime, which doesn't insult common sense, and which most people can accept—demands that all available evidence be seen and analyzed. It's impossible to reach a conclusion about Lee Harvey Oswald's funding and finances without seeing his tax returns, yet these remain a secret, courtesy of the federal government. All the evidence still suppressed needs to be made available to the public. "Destroyed" and "lost" records need to be undestroyed, and found.

And there are still numerous avenues for obsessive researchers to explore, including the full facts of the Chicago case; the history of Hunter C. Leake, who claimed to hold high rank in CIA, and to have been the paymaster of Oswald and Banister; Jose Rivera and his activities; Senator Dodd's subcommittee, and its alleged use of the "Hidell" alias to order weapons; the NSRP/military nexus that was General Walker's circle; E. Howard Hunt's "deathbed confession"; researcher Joan Mellen's claim that Oswald, while in Russia, communicated with CIA via an American Express employee, Michael Jelisavcic; Bill Kelly's and James W. Douglass' detailing of assassination links to a CIA contractor, Collins Radio; and Douglass' tale of a CIA flight which landed in Dallas after the assassination;[3] plus the Russian intelligence story (cynical propaganda or heartfelt belief?) that Dallas oil men, specifically the Hunts and the Murchisons, were behind the hit.[4]

Which avenue to follow? For me, General Walker is a prime suspect for at least five reasons: 1) his previous encouragement of extreme right-wing violence, involving snipers, in Mississippi; 2) the security-stripping at Ole Miss and Dallas, which enabled the snipers to enjoy a free firing range; 3) Walker's organization of the violent anti-Adlai Stevenson demonstration in Dallas; 4) his failure to organize an anti-Kennedy demonstration in Dallas, coupled with his decision to be far from home on the day the president came (this is what Donald Rumsfeld would call "evidence of absence"); 5) Walker's documented support for right-wing political assassins, especially Byron de la Beckwith (both *Time* and *Newsweek* reported Walker and the former governor, Ross Barnett, ostentatiously "dropping in" on de la Beckwith's trial "with a handshake and a cheery word" in February 1964).

Walker's support for de la Beckwith was detestable. But he was not alone. As a Bircher and a NSRP supporter, the General was part of a national network involving military officers, policemen and armed good ol' boys. Among them was Barnett, governor of Mississippi when whites rioted at Ole Miss. Barnett issued the order to withdraw state troopers, consigning federal marshals to the snipers, while General Walker urged the white mob on: "Protest! Protest! Keep it up!" Bill Decker's instructions to the Dallas sheriffs not to participate in the president's security was on a par with Barnett's pulling the state troopers. Emory Roberts' instruction to the Secret Service detail not to protect the president, and his removal of the motorcycle outriders, are similar examples of deliberate security stripping, which led to avoidable deaths. Thanks to Abraham Bolden, we know the president's Secret Service detail shared the white, racist worldview of Walker, Barnett and the NSRP. As Martin Luther King observed, after Jack Kennedy's murder, "We have seen children murdered in church, men shot down from ambush in a manner so similar to the assassination of President Kennedy, that we must face the fact that we are dealing with a social disease that can no longer be neglected or avoided."

On February 22, 1978, HSCA investigators interviewed John Marshall, former Secret Service SAIC, Miami. They reported:

> "Twice during the interview, Mr. Marshall mentioned that, for all he knew, someone in the Secret Service could possibly have been involved in the assassination. This is not the first time an Agent has mentioned the possibility that a conspiracy existed, but it is the first time that an Agent has acknowledged the possibility that the Secret Service could have been involved."

Jack Kennedy and Lee Harvey Oswald were enigmatic individuals. One had almost all the advantages in the world, the other had almost none, beyond his cleverness. Both had a dominating, flawed parent. Both married beautiful, exotic women, and neglected them. Both served their country at sea. Both liked reading James Bond books, and weightier tomes. Both enjoyed the movies. Both took a keen interest in foreign affairs. Both made the most of their short lives, though they were often misguided by others. Both died in brutal, unjust ways. That the system did not arrest and punish the guilty, but merely blinked, and moved on, shows that both men—Jack and Lee—were small potatoes in the greater scheme of things. James DiEugenio recalled a story told by the American satirist Mort Sahl:

> "...before the 1960 election, [Sahl] liked to kid Kennedy about being the scion of a multimillionaire. Kennedy cornered him once on this topic and asked him point-blank how much he thought his family was worth. Sahl replied, 'Probably about three or four hundred million.' Kennedy then asked him how much he thought the Rockefellers were worth. Sahl said he had no idea. Kennedy replied sharply, 'Try about four *billion*.' JFK let the number sink in and then added, 'now *that's* money, Mort.'"[5]

Schoolchildren in Texas and the South cheered when their teachers told them Kennedy was dead. Elsewhere, the reaction was different. Pete Hamill, the author, recalled:

> "I let out a wail, a deep scary banshee wail, primitive and wounded... full of fury and pain... kids were wailing now... but I turned, ashamed of my pain and my weeping, and rushed into the night. All through the Catholic neighborhood called Andersonstown, doors were opening and slamming and more wails came roaring at the sky, wails without words, full of pagan furies and old as bogs. I wanted to find my father, wanted to have him hug me. But I careened around dark streets, in the midst of the wailing. I saw a man punch a tree. I saw a stout woman fall down in a sitting position on a doorstep, bawling. I ran and ran, trying to burn out my grief, my anger, my consciousness. I found myself on the Shankill Road, main avenue of the Protestant district. It was no different there... I saw a man kicking a garbage can over and over and over again in primitive rage. I saw three young women heading somewhere, dissolved in tears..."[6]

Fifty years later, what can be done? So many years after the assassination, the only remedy for this still-open wound must be a Truth Commission, similar to the ones which operated successfully in South Africa and South Korea. Such a commission—like Bertrand Russell's project—would be citizen-run. It would be based in the United States, probably as part of a larger enterprise, investigating the whole imperial project: why America took that route, who gained, who lost, and who just "went along."

A Truth Commission into the imperial project would empower witnesses to speak, and journalists to own up to their intelligence connections.[7]

Writers and reporters who have, for many years, deliberately told lies fed to them by government or corporate sponsors, would be encouraged to speak the truth about what they did, and for whose benefit. Those who hacked phones, wrote opinion pieces on demand, and promoted war, the invasion of foreign countries, and the perversion of democracy, would have a safe forum in which to talk about the work they did, and who they did it for.

Such a Truth Commission couldn't limit itself to the Kennedy assassination, or the assassinations of Martin Luther King, or Robert

Kennedy. Nor could it be confined to WMD, or to who profits from the drug trade and the drug war, or to what took place on September 11, 2001, or to issues of corporate personhood, or to the environmental consequences of warfare, or to why taxpayers must fund extrajudicial killing and bail out billionaires. It would need to address the entire imperial deal, no less, no more.

It's a tall order.

So let's roll.

notes

1   Attempts, in the NORTHWOODS manner, to link Fidel Castro to the Kennedy assassination have been numerous over the years and still continue: On March 18, 2012, *The Guardian* reported on a former CIA analyst's claim that Castro had advance knowledge of an Oswald assassination plot in Dallas: "Fidel Castro May Have Known of Oswald Plan to Kill JFK" by Richard Luscombe.

2   Jerry D. Rose, "Agent 179: The Making of a Dirty Rumor," *The Third Decade*, Vol. 1, No. 4, May 1985, pp. 14–20.

3   Douglass, *JFK and the Unspeakable*, pp. 294–296, 298–301.

4   Fursenko and Naftali, *One Hell of a Gamble*, pp. 347–348.

5   James DiEugenio, "The Posthumous Assassination of John F. Kennedy," *The Assassinations*, p. 35.

6   Pete Hammill, *A Drinking Life*, New York: Little, Brown, 1994, pp. 241–242.

7   DiEugenio, in *Destiny Betrayed* (pp. 310–321) reprints two lengthy CIA memoranda, obtained by Mark Lane in an FOIA suit, dated April 1, 1967, and July 19, 1968, proposing ways friendly journalists should respond to Lane, Russell, Epstein, and other critics of the Warren Report. Fletcher Knebel is cited as a "useful" journalist in this context, as John Sparrow was in the U.S. Embassy cables. The Agency also prepared a series of psychological profiles of Lane, and issued a Lane Psychological Report, predicting Lane's reaction to various stimuli and the best way to derail him (Lane, *Plausible Denial*, p. 77).

FROM THE HISTORIC DIARY OF
LEE HARVEY OSWALD

★ ★ ★ ★ ★ ★ ★ ★ ★ ★ ★ ★

"My fondes dreams are shattered because of a petty offial; because of bad planning I planned to much! 7.00 P.M. I decide to end it. Soak rist in cold water to numb the pain. Then slash my left wrist. Than plaug wrist into bathtub of hot water. I think, "when Rimma comes at 8. to find me dead it will be a great shock. somewhere, a violin plays, as I wacth my life whirl away. I think to myself. "how easy to die" and "a sweet death, (to violins) …""

October 22 1959

BIBLIOGRAPHY

The material in this book about Jack Kennedy and his presidency is drawn from mainstream histories: Richard Reeves' *President Kennedy*, Nigel Hamilton's *Reckless Youth*, Robert Dallek's *An Unfinished Life*, Gary Wills' *The Kennedy Imprisonment*, Bruce Miroff's *Pragmatic Illusions*, Herbert S. Parmet's *Presidency of John F. Kennedy*, Ronald Kessler's *Sins of The Father* (a biography of Joe Kennedy Sr.), and the *New York Times*. I haven't relied on authors such as Noam Chomsky or Seymour Hersh, who display a significant animus toward Kennedy. What follows is a far from exhaustive list of other books, which relate in some other way to Oswald, the Kennedy presidency or assassination. Most of them I bought or borrowed; the rest were donated by my dear friend Hercules Bellville, who generously bequeathed me his Kennedy files.

Mark Lane, *Rush to Judgment*
Mark Lane, *Plausible Denial*
James W. Douglass, *JFK and the Unspeakable*
David Talbot, *Brothers*
Michael L. Kurtz, *The JFK Assassination Debates*
Jim Marrs, *Crossfire*
Thomas Michael Evica, *And We Are All Mortal*
Abraham Bolden, *The Echo From Dealey Plaza*
Robin Ramsay, *Who Shot JFK?*
Henrik Kruger, *The Great Heroin Coup*
Joaquin Joesten, *How Kennedy Was Killed*
Joaquin Joesten, *Oswald—Assassin or Fall Guy?*
Joaquin Joesten, *Oswald The Truth*
Josiah Thompson, *Six Seconds in Dallas*

Penn Jones, Jr. *Forgive My Grief* Vol. 1, Vol. 3

Harold Weiseberg, *Whitewash*

Harold Weiseberg, *Whitewash II*

Sylvia Meagher, *Subject Index To The Warren Report*

Sylvia Meagher, *Accessories After The Fact*

Dick Russell, *The Man Who Knew Too Much*

John Newman, *Oswald and The CIA*

Nick Bryant, *The Bystander*

Tom Miller, *The Assassination Please Almanac*

Carl Oglesby, *The Yankee and Cowboy War*

Gerard Colby and Charlotte Dennett, *Thy Will Be Done*

Peter Dale Scott, *Deep Politics and the Death of JFK*

Ray and Mary La Fontaine, *Oswald Talked*

Paris Flammonde, *The Kennedy Conspiracy*

Jim Garrison, *On The Trail of The Assassins*

Edward J. Epstein, *Legend—The Secret World of Lee Harvey Oswald*

Philip Melanson, *Spy Saga*

James DiEugenio and Lisa Pease, *The Assassinations*

James DiEugenio, *Destiny Betrayed*

Thomas G. Buchanan, *Who Killed Kennedy?*

Anthony Summers, *Conspiracy* (revised as *Not In Your Lifetime*)

Anthony Summers, *Official and Confidential: The Secret Life of J. Edgar Hoover*

Robert Sam Anson, *"They've Killed The President!"*

Report of the Warren Commission on the Assassination of President Kennedy

Final Assassinations Report of the HSCA

Edward T. Haslam, *Mary, Ferrie & the Monkey Virus*

Tom Mangold, *Cold Warrior: James Jesus Angleton*

James Kirkwood, *American Grotesque*

Anthony Frewin, *The Assassination of John F. Kennedy: An Annotated Film, TV and Videography*

Fletcher Knebel and Charles W. Bailey II, *Seven Days In May*

Frank L. Kluckhorn, *America: Listen!*

Theodore H. White, *The Making of The President, 1960*

John A. Stormer, *None Dare Call It Treason*

Kent and Phoebe Courtney, *The Case of General Edwin A. Walker*

William W. Turner, *Power On The Right*

Aleksandr Fursenko and Timothy Naftali, *"One Hell of a Gamble"*

Jefferson Morley, *Our Man In Mexico: Win Scott & the Hidden History of the CIA*

John Bainbridge, *The Super-Americans*

James Reston, Jr., *The Lone Star: The Life of John Connally*

Jane Wolfe, *The Murchisons*

Lamar Waldron and Thom Hartmann, *Ultimate Sacrifice*

Richard Bartholomew, *Possible Discovery of an Automobile Used in The JFK Conspiracy (The Nash Rambler)*

Vincent Palamara, *Survivor's Guilt*

Christopher Simpson, *Blowback*

Deborah Davis, *Katherine The Great*

James Bamford, *Body of Secrets*

Donald Gibson, *Battling Wall Street*

Donald Gibson, *The Kennedy Assassination Cover-Up*

Back issues of Prof. Jerry D. Rose's *Third* and *Fourth Decades*, and *PROBE*, the CTKA magazine, were vital resources for this book. The best resources of all are often the original documents on which the Warren Commissioners may or may not have based their conclusions. These were originally published in expensive, multi-volume sets; today, painstakingly scanned, they're freely available on the Internet, as are many HSCA and ARRB releases. When in doubt, refer to the original materials. The doubt may persist, but at least you'll be looking at the closest thing there is to evidence.

ACRONYMS

ACLU	American Civil Liberties Union
AFB	Air Force Base
ALPHA 66	CIA-connected Cuban terrorist group, violently opposed to Fidel Castro
AP	Associated Press
ARRB	Assassination Records Review Board
ATTD	Alcohol and Tobacco Tax Division (later ATF: Alcohol, Tobacco & Firearms Division)
ATU	Alcohol and Tax Unit (of the Treasury/IRS—later ATTD)
BBC	British Broadcasting Corporation
CAP	Civil Air Patrol
CBS	Columbia Broadcasting System
CE	Warren Commission Exhibit
CEEO	Committee on Equal Employment Opportunity
CIA	Central Intelligence Agency
CORE	Congress on Racial Equality
CRC	Cuban Revolutionary Council, CIA-connected Cuban exile organization
CUSA	Conservatism, USA, Walker-linked group opposed to communism in Europe and United States
DIA	Defense Intelligence Agency
DPD	Dallas Police Department
DRE	Student Revolutionary Directorate (Directorio Revolucionario Estudiantil), CIA-connected Cuban exile organization
FBI	Federal Bureau of Investigation
FPCC	Fair Play for Cuba Committee, CIA-infiltrated, initially funded by Cuban government
HSCA	House Select Committee on Assassinations
HUAC	House Committee on Un-American Activities
ICBM	Intercontinental ballistic missile
INCA	Information Council of the Americas, CIA-connected anticommunist organization

IRS	Internal Revenue Service
JM/WAVE	CIA operations and intelligence gathering station, Miami, FL
JURE	Cuban Revolutionary Junta, CIA-connected Cuban exile organization
KGB	Committee for State Security (Komitet Gosudarstvennoy Bezopasnosti), Russian national security agency
KKK	Ku Klux Klan, white racist organization
MDC	Christian Democrat Movement (Movimiento Democratico Cristiano), CIA-connected Cuban exile organization
MIT	Massachusetts Institute of Technology
MVD	Ministry of Internal Affairs (Ministerstvo Vnutrennikh Del), Russian domestic national police
NAACP	National Association for the Advancement of Colored People
NACIREMA	"American" spelled backwards, the Dixie Clan of Georgia
NASA	National Aeronautics and Space Administration
NATO	North Atlantic Treaty Organization
NOPD	New Orleans Police Department
NPIC	National Photographic Interpretation Center, CIA's photo lab
NRO	National Reconnaissance Office, spy satellite agency
NSA	National Security Agency
NSAM	National Security Action Memo
NSC	National Security Council
NSRP	National States Rights Party, white supremacist group overlapping with American Nazi Party
OAS	Organization of American States
ONI	Office of Naval Intelligence
OSS	Office of Strategic Services
PBS	Public Broadcasting Service
SAC	Strategic Air Command (U.S.)
SAC	Special Agent in Charge (FBI)
SAIC	Special Agent in Charge (Secret Service)
SIOP	Single Integrated Operating Plan for nuclear war (Pentagon)
SWP	Socialist Workers Party
TSBD	Texas School Book Depository
UPI	United Press International
USAF	United States Air Force
USMC	United States Marine Corps
USSR	Union of Soviet Socialist Republics

USSTRICOM	U.S. Strike Command, MacDill Air Force Base, Florida
WH	Warren Commission Hearings and Exhibits (26 volumes)
WDSU	New Orleans Radio Station

Code Names for Covert Operations

APHRODITE	U.S. Army and Navy project to create flying bombs (drones)
AMTRUNK	CIA operation to cultivate coup leaders in Cuba
AMLASH	CIA operation to assassinate Fidel Castro and other Cuban leaders
COINTELPRO	FBI program to infiltrate and subvert leftist political organizations and discredit individuals
HADES	Army/Air Force program to defoliate the jungles of Vietnam
IOP	Ideological Operations Project: IRS/Justice Dept. program to investigate tax status of political organizations
LCIMPROVE	counterespionage designed to penetrate Soviet intelligence
MOCKINGBIRD	covert CIA campaign to influence foreign and domestic media with well-placed reporters
MONGOOSE	covert operation of Pentagon and CIA to undermine the Cuban government
NORTHWOODS	Pentagon plan to stage terrorist attacks against Americans, on U.S. soil, to justify invasion of Cuba
PAPER CLIP	operation to recruit former Nazi scientists for the U.S.
RANCHHAND	renamed Operation HADES, expanded to destroy "enemy" crops
RUSTY	operation to acquire the Nazis' secret police network

Warren Commission documents, HSCA and ARRB documents and records are available at **www.aarclibrary.org**
(The same site also contains files from the Garrison investigation, certain FBI and CIA records, and records of LBJ's phone calls.)

Copies of Warren Commission documents, plus journals including The Third Decade and Fourth Decade, are at the Mary Ferrell site: **http://www.maryferrell.org**

CTKA, a valuable assassination and parapolitics related site is at **http://www.ctka.net**. Back issues of its journal probe Probe are available there.

John Simkin ran a very useful forum dedicated to the Kennedy assassination (now closed) here: **http://educationforum.ipbhost.com/ index.php?s=0973a965eed0d8527573c585e7bbf770&showforum=126** and runs a detailed British-hosted forum at **http://www.spartacus. schoolnet.co.uk/JFKindex.htm**

There is a lively forum at **jfklancerforum.com**.

The Assassination Research site is a useful resource - **assassination- research.com** - as is Douglas Horne's blog Inside The ARRB: **http:// insidethearrb.livejournal.com/**

Edwin Black's original article about the Chicago plot to murder President Kennedy can be read at **http://www.scribd.com/doc/49710299/ The-Chicago-Plot-to-Kill-JFK**

Vincent Palamera's important book about Secret Service ineptitude/ complicity, Survivors' Guilt, is available as a free download from **http://www.assassinationresearch.com/v4n1.html**

Mark Lane's original book Rush to Judgement can be downloaded
here: **http://www.balderexlibris.com/public/ebook/Lane_Mark_-_Rush_
to_Judgment.zip** or at **http://ewhoedge.blog2009.com/The-first-blog-b1/
Rush-to-Judgment-book-b1-p58.htm**

The documentary film *Rush to Judgement*, by Lane and Emile
DiAntonio, is available from the wonderful archive.org here: **http://
archive.org/details/RushToJudgment_608**

A.J. Webermann's site about Oswald, the assassination and the "Three
Tramps" is at **http://ajweberman.com/** This website has been closed
down as we go to press but we have left the link in case it is reactivated.

JFK's speeches can be watched, heard or read at **http://www.jfklibrary.
org/JFK/Historic-Speeches.aspx**

The **jfklibrary.org** site also contains various chronologies, including
that of the *New York Times*.

Oswald's radio "debate" with Ed Butler and others in New Orleans,
can be heard at **https://www.youtube.com/watch?v=Ao2a9mRWkso**

The Kennedys' arrival at Dallas Love Field Airport can be seen at
https://www.youtube.com/watch?v=twKRh2uKkPE. (This video contains
footage of a Secret Serviceman being abandoned by his colleagues on
the tarmac.)

There are various 'stabilized' versions of the Zapruder film on the
Internet. Two of them are here:
https://www.youtube.com/watch?v=QTBInhsKW3E
https://www.youtube.com/watch?v=Zmz4lz6l8Fs

Jack White's take on the 'faking' of the Zapruder movie can be seen
here: **https://www.youtube.com/watch?v=PNsrGgyoIgo**

Larry Florer's arrest in Dealey Plaza can be seen here:
https://www.youtube.com/watch?v=G3lPAL8BBOs

Florer was also filmed being interviewed by DPD detectives:
https://www.youtube.com/watch?v=qbqKJ2PDU3A

Other mysterious characters in Dealey Plaza are profiled here:
https://www.youtube.com/watch?v=z32v9dJABw8

There is a long article about the Umbrella Man, by Ronald L. Ecker, at **http://hobrad.angelfire.com/umbrella.html**

Raw footage of Lee Oswald in the custody of the Dallas police (including a clear shot of Jack Ruby in the hallway) is here: **https://www.youtube.com/watch?v=4FDDuRSgzFk**

There is video of Oswald's midnight press conference at
https://www.youtube.com/watch?v=IcTwch9oIMo
https://www.youtube.com/watch?v=yaS-UV-BsdY

His police station hallway "interviews" can be seen here:
https://www.youtube.com/watch?v=yaS-UV-BsdY
https://www.youtube.com/watch?v=u6ELsuoEc2w

Oswald complains to reporters on his way to the line-up here:
https://www.youtube.com/watch?v=20SzdIBn51Q

Alex Cox: Case Not Closed: The Umbrella Man
http://vimeo.com/70200324

Alex Cox: Case Not Closed: The Zapruder Film
http://vimeo.com/71655165

INDEX